The Blues Detective

THE BLUES DETECTIVE

A Study **of**
African **American**
Detective **Fiction**

Stephen F. Soitos

The University of Massachusetts Press
Amherst

Printed in the United States of America
LC 95-43872
ISBN 0-87023-995-3 (cloth); 996-1 (pbk.)
Designed by Dennis Anderson
Set in Sabon by dix!
Printed and bound by Braun-Brumfield, Inc.

Library of Congress Cataloging in Publication Data

Soitos, Stephen F., 1947–
   The blues detective : a study of African American detective
fiction / Stephen F. Soitos.
      p.   cm.
   Includes bibliographical references and index.
   ISBN 0-87023-995-3 (cloth : alk. paper).—ISBN 0-87023-996-1
(pbk. : alk. paper)
   1. Detective and mystery stories, American—Afro-American authors—
History and criticism.   2. Afro-Americans in literature.
I. Title.
PS648.D4S577   1996
813'.087208896073—dc20   95-43872
                                                    CIP

British Library Cataloguing in Publication data are available.

Dedicated to my mother, Ledora,
my sister Francine,
my daughter Stefana,
and Anne Marie Mascaro.
In memory of my father.
To Jimmy

Contents

Preface

The Blues Detective, like many a good mystery, evolved out of a coincidence of factors when, as both student and teacher, I concentrated my field of study on twentieth-century art forms. In analyzing African American expressive arts as well as the popular culture field of detective fiction, I saw a number of clues that suggested a connection between the two. *The Blues Detective* represents a dovetailing of my study of these two important American cultural creations, brought to fruition or, if you will, solution in a satisfying way.

One of my early surprises was realizing how quickly African Americans had adapted detective formulas to their own ends. One of the clues that put me on the trail of the blues detective was a repeated reference to a detective story that had been published early in the twentieth century in an obscure magazine or newspaper. Apparently, this novel not only was written by a black author but also had a black detective as hero. If I could find the story, I thought, it might predate *The Conjure Man Dies* (1932) by Rudolph Fisher and consequently might be the first known black detective novel. With help from Henry Louis Gates's Black Periodical Literature Project and Professor John Gruesser, I was able to locate this mysterious story as well as to uncover some additional interesting clues to the origins of black detective fiction. One of these discoveries was Pauline Hopkins's African American female detective, who appears in a work that predates all known black detective novels.

As the co-author of three mystery novels, as well as a teacher who designed and taught a course entitled Great American Mysteries, I had been fascinated with the detective formula for some time. In particular, I had closely studied the detective story as created by

Edgar Allan Poe and given new dimensions by the American hard-boiled school. The detective genre had established a tradition in its own right, and I was well aware of its increasing influence on American literature.

Therefore, I was intrigued by the possibility of a black author/black detective for a number of reasons. What made this study interesting for me was the discovery of a particular tradition of African American detective tropes that appeared as I studied the texts. In a literary landscape deluged with vast numbers of white male and female detectives, I wondered what new perspectives on race, gender, and class these black detective writers would bring to the Euro-Americentric world of detective fiction, that is, work expressing white European and American value systems. Certainly, blacks had entered this detective landscape—but usually only through rear service doors, employed as incidental and racial character types. This was an impression gained from my own reading in detective fiction and further supported by such fascinating works as Frankie Y. Bailey's *Out of the Woodpile: Black Characters in Crime and Detective Fiction* (1991). Furthermore, I wondered how detective novels written by African Americans at the very genesis of the hardboiled school would compare to Carroll John Daly's Race Williams or Dashiell Hammett's Continental Op, whose stories of the same vintage were published in *Black Mask* magazine.

Thanks to Professor Bernard Bell, who encouraged and supported this unusual undertaking, I was put in contact with other people who could help me with my research, and my initial clues eventually led me to a larger set of associations that needed verification and validation. *The Blues Detective* presents the progression of that process in what I hope is both an interesting and an enlightening way. My first clues remained isolated and without pattern until a number of other factors began to influence how I looked at the problem. James Baldwin, then Visiting Professor of Literature at the University of Massachusetts in Amherst, helped reorient my interest in detective motifs in African American fiction. After discussions with Baldwin about the structure of Richard Wright's *Native Son* and, in particular, "The Man Who Lived Underground," it became obvious to me that Wright had been heavily influenced by detective fiction. Further research proved this to be so, as readers of Michel Fabre's works on Wright can attest. Also, black female writers such as Toni Morrison, Ann

Petry, and Gayl Jones have employed the strategies of detective fiction in their works. The questions that Baldwin helped me to consider are at the root of *The Blues Detective*. Among these questions are: How many African American authors had written detective novels with conscious reworking of detective tropes? Why had African American authors chosen the detective form? Did the evidence of the black detective novel suggest important revisions of the detective personas and use of what I call double-consciousness detective themes?

The Blues Detective is a work of literary history and criticism that attempts to answer these and other questions concerning the use of common detective tropes by African Americans. However, it was impossible for me to approach this subject without focusing solely on *African American authors* whose works include or make strong reference to *black detectives* and *the detective tradition*. In doing so I began to notice a pattern in African American writing using popular detective story motifs. In the initial stages of this research, the late Professor Emeritus Sidney Kaplan provided yet another piece of the puzzle by offering information concerning African Americans and popular culture interpretations. It became clearer to me, as I started to put these various strands together, that an important aspect of popular culture transformation was contained in African American creations using detective motifs and formulas. By using a white Euro-American popular culture form, black authors created important new tropes in black detective fiction.

At this point, like a person in a maze, I had a number of interconnected links or clues leading to some unknown solution. What I lacked was a theoretical approach to my intuitions and discoveries. In this capacity I was immensely helped by Professor Bell, who pointed me in the direction of important new work on African American literature and critical theory. My reliance on and application of African American critical theories will become apparent in the following pages. I hope that will not dissuade a reader from further inquiry into *The Blues Detective*, since I should like to emphasize the beauty and validity of an approach that judges African American detective texts on their own merits. In this regard, I am indebted to Professor Houston Baker for the title of this work, which was suggested by the broader use of the term "blues detective" in his book *Blues, Ideology, and Afro-American Literature*.

I believe that new critical theory, rather than alienating the perceptive reader, enriches the appreciation of African American expressive arts creations. The recognition of a vernacular tradition in black expressive arts is not necessarily new. Certainly, Zora Neale Hurston utilized and interpreted diverse facets of the cultural creations of black folk, especially religion, music, and dance. In addition, Ralph Ellison in *Shadow and Act* provided seminal work in vernacular theory and criticism. What is new is the creation of a vocabulary that interprets works in an African American way, that is, pertaining to the cultural tradition based on African American value systems with connections to the African past. These values can be ascertained by a number of disciplines in an assortment of African American creations and vernacular arts, including, but not limited to, language, music, and literature.

Vernacular criticism is an exciting and enlightening tool that can be used for support and defense of the heritage of African Americans and their humanitarian and community values. This type of criticism helps to connect the varied and powerful creations of African Americans by developing a critical vocabulary based not on Euro-Americentric models but on African American and Afrocentric worldviews. Vernacular criticism challenges negative attacks on black Americans which suggested or suggest that African Americans have no real culture of their own. Furthermore, rather than divorce itself from the social value of African American texts, it enhances these values by demonstrating ways in which average rural and urban African American people transformed the dominant folk and formal cultural formulas, indicating their own cultural survival and triumph over oppression.

I believe vernacular criticism illuminates rather than obfuscates texts by focusing on a matrix of African American expressions that conclusively affirm the positive and unique contributions of African American culture. This allows further assessment concerning the social importance of African American expressive arts to American culture as a whole. Writing *The Blues Detective* enabled me to discover ways that postmodern criticism can be applied to popular culture forms. I see *The Blues Detective* as reinforcing structuralist examiners of mystery/detective fiction such as Dennis Porter and John Cawelti. I hope also to support the validity of African American vernacular criticism by opening up new avenues of textual exploration connected to sociohistorical and socioreligious value systems.

Perceptive critics and readers should find that vernacular criticism liberates black scholarship from the fetters of restrictive methodologies ordained by others. I believe indigenous art forms deserve indigenous creative critical theories. This seems to me particularly appropriate when analyzing how African Americans took detective formulas and made them into new creations. In this way African American culture progresses not only in reinterpretations of its past but in preparation for its future.

Acknowledgments

The author would like to express heartfelt thanks to Professor Bernard Bell of Pennsylvania State University for his continued encouragement and support. The late Professor Emeritus Sidney Kaplan offered professional advice and personal anecdotes of an unparalleled nature, and Professor John Gruesser of Kean College of New Jersey aided my research in the writing of Chapter 1. Esther Terry and the Afro-American Department at the New Africa House at the University of Massachusetts in Amherst provided additional needed support. Thanks to Ben Davis. Special appreciation is due to the late James Baldwin whose encouragement and friendship touched so many people during his stay at the University of Massachusetts in Amherst.

The Blues Detective

Introduction

The conflation of African American literature and the detective fiction genre demands explication on a number of different levels.[1] For example, on the surface African American sensibilities and the hardboiled school of detective fiction would seem to have little in common. However, it is my contention that black detective writers use African American detective tropes on both classical and hardboiled detective conventions to create a new type of detective fiction. Through the use of black detective personas, double-consciousness detection, black vernaculars, and hoodoo creations, African American detective writers signify on elements of the detective genre to their own ends.

The primary issue is how African American authors create what I see as new variations of the detective form through the use of the tropes of black detection. In approaching the specific issues of African American literature and detective conventions, it is important to reconsider some root questions pertinent to my analysis. It is hoped that *The Blues Detective* will contribute to the ongoing debate about African American culture by suggesting that the shared use of detective fiction tropes by black writers supports the argument that African Americans do have a distinct culture.

The overall assessment of black detective fiction suggests socially, politically, and culturally affirmative ends as black writers expanded the scope of a popular culture form in the areas of race, gender, and class. In what follows I shall attempt to show how African American authors such as Pauline Hopkins, J. E. Bruce, Rudolph Fisher, Chester Himes, Ishmael Reed, and Clarence Major have altered the formulas of detective fiction in significant ways.[2] Their adaptation of detective conventions forms a matrix of four tropes whose implementation

3

changed standard detective expectations. My conception of "tropes" somewhat amplifies M. H. Abrams's definition as "words or phrases . . . used in a way that effects a conspicuous change in what we take to be their standard meaning" (64). In my usage tropes are associated with figures of thought, and effect conspicuous changes on detective conventions in the areas of the detective persona, double consciousness, black vernaculars, and hoodoo, as well as presenting issues of black nationalism and race pride in new ways. These four tropes help to define a coherent worldview shared by African American authors using the detective form.[3]

Through the tropes of black detection, common Euro-Americentric ideological and literary expectations are subverted. Black detective writers manipulate conventional detective structure and characterization, which in turn alters the moral message. In this sense, I hope to contribute to the black vernacular tradition of literary criticism by way of a close textual analysis of detective novels written by African Americans. Recent African American critics such as Houston Baker (*Blues, Ideology, and Afro-American Literature: A Vernacular Theory*, 1984), Bernard Bell (*The Afro-American Novel and Its Tradition*, 1987), and Henry Louis Gates, Jr. (*The Signifying Monkey: A Theory of Afro-American Literary Criticism*, 1988) have defined the specifics of black vernaculars and have shown how they represent characteristics of both Afrocentric and Euro-Americentric culture. These critics and others—for example, Robert Thompson in *Flash of the Spirit* (1983) and John W. Roberts in *From Trickster to Badman: The Black Folk Hero in Slavery and Freedom* (1989)—are contributing to the creation of a new hermeneutics of literary criticism based on African American models that reassess African American social systems and literary creations. Consequently, the most exciting breakthroughs in recent criticism achieve perspectives through a cross-discipline interpretation of African American cultural contributions.

Moreover, the growing critical work done by both women and men in such works as Hazel Carby's *Reconstructing Womanhood* (1987) and Michael Awkward's *Inspiriting Influences* (1989) opens up the field of female black authorship. These works have broadened the perspective on feminist interpretations by considering gender, class, and race in relation to earlier African American critics, as well as increasing the spectrum of black female contributions to black culture. In *The Blues Detective* I examine black detective fiction in relation to race, class, and gender because I believe these novels were written with these issues in mind. Consequently, I analyze closely Pauline Hopkins's *Hagar's Daughter*, J. E. Bruce's *Black Sleuth*, Rudolph Fisher's *Conjure Man Dies*, Chester Himes's series of Harlem detective novels and his short stories, Ishmael Reed's *Mumbo Jumbo*, and Clarence Major's *Reflex and Bone Structure*, assessing their sociopolitical achievements.

Recent attempts to apply new critical methodologies to the accepted (as well as neglected) classics of African American literature have produced interesting results. Often it becomes obvious that African American writers consciously used narrative techniques of a very sophisticated structure at the origins of African American discursive creations. My own work on narrative discourse in Charles Waddell Chesnutt's Uncle Julius tales is a case in point. I used the structuralist critical theory of Gerard Genette to show how Chesnutt fashioned an intricate narrative structure to explore and explode late-nineteenth-century conventional expectations of black and white relationships, as well as to comment on the sociohistorical aspects of slavery. I delivered this paper at the annual Langston Hughes Festival at City College in New York in 1990, in a forum entitled Afro-American Literature and Critical Theory. The reception was positive, but a number of participants were concerned about the application of Euro-Americentric critical terminology to African American material and the usurpation of indigenous value systems which that terminology might entail.

Consequently, I believe it is important, as do Baker, Bell, and Gates, to defend the application of different critical methods in analyses of African American cultural creations. My development of a system of critical terminology, which I call the tropes of black detection, will, I hope, be a positive case in point. One result of my thesis should be more evidence for a distinct African American culture. The issue of African American cultural identity has long been debated, and the debate is far from over. Current African American vernacular criticism attempts to establish a coherent system of principles derived from the rural and urban culture of everyday African Americans. Therefore, an important question lies at the root of any discussion of African American accomplishments: Is there an African-American culture? If so, how does one define it?

Berndt Ostendorf pinpoints the problem in his book *Black Litera-*

ture in White America (1982): "The history of blacks in America has too often been treated as a progress report on acculturation" (7). I believe it is a mistake to look at African American culture as purely one of transference or absorption of white or Euro-American cultural patterns. Not only does such an assimilationist approach severely limit the understanding of black culture in America, but it lends itself to hierarchal and essentially distorted, racist attitudes. Social scientists and historians using this limited model tend to denigrate what blacks have achieved outside and in spite of white dominant modes. In 1929 Ulrich Bonnell Phillips, the influential historian of the southern plantation tradition, commenting on the slave system, wrote that "Negroes in America . . . were as completely broken from their tribal stems as if they had been brought from the planet Mars" (*Life and Labor* 160). Gunnar Myrdal, the Swedish author of the classic *American Dilemma,* suggests that Negroes are "a caste of people deemed to be lacking a cultural past and assumed to be incapable of a cultural future" (54). Kenneth Stampp, the revisionist historian of southern slavery, says that "innately Negroes are, after all, only white men with black skins, nothing more nothing less" (viii), and Harvard sociologists Nathan Glazer and Daniel Moynihan write that "the Negro is only an American and nothing else. He has no values and culture to guard and protect" (53). The often quoted Howard University black sociologist E. Franklin Frazier states: "Probably never before in history has a people been so nearly completely stripped of its social heritage as the Negroes who were brought to America" (15). As recently as 1991 a black critic writing on the concept of multiculturalism stated:

> Multiculturalism cannot possibly be the goal of affirmative action because blacks have no distinct culture. They have no distinct cuisine (except the malnutritious diet of the poor); they have no language except the patois that some liberal educators have tried to fashion into a discrete language; they have no separate art. . . . blacks have made their contributions in the absence of any rooted sense of an alternative nationality or culture.[4]

Perspectives such as these demean African Americans by suggesting that their historical reliance on white culture was their only motivation. In essence this line of argument denies a distinct heritage of black culture, rejects the possibility that the African past had any psychological or cultural influence on American blacks, and implies that African Americans were completely fragmented and destroyed as social entities in the Americas. No other subdominant group in the Americas, except perhaps women and American aborigines, has been relegated to this consistently inferior and nonspecific status. What is lacking in these black cultural analyses is insight into the subdominant *methods* of distinct cultural exchange leading to a shared worldview.

Bernard Bell helps refocus the critical interpretations of African American creative expression by foregrounding important new methods of analysis. In direct refutation of the sentiments outlined above, Bell writes that

> recent research in anthropology, sociology, history, folklore, musicology, and linguistics not only challenges these conclusions but convincingly supports the beliefs long held by many Afro-Americans that the conflicts between black culture and white society have resulted in creative as well as destructive tensions in black people and their communities. (9)

Melville Herskovits, an anthropologist and Afrocentrist interested in establishing a connection between blacks in the New World and their African past, did pioneering research to reorient cultural critics to a new perspective. This important link between Africa and the New World is the first step in creating a comprehensive African American worldview. Herskovits's theory of social science confronts the alienated approach of historians like Phillips and sociologists like Frazier by referring to a continuity of African culture found in new environments such as the Caribbean and the Americas. Herskovits, in *The New World Negro* (NWN) and *The Myth of the Negro Past,* posits the idea that the African heritage can be traced in New World culture:

> Music, folklore, magic, and religion on the whole, have retained more of their African character than economic life, or technology, or art, while language and social structures based on kinship and free association tend to vary through all the degrees of intensity that are noted. (NWN 53)

Herskovits suggests three ways in which this was accomplished:

> *Retention*—the continuity of some African interpretations of phenomena.
>
> *Reinterpretation*—the interpretation of white cultural patterns according to African principles.
>
> *Syncretism*—the amalgamation of African and American cultural patterns and sign systems. (NWN 53)

Sociologist Robert Blauner, in his essay "Black Culture: Myth or Reality?" continues this line of argument: "But at the same time, beginning with slavery, the group and culture building process began among the black population and the development of an ethnic group identity and distinctive culture has been going ever since" (351).

Zora Neale Hurston, as writer and anthropologist, is one of the pioneers of the anthropological approach to black culture. Hurston demonstrated in her fiction how black expressive arts such as language, music, dance, and hoodoo specifically contribute to the wholeness of black culture, and how the repeated use of these African American adaptations forms what Gates calls "the traditional recurring canonical metaphors of black culture" (Hurston, *Tell My Horse* 295).

Later, Ralph Ellison in *Shadow and Act* (1964) supported the expansion of black cultural analysis. His pioneering efforts opened up a new direction in critical discourse. Ellison's book of essays is concerned with three general themes: "Literature and folklore, Negro musical expression—especially Jazz and the blues, and . . . the complex relationship between Negro American subculture and North-American culture as a whole" (xviii). By demonstrating that black Americans had repositories of cultural creations yet untapped, Ellison pointed the way toward a multidiscipline approach to critical theory. He suggests that the elements of African American culture must be enlarged to include diverse vernacular attributes.

> This "American Negro culture" is expressed in a body of folklore, in the musical forms of the spirituals, the blues and the jazz; and idiomatic versions of American speech (especially in the Southern United States); a cuisine; a body of dance forms and even a dramaturgy which is generally unrecognized as such because still tied to the more folkish Negro churches. (263)

His suggestion then is to turn to the indigenous art forms themselves to judge a people's unique cultural contribution. Primary examples of two art forms uniquely transformed through African American vernacular experimentation are, of course, music and language.

Houston Baker, Jr., continues this line of thought when he writes about developing a new system of literary analysis called the "anthropology of art." He is interested in "*how* black narrative texts written in English preserve and communicate culturally unique meanings"

(*Journey* xii). One way to interpret this textual evidence is to use a variety of disciplines to derive coherent interpretations of black American literature and culture. Baker sees the vernacular or expressive arts of the people as paramount in this quest, and he isolates and identifies the blues as the preeminent trope of black American culture. In speaking of the connection between literary analysis and cultural anthropology, he makes the insightful observation that "each must strive . . . to *interpret* the manifestations of a culture in accordance with the unique, richly symbolic, and meaningful contexts within which such manifestations achieve their effects" (xv). Baker refers to Ellison: "At the vernacular level, according to Ellison, people possess a cultivated taste that asserts its authority out of obscurity" (*Blues* 12). For Baker, the blues "forms a matrix for Afro-American culture." It is an indigenous African American art form that suggests for Baker an all-encompassing trope for the whole of black American culture: "The subtle, parodic, inversive, completely reflexive blues texts of black writers testify to the vitality of an Afro-American matrix as they fulfill the long-standing dream of an American form," (*Blues* 114).

Houston Baker sees the blues as the result of African American transformations of Euro-Americentric musical structure and in so doing develops a strong argument for the *blues* as the primary metaphor for all African American expressive arts. The Blues then, for Baker, becomes a matrix-establishing sign that stands for the ability of African Americans to re-create Euro-Americentric art forms for their own benefit. Baker argues for a new definition of criticism that is broader in scope and deeper in analysis than traditional approaches. By recognizing the continuous use of tropes in African American literature, he "seeks the historical, mythic, or blues force of the narrative" (*Blues* 123). He writes: "Tropological thought is a discursive mode that employs unfamiliar (or exotic) figures to qualify what is deemed traditional in a given discourse." (*Blues* 28). Critics employing this method of analysis are in effect the "blues detectives" of black culture—hence the title of this work. Most important, this vernacular method of criticism places the locus of the apparatus of theory dead center in the manifestations of the culture itself.

Henry Louis Gates does the same for language, transformed as it is by African Americans into a unique art through "signifyin(g)"— an African American language art that foregrounds the ironic and parodic rhetorical oral elements of African American culture and its African origins or cognate. In *The Signifying Monkey* Gates attempts to "demystify the curious notion that theory is the province of the Western tradition, something alien or removed from so-called non-canonical tradition such as that of the African-American" (xx). To accomplish this he too turns to the vernacular in the form of the linguistic tradition of signifyin(g): "The theory of Signifying arises from . . . moments of self-reflexiveness. . . . The Signifying Monkey is a *trope* . . . in which are encoded several other peculiarly black rhetorical tropes" (xxi). Gates analyzes these tropes in their relation both to past African traditions and to their ever-changing and challenging position in African American expressive culture.[5] The African trickster figure Esu-Elegbara and the African American Signifying Monkey are two sources of the signifying tradition in African American culture, a tradition that is carried forth into black detective texts in a number of interesting ways. In relation to Baker's *Blues* book, Gates writes: "My reading of his ms. convinced me that in the Blues and in Signifying were to be found the black tradition's two great repositories of its theory of itself, encoded in musical and linguistic terms" (x). Finally, Gates makes an important point concerning repetition and continuity, which gives particular emphasis to his theory.

> Black texts employ many of the conventions of literary form that comprise the western tradition . . . but black formal repetition always repeats with a difference, a black difference that manifests itself in specific *language* use. And the repository that contains the language that is the source and the reflection of black difference is the black English vernacular tradition. (xxii)

Such black vernacular re-creations are, of course, made up of a number of distinctive techniques. A simplified example in music structure involves use of a basic twelve-bar repetitive pattern created by black Americans. Accordingly, we recognize the Afrocentric call-and-response echoes in the verse-and-chorus repetitions. These elementary transformatives only suggest the complex adaptation of Euro-Americentric musical forms by black Americans.[6] Similarly, Gates establishes through signifying a direct connection to the African past primarily focused on the basis of his understanding of Yoruba culture. In a masterful analysis of the trickster god Esu-Elegbara, he shows how African American language arts have incorporated oral traditions and established distinct Afrocentric linguistic conventions.[7]

Vernacular creations like the blues and signifying are closely connected in cultural context to the general term "folklore," a sweeping term that encompasses many manifestations of cultural interplay. In particular, folklore is an extremely important component of black culture in the New World, as blacks made use of oral tales, hoodoo, and music to develop and maintain a distinct socioreligious worldview. Keith Byerman in *Fingering the Jagged Grain* (1985) redefines folklore and attempts to show how "folklore serves in the literature as the antithesis of closed oppressive systems" (3). He develops a comprehensive definition, which includes many heretofore neglected aspects of black culture:

> Black folk culture is used in this study in a very broad sense to mean both the history of the black masses and the primarily oral forms of expression that have developed over that history. These forms comprise blues; jazz; spirituals; sermons; toasts; the dozens; cautionary tales; trickster tales; legends; memorates; rural and urban speech patterns; folk beliefs such as voodoo, conjure, and superstition; and folk characters such as Brer Rabbit, stagolee, John Henry, the loup garou, flying Africans, the conjure woman, the good-time woman, and the aunt. (2)

Vernacular contributions are what I would call the substantive building blocks of African American culture. *The Blues Detective* will show how African American writers have taken the detective tradition and transformed it through use of the four major tropes: the detective persona, double-consciousness detection, black vernaculars, and hoodoo. By closely defining and examining these four areas I hope to show how black detective writers joined together to create a new type of detective novel. In one of the most interesting aspects of new critical theory application black Americans are shown to have subverted or transformed the available literary forms to serve their purposes. This is never more evident than in the way that African Americans have used the Euro-American detective tradition for their own ends.

1

The Paradigmatic Gesture

The detective fiction genre has developed in a number of different ways in the century and a half since Edgar Allan Poe wrote the first detective stories for the popular press of the 1840s. "The Murders in the Rue Morgue" (1841), published in *Graham's Magazine,* introduced the brilliant amateur detective Dupin. Since then, detective fiction has expanded in variety and scope, undergoing a number of transformations in the process. Detective genre conventions now command multimedia attention and always appeal to a large audience. Although it remains one of the most popular forms of fiction published in the United States, the detective story has only recently begun to receive the academic and critical attention it deserves.

A large percentage of all books published each year in the United States are in the detective field. Julian Symons claims that the detective genre is "almost certainly more widely read than any other class of fiction in the United States [and] the United Kingdom" (17), and authors like Agatha Christie and Mickey Spillane have published millions of books in various editions.[1] Numerous regional popular culture conventions occur yearly in all sectors of the country, and as part of the larger popular culture field, detective fiction categories are represented by large contingents not only at the conventions but in the pages of journals devoted to serious study of popular culture.

The detective genre has proven to be of interest to scholars and academics. Dennis Porter, professor of French critical theory at the University of Massachusetts, has written one of the best structural critiques of detective fiction, *The Pursuit of Crime: Art and Ideology in Detective Fiction* (1981). Umberto Eco, an Italian professor of linguistics, has written extensively on detective fiction as well as writing a major best-selling mystery novel, *The Name of the Rose*. Robert Parker, author of the Boston-based "Spenser" detective series, wrote a doctoral dissertation on Dashiell Hammett and Raymond Chandler. Amanda Cross, who writes the "Kate Fansler" mystery series, is actually Carolyn Heilbrun, a former professor of English at Columbia University. Modern critics of the detective form such as Dennis Porter, John Cawelti in *Adventure, Mystery, and Romance* (1976), and Tzvetan Todorov in *The Poetics of Prose* (1977) have helped to redefine the importance of detective fiction. Porter points out that "Poe showed how in fiction crime might cease to be regarded as a social problem in order to become a philosophic and even aesthetic one" (28). He also writes that

> a critic's attitude toward a work of literature is comparable to that of a detective at the scene of a crime. . . . The activities of both literary critic and detective involve a process of selecting from a multiplicity of soliciting signs those that may be organized into an interpretation. (226)

Popular culture forms are receiving recognition in major university programs on film, literature, music, and television. These forms are proving more and more useful in expanding approaches to interpretations of cultural and social issues, although, as might be expected, the quality of production is uneven in a field as diverse and voluminous as the detective novel. Unfortunately, detective reading as well as writing can become addictive and less than enlightening. Therefore, I have limited the focus of this study to black authors who utilize black detectives in works that alter recognized detective formulas through use of the four tropes of black detection: black detective personas, double-consciousness detection, black vernaculars, and hoodoo.

As a relatively new literary form, detective fiction has proven popular not only with readers but with writers who use it for diverse ends. To understand the full implications of African American use of the detective form, we should consider some important attributes of detective conventions as they developed in the last century and a half. Detective fiction shares many characteristics with what is termed the romance tradition. In *Secular Scripture* (1976), the eminent critic Northrop Frye defines the romance tradition and traces its origins back to and beyond Greek literature:

> Romance is the structural core of all fiction: being directly descended from the folktale, it brings us closer than any other aspect of literature to the

sense of fiction considered as a whole, as the epic of the creature, man's vision of his life as quest. (15)

Frye isolates certain romance conventions which are also part of detective fiction conventions: a mysterious birth, oracular prophecies about future contortions of the plot, adventures that involve capture, narrow escapes from death, recognition of the true identity of the hero, eventual marriage, or restoration of order. Detective fiction is easily recognized as urban romance in the way that it transforms these tropes. The detective genre is a modern, usually urban romance because the structural core of the detective form mimics romance conventions. Frye's romance conventions are seen in reverse in detective fiction: Mysterious death is substituted for mysterious birth. Oracular prophecies are replaced by witnesses, police officers, and others with "predictions" of the nature of the crime and the criminal. Narrow escapes from death are self-explanatory, especially in relation to the hardboiled detective novel. Finally, the true identity of the hero is replaced by the true identity of the murderer in the important climactic ending common to both romance and detective fiction known as the recognition scene.

Poe's fascination with popular forms, such as the German gothic romance, suggests his ability to translate romance conventions to his creation of detective fiction. As urban romance, detective fiction's antecedents have been connected to the criminal romances that came into prominence at the end of the seventeenth century in the English rogue novel as well as the Spanish picaresque tradition.[2] The early confessional criminal romances, such as Daniel Defoe's *Moll Flanders,* were most often fictions, ghost-written, and structured around the romance conventions. Furthermore, the episodic structure of the romance relied on plot for adventure, coincidence for surprise, disguise for secrecy, reversals of identity for recognition, and a cyclical rather than a linear movement toward the restoration of moral order. A perfect example of this type would be *Tom Jones* by Henry Fielding. These early novels in English literature suggest a cultural need that was satisfied by creation of new genres of narrative. Michael McKeon argues that

> the novel emerged in early modern England as a new literary fiction designed to engage the social and ethical problems the established literary fictions could no longer mediate—which is to say, both represent and conceal—with conviction. (133)

Detective fiction as a new genre creation in the nineteenth century would continue this process.

We have noted that Northrop Frye recognizes romance literature as having folklore roots. By extension, detective fiction shares some of these same roots. The tradition of oral narrative and storytelling plays an important role in the structure of detective fiction. Both classical and hardboiled detective fiction utilize techniques closely associated with romance narrative. It is not my purpose here to discuss the intricacies of narrative approach, but the folk roots of the detective narrative are worth mentioning. Suffice it to say that the first-person narrative construction of hardboiled fiction and its heroic mythology of the detective persona can easily be seen as reflections of an oral tradition. As David Geherin notes in *Sons of Sam Spade* (1980),

> the narration of the action provides much more than a mere summary of the events of the case; it also provides a substantial portrait of the narrator. When the narrator speaks, he communicates a tone, an attitude, a sensibility, even a sense of values. (14)

The value of genre in reflecting community values is analyzed quite closely in Mikhail Bakhtin's *Dialogic Imagination* (1981). Examining the origins of genre, Bakhtin writes:

> There exists in addition a special group of genres that play an especially significant role in structuring novels, sometimes by themselves even directly determining the structure of a novel as a whole—thus creating novel types named after such genres. (Examples of such genres could be confession, the diary, travel notes, biography, the personal letter and several others). (321)

The formulas of romance literature provide primary models for detective genre structure. The creation of detective fiction as yet another new genre suggests a cultural need for that type of fiction.

The detective story, as we know it, is usually seen as simply a story about a murder or murders containing a detective. Erik Routley in *The Puritan Pleasures of the Detective Story* (1972) posits a more comprehensive definition:

> For a detective story, properly so called, is a story involving crime, a police force, a detective (who may or may not be a member of the force) and a solution. It must evoke a major interest in the finding of the solution. Without these properties any story that appears to be "detection" is so called only by analogy. (19)

Stefano Tani in *The Doomed Detective* (1984) emphasizes the need for "a detective, the process of detection, and the solution" (41). Of course, there are many variations on these primary themes. The investigation of the murder can take any number of routes: tracking of the criminal, examination of the atmosphere of the crime, investigation of the pathology of the criminal, and in the best detective novels investigation of race, class, and gender in relation to cultural and criminal milieus.

Dorothy Sayers in her introduction to *The Omnibus of Crime* (1929) makes a plea for recognizing detective elements in literature from Aristotle and the Bible down through Voltaire's *Zadig*.[3] However, major literary critics of the detective novel, such as Julian Symons in *Mortal Consequences* (1972), Russel Nye in *The Unembarrassed Muse* (1970), and Howard Haycraft in *The Art of the Mystery Story* (1947), generally agree that the detective story genre was invented by the American Edgar Allan Poe in the first half of the nineteenth century with such classics of ratiocination as "The Murders in the Rue Morgue" (1841). "The Mystery of Marie Roget" (1842), and "The Purloined Letter" (1845). Poe is generally credited with creating many of the now accepted conventions of the detective form. These include, but are not limited to, the amateur detective who is both highly rational and curiously intuitive and eccentric, the first-person narrator who is usually a friend or associate of the detective, the baffled and thick-headed police, the analytical examination of clues and details, the locked-room mystery, and the cleverly hidden object or clue needed for the investigation.

Perhaps the most interesting aspect of Poe's creation was the prototypical Dupin, who established the complicated detective persona. Poe's unnamed narrator catalogues for the reader Dupin's character at the moment of his most intense reflection on the mystery:

> His manner at these moments was frigid and abstract; his eyes were vacant in expression. . . . Observing him in these moods, I often dwelt meditatively upon the old philosophy of the Bi-Part Soul, and amused myself with the fancy of a double Dupin—the creative and the resolvent. ("Murders in the Rue Morgue")

This essential split in personality is a trademark of detective fiction: the double nature of detective character necessary to solve crimes. The classical detective must be highly intuitive and creative as well as highly rational. Interestingly, Stefano Tani points out that the essential duality of the detective was also mirrored in the duality of the plot—simply stated, good versus evil. Therefore, the detective story as firmly established in Poe's models includes the dual nature of the detective as well as the detective/criminal split. "Duality is the basic principle of detection, since the sine qua non requirements of the detective story are a detective and a criminal" (Tani 4).

Sherlock Holmes carries these intense dual character traits to extremes. As a user of cocaine and a brooding melancholic violin player when not on a case or when baffled, Holmes represents a dramatic split personality. These personality characteristics are furthered by Holmes's love of costume and masquerade. He is able to alter his appearance and accent so as to infiltrate even the most closed society, such as a seamen's bar. This essential ingredient of disguise and masking in early detective fiction is later expropriated by black writers. Black detectives use their own blackness to mask their true identities as detectives, connecting the trope of double consciousness to the trickster tradition.

Because the detective novel has always been related to crime, some of its antecedents certainly lie in the rogue novel, the Newgate Calendar, and other literature such as the criminal confessional and police memoirs.[4] The detective novel has also been generally associated with the city. The London Bow Street Runners and nascent urban police forces were integral parts of early crime stories. Most critics consider François Eugène Vidocq's *Mémoires* of 1829 to be the best early material on the urban police force. Vidocq was a criminal before becoming a police detective in Paris. An apocryphal source has it that Wilkie Collins and Charles Dickens were rumored to have fought over a copy of his memoirs found in a used-book bin in London, Collins exclaiming that it contained enough plots for a lifetime of writing.

Between Poe and the period of the hardboiled school in America (1920s-30s) there were many important milestones in the development of the detective novel. Although there is some argument about the real "first" detective novel, the following books are considered forerunners in the field. In England there was Charles Dickens's *Bleak House* in 1853, and in France Emile Gaboriau's *L'Affaire Lerouge* published in 1866. Wilkie Collins's *Woman in White* was published in 1860, and his *Moonstone* appeared in 1868. In America two women were in the forefront of the development of the detective novel: Seeley Regester (Metta Victoria Fuller Victor) published *The Dead Letter* in 1864, and Anna Katherine Green published *The Leavenworth Case* in 1878, a book long thought to be the first American detective novel published by a woman.[5] The dime novels were quick to pick up on the detective novel, albeit in its most unoriginal form. These cheap paper publications were available on newsstands in the late 1800s. Typically, they were poorly written adventure and Western tales published on inferior yellow paper stock, with a stiff illustrated cover. Civil War soldiers on both sides carried, traded, and read and reread all varieties of these elementary mass publications. The Old Sleuth series began in 1885. Nick Carter was on the stands soon after. These and other series such as Doc Savage and the Shadow went through numerous editions and authors over the next fifty years.

In 1887 Arthur Conan Doyle's archetypical detective Sherlock Holmes made his first appearance in *A Study in Scarlet*. Doyle's detective stories emphasized Holmes's reasoning powers as well as his brilliant character analysis. His most obvious talent was his ability to determine a character's personal history and occupation through observation of apparently incidental clues. The first-person narration by Holmes's assistant Watson became a classic convention. Doyle also followed Poe's plotting example and developed the narrative around discovery of the crime and pursuit of the criminal. The bumbling police force became a stock foil to Holmes's analytical ability. Poe provided the primary example of this type of detective showmanship in his story "The Purloined Letter," where the police prefecture has to ask Dupin for his help and remains baffled throughout the case. As Gloria Biamonte points out in her dissertation "Detection and the Text: Reading Three American Women of Mystery," six typical elements make up the conventional plot as instigated by Poe and institutionalized by Doyle:

> 1) the crime occurs; 2) the investigator, often a bit eccentric, takes on the case; 3) the finger of suspicion points at several characters; 4) mystery and confusion abound; 5) the seemingly guilty are proven innocent; 6) the seemingly innocent are proven guilty; 7) the detective provides an explanation at the denouement clarifying what has happened and revealing how she/he has arrived at the discovery. (24)

After Doyle's tremendous popular success with Sherlock Holmes, whose very outfit (pipe, hat, and cloak) has become a detective icon, detective fiction waned for a considerable period of time. E. C. Bentley's *Trent's Last Case* (1913) resurrected the genre and is often considered the beginning of the modern classical detective story. This strong tradition was continued in England by Agatha Christie, Dorothy Sayers, and many others.

In the United States, the detective novel took a new turn. Dashiell Hammett, Carroll John Daly, and Raymond Chandler are generally credited with returning the detective form to American hands. They were published in the magazine *Black Mask,* which first appeared in 1920, and according to David Geherin, "Soon the pulps supplanted the dime novel as the most popular form of cheap, mass-produced reading entertainment for millions of Americans" (*Private Eye* 27). Although Dashiell Hammett and Raymond Chandler have received most of the critical attention as creators of the hardboiled school, critic Ron Goulart in *The Dime Detectives* (1988) argues that Daly, Raoul Whitfield, Frederick Nebel, and other pulp writers were equally responsible for this American variation. *Black Mask* was published by Henry L. Mencken and George Nathan. Its editor, Capt. Joseph T. Shaw, assumed the position in 1926 and is credited with encouraging and formalizing what is now called the hardboiled school of writing. "Hardboiled" is an adjective used from the beginning to describe writers who shared writing styles and a white male worldview. In general the writing was terse, direct, and violent, and the worldview reflected the sentiments of a white middle-aged man, who was shrewd but not formally educated, dedicated to his task, and extremely alienated in a threatening urban atmosphere. The hardboiled detectives shared a commonality of disillusionment with the police and government. They were fatalistic, violent, and chauvinistic toward women. These writers, as Philip Durham notes in his essay "The *Black Mask* School," had detective heroes who

> acted as rugged individualists while they brought justice to the deserving. . . . their violence was not merely that of sensationalism. It was rather a kind of meaningful violence, sometimes symbolic of a special ethical code or attitude, sometimes an explicit description and implicit criticism of a corrupt society. (51)

In the very beginning, the hardboiled school of writers set certain standards for this form of detective novel. The primary change from classical detective fiction occurred with the creation of a new type of detective. The classical detective was a person of the upper class, an amateur who spoke and acted with aristocratic grace. The hardboiled detective was a man of the streets, a professional who spoke and acted with American vernacular crudeness. In classical detection the stories were told either by a sidekick narrator or from the third-person point of view. The hardboiled school used direct first-person narration, which made the action much more dramatic, and the style became equal in importance to the plot. David Geherin writes:

> It is important to note that, with a few exceptions such as *The Maltese Falcon*, virtually every hard-boiled novel is narrated by the detective himself and narrated *after the fact*. Hence everything is filtered through his consciousness and sensibility. (*Sons of Sam Spade* 13–14)

Writers for *Black Mask,* in particular Daly, Hammett, and Chandler, set the pattern for much of American detective fiction after the 1920s. Raymond Chandler became a spokesman for the hardboiled detective worldview and created the romantic image of the hardboiled detective in his essay "The Simple Art of Murder" (1934): "But down these mean streets a man must go who himself is not mean, who is neither tarnished nor afraid. He is the hero; he is everything. He must be a complete man and a common man and yet an unusual man" (20).

With such important novels as Hammett's *Red Harvest* (1929) and *Maltese Falcon* (1930) and Chandler's *Big Sleep* (1939), a new way of writing enters the American literary scene. Kenneth Rexroth, as quoted by David Madden in his introduction to *Tough Guy Writers of the 30s,* has suggested: "The only significant fiction in America is popular fiction. It is from Chandler and Hammett and Hemingway that the best modern fiction derives" (xxiii). Madden adds:

> Of course, in an important sense, the best of the tough writers are not second-rate writers, but first-rate practitioners of a minor genre. Chandler suggests that if Hammett learned from Hemingway, perhaps Hemingway also learned from Hammett. (xxii)

The position of detective novelists in the literary canon is an issue that is as yet unresolved. According to Madden,

> Perhaps we ought to assess more fully the consequences of the fact that popular writers, perhaps more than writers whom critics admire, affect the nerve centers of mass experience and shape the attitudes and predispositions of the mass of men. (xxii)

The connection between detective fiction and popular beliefs becomes interesting when we examine how black writers used the form to reflect their concerns. The term "genre" is often used to describe detective fiction, the implication being that detective fiction shares certain characteristics. Genre is a useful term in that it does suggest a series of recognizable formulas that create the structure and meaning of the narrative. John Cawelti in *Adventure, Mystery, and Romance* bases much of his analysis on the patterns of repetition of formulas in popular forms: "The concept of a formula as I have defined it is a means of generalizing the characteristics of large groups of individual works from certain combinations of cultural materials and archetypal story patterns" (123). Tzvetan Todorov in his *Poetics of Prose* devotes a chapter to detective fiction in which he stresses the importance of genre to a structural analysis of what he recognizes as a cross-cultural popular literary form. As a genre it is based on what he terms "norms" or structural aspects similar to bound-and-free motifs, which Porter analyzes so effectively in *The Pursuit of Crime*. Todorov writes:

> Detective fiction has its norms; to "develop" them is also to disappoint them: to "improve upon" detective fiction is to write "literature," not detective fiction. The whodunit par excellence is not the one which transgresses the rules of the genre, but the one which conforms to them. (43)

Several critics recognize, then, the existence of what I call the paradigmatic gesture in detective fiction. The conditions of this paradigm are important to any discussion of detective fiction, and since we are dealing primarily with ways in which African Americans transformed the paradigm, it is worthwhile to note some of the major characteristics of the paradigmatic gestures that have given the form continuity as a genre.

The detective paradigm, for my purposes, breaks down into two large categories, classical and hardboiled. *Classical* refers to both European and American detective novels modeled on the Poe/Doyle formula, utilizing an amateur detective investigating a crime, and generally following a narrative structure based on the six elements listed by Biamonte. *Hardboiled* refers to an American school of detective writing that is typically a first-person narration involving a professional private detective investigating a murder on his or her own terms. Hardboiled detective writing lacked female detectives until the recent creations of Sara Paretsky (*Bitter Medicine*, 1987; and *Blood Shot* 1988) and Sue Grafton (*"F" is for Fugitive*, 1989; *"G" is for Gumshoe*, 1990). The relationship of female detectives to the hard-boiled tradition is an interesting one which has been analyzed quite effectively in the opening pages of Gloria Biamonte's chapter on Seeley Regester in her dissertation.

Although there are of course many deviations from these norms, my concern here is simply to sketch out some of the essential differences and similarities of these two camps without delving deeply into the nuances of either. The categories share a number of conventions developed through the progression of the genre. We find that detectives from both categories are solitary, secretive, eccentric, and supremely self-confident. Their behavior is idiosyncratic and often antisocial. They use drugs and/or alcohol frequently, manifest no overt sexual behavior, and often make amoral decisions. Classical and hardboiled novels also use similar conventions of plot, character, and scenic development. These include:

Analytical reasoning. The detective generally works a path of detection back from the effects of the crime to its solution. Along the way the detective is a close observer of *details*, which helps to define setting, character, and motive.

Narrative approach. Narration is usually from the viewpoint of a close associate or friend told in the first person or from the viewpoint of the detective told in the first person.

Conflict with official police. The detective is normally not part of the official police who, in fact, have difficulty with the crime or case. The detective often ridicules and argues with the official police.

Urban landscape. The detective primarily works in or comes from the city. The landscape of the city can often contribute important elements to the story in terms of mystery and motivation. (A significant exception is the rural character of much of English classical detective fiction as exemplified by Agatha Christie.)

Plot over character. The plot is the main structural device of the detective novel. Plot development is generally emphasized more than character analysis or character development, particularly in the classical form.

Worldview—individual over group. Although generally the detective restores moral order in solving the case, the detective character is mysterious in terms of personal history, religious values, and community orientation. Detectives are solitary figures in the romantic tradition of individual alienation from normal social values like marriage, religion, and community.

Although there are many creative interpretations of these norms, the essential attributes of the detective hero are the same down through the history of the form. It is not within the scope of this elementary survey to do justice to the variety of women detectives or to variations on the above themes in male detective novels. The primary split that concerns my analysis is, of course, the difference between the classical detective hero and the hardboiled detective hero. We will find that the black detective is a curious amalgam of the two. Therefore, it is interesting to compare some of the attributes of these two types in our initial survey of the form.

Classical	Hardboiled
Aristocratic/upper-class	Democratic/classless
Amateur detective	Paid professional/private eye
Plot emphasized	Narration/language/character emphasized
Deductive/rational	Inductive/instinctive
Observer detached	Observer involved
Scientific investigation/ psychology of behavior	Gut-reaction investigation/ coincidence
Urban/rural settings	Urban; rural setting rare
Murder as "clean" puzzle	Murder as "dirty" muddle
Perpetrator acts alone	Perpetrator acts as part of group or gang conspiracy
Physical violence minimal in description and act	Physical violence pervasive in description and act
Critique of society from above	Critique of society from below
Closure with restoration of moral order	Closure often morally ambiguous

The patterns that I have isolated concerning the detective persona are important because they were instrumental in first defining the form for the public *and for other authors*. Perhaps more than any

other popular culture genre, the detective novel is a shared and re-
vered literary set that is handed down from generation to generation.
In 1928 the popular American author S. S. Van Dine went so far as
to dictate a series of twenty rules to which the classical detective novel
must conform. For example, (1) the novel must have at most one
detective and one criminal, and at least one victim (a corpse); (2) the
culprit must not be a professional criminal, must not be the detective,
must kill for personal reasons; (3) love has no place in detective
fiction; (4) there is no place for descriptions or for psychological
analyses ("Twenty Rules" 189–93).

Of course, rules are made to be broken. This is particularly true
in the case of the detective novel because "formulas" thrive on the
challenges presented by the specifics of their conditions. What I have
outlined in general are the initial paradigmatic gestures of the detective form that by definition created the genre in the first place. Many
of these generalities still hold true in detective fiction. Others have
been altered dramatically by the tremendous variety and adaptability
of the form to specific agendas down through the years. Specifically,
female authors and female detectives have actively worked to displace
and enlarge many of the narrow parameters of white-male-oriented
detective fiction, as have postmodern experimenters with the form.
Detective fiction as a genre with recognizable conventions established
itself through time as a form that suggests certain expectations. Readers as well as scholars of detective fiction acknowledge the basic
paradigms every time they recognize a creative interpolation. That is
to say, like a chess match between two masters, detective authors
make moves that suggest other patterns that the reader expects. Good
detective fiction surprises and sometimes frustrates these expectations, thereby creating new moves that become part of the canon.
Most importantly, revisions can be acknowledged only as deviations
from the norm. Dennis Porter writes:

> In the language of the formalists, one important source of literary pleasure
> is in the artful deviation from the norm. In this respect, a detective novel is
> not less literary than a major work of highbrow culture but more so. No
> other genre is more conscious of the models from which it borrows and
> from which it knowingly departs. (54)

The norm, of course, has expanded as more and more subcategories
are added to the overall genre. The police procedural for instance,

appeared relatively late in the detective canon. According to George N. Dove in *The Police Procedural* (1982), Lawrence Treat's *V as in Victim* (1945) is the first authentic example.

The continuity and strength of detective fiction are directly related to popular culture, as evidenced by the pulp origins of the hardboiled school. The early stories by Dashiell Hammett and Raymond Chandler, recognized masters of the form, could be found only in the issues of *Black Mask* sold at newsstands. Detective fiction in the United States was, and to some degree remains, a vernacular art form. Vernacular in this sense means "belonging to, or developed in a particular place, region, or country; native, indigenous." The term also suggests the use of native language as opposed to literary language in describing the characteristics of a particular locality.

Detective fiction has proven itself to be a dynamic literary device for the implementation of cultural worldviews. Its continuous popularity supports this contention, as does the frequency of experimentation with the form. Even with constant elaboration, the detective "style" is recognized throughout the world by its characterizations, its use of language, and its iconic images—trenchcoat, hat, magnifying glass, etc. The myriad combinations of these fields of reference create the world of the detective. Out of this fantasy landscape derives a worldview that is commonly associated with the detective. The patterns of these conventions were effectively challenged by African American authors who altered the conventions for their own use, infusing the text with black tropes that led to the creation of an African American detective tradition.

2

The Tropes of Black Detection

Through constant applications, the formulas of classical and hardboiled detective fiction have created a tradition of detective writing. African Americans from the beginning have fearlessly altered these formulas in their own way and to their own ends. Specifically, black authors were interested in using detective fiction to present African American social and political viewpoints and worldviews. They signified on detective fiction through the four tropes we have listed earlier: alteration of detective persona, double-consciousness detection, black vernaculars, and hoodoo.

Many authors, such as Baker and Gates, use "vernacular" as an all-inclusive term covering a range of black expressive arts in the folk tradition. For example, Houston Baker in *Blues, Ideology, and Afro-American Literature* defines vernacular as "arts native or peculiar to a particular country or locale" and mentions that, interestingly, vernacular originally meant "a slave born on his master's estate" (3). Baker expands on both definitions to suggest the primary importance of vernacular to understanding the specificity of African American culture:

> In my study as a whole, I attempt persuasively to demonstrate that a blues matrix (as a vernacular trope for American cultural expression in general) possesses enormous force for the study of literature, criticism and culture. (Blues 14).

In his conclusion Baker challenges scholars to search further for other manifestations of vernacular: "The task of present-day scholars is to situate themselves inventively and daringly at the crossing sign in order to materialize vernacular faces" (202).

Consequently, I expand on the plural "vernaculars" to suggest the similarities and the *differences* between these folk arts. Obviously, the vernacular is a group made up of individual aspects of black folk culture. By calling them vernaculars I make each available for discussion. Thus I purposely make a distinction among the vernaculars of music, language use, hoodoo, and others because they share common roots in folk tradition but have expanded into distinct realms of their own. For example, hoodoo is more akin to a philosophical and sociopolitical worldview that demands a detailed examination, not just a cursory glance under the rubric "voodoo." Zora Neale Hurston confirms this approach when she writes in *The Sanctified Church* (1983):

> While the [African American] lives and moves in the midst of white civilization, everything that he touches is re-interpreted for his own use. He has modified the language, mode of food preparation, practice of medicine, and most certainly the religion of his new country. (58)

The detective novel is simply another example of this reinterpretation, as each of the four black detective tropes infuses the detective text with African American cultural expressions and value systems.

African American detective novels share much with other African American novels—in particular, a creative reuse of already established forms. Bell sees the African American novel as a: "hybrid narrative whose distinctive tradition and vitality are derived basically from the sedimented indigenous roots of black American folklore and literary genres of the Western world" (xii). African American novels are for Bell a "socially symbolic act . . . a rewriting of the survival strategies . . . especially the use of the vernacular, music and religion" (xii). As we shall see, the vernaculars of black culture will prove instrumental in defining the difference between detective and black detective texts. However, use of vernaculars is only part of this transformation. It is the interconnection between the four tropes that gives African American detective fiction its uniqueness. Consistent use of the four tropes indicates a comprehensive alteration of detective formulas by black writers leading to a black detective tradition.

Detective Persona

From the beginning black writers created their own versions of the detective persona. They relied, in part, on some of the accepted conventions from classical and hardboiled traditions, but more importantly they forged new images of the detective based on African American needs. First, they made the detectives—both male and female—black, and their blackness is an integral ingredient for the success of the investigation. Second, the blues detective's identity is directly connected to community. The detectives studied herein range from servants to intellectuals, but all of them are aware, and make the reader aware, of their place within the fabric of their black society.

In some of the texts studied, such as Major's *Reflex and Bone Structure,* the blues detective is an elusive character. The trail he leaves is thin, and the clues to his identity confound expectations. His motives, on the surface, remain unclear. In other texts, such as Himes's Harlem series, the detective is brash and violent in the manner of the hardboiled detective. However, in the long tradition of the detective, stretching back to Poe's Dupin, there is no detective protagonist as collectively complex as the blues detective. This is due in part to the cultural heritage of their own complicated personalities and to the varieties of black vernaculars represented in the text. Both the classical and the hardboiled detective manifested certain recurring conventions of the detective persona. Primarily, the detective by name suggests relentless pursuit of the truth, usually in relation to a murder and discovery and conviction of the perpetrator of the crime. This distinction holds whether the detective is a brilliant amateur or a hardworking professional, aristocratic or classless, continental or American. The persona of the detective may be whimsical, detached, aloof, and insulting, or it may be industrious, sad, violent, and brutal; in any case, it is always obsessed with figuring out the puzzle of human behavior in relation to a crime. However, in both classical and hardboiled, the general pattern of the detective's own life, beliefs, and personal attachments is sketchy to nonexistent. The detective's personal life is somewhat relevant to the quest, but his or her notion of cultural community is subjective and idiosyncratic. When we consider how the detective is presented in the texts, it is not such a long way from 221B Baker Street in London to a third-floor walkup office in Los Angeles. Both cityscapes, although culturally dissimilar, are essentially lonely outposts for the alienated romantic detective. Classical and hardboiled detectives are dedicated to determining life on their own terms. Like priests of a new religion, detectives outline the dogma of participation in their world through highly subjective qualifications. The detective's world is defined through the detective's eyes, or the eyes of an acolyte—the Watson-like observer. The only really distinct personal attribute that most detectives share is doggedness in pursuit of a solution that doesn't leave much room for casual concerns, romantic infatuation, or personal history. Thus we have the "No-Name" detective created by Bill Pronzini, the ultimate in glass-wall characterization, who is predicated by Hammett's nameless Continental Op and Chandler's nameless prototype for Marlowe (although in one short story, "Try the Girl," the detective was named Carmady). The irony of this type of persona is that it creates rather than prevents reader identification. The character of the detective becomes essentially an overriding rationality surrounded by the icons of the detective world. The detective has no personal past, only the personal present—hence, the often offered criticism of "cardboard" characterization.

This essential detective persona is what Todorov and Vladimir Propp (in his *Morphology of the Folktale*) would call "bound" motifs, or motifs that remain constant through numerous works. Whereas the bound motifs in folktales, such as the heroic sword slayer, evolved out of the mists of time into archetypal figures, the conventions of the detective persona were created quite recently as part of the structural poetics of the form. Some of the primary purposes of this poetic are easy identification in terms of character, simplified access to plot, and serial repetitions. Complicated characterizations take away from the structural primacy of detective fiction. Consequently, simplified characterization is attractive because readers can fill the void imaginatively. The detective acts as a lighthouse for the reader, providing direction through the maze of red herrings and false clues in most detective novels. By remaining uncomplicated, the detective persona becomes a structural tool. This is a device that is used repeatedly in detective novels. The personas of the classical detectives Sherlock Holmes and Hercule Poirot have been duplicated in an almost endless series of novels. The hardboiled tradition also has its formulas, which are based on a subjective rationality in the face of overwhelming odds. The hardboiled detective is a paid professional who invariably gets more involved personally in the case than the classical detective. Through the use of highly developed observational skills, courage, curiosity, and, in many cases, violence, the hardboiled detective inhabits a recognizable world handed down from author to author. Furthermore, both classical and hardboiled detective personas are accentuated by the familiar icons of the trade, including such items as the magnifying glass, the pipe, the trenchcoat, slouch hat, cigarette, and bottle of whiskey in the top desk drawer. *Difference*

The blues detective is not so easy to label because, to a large degree, African American writers ignore standard, repeated personification. Black authors opted from the beginning to create nonstandard detectives who appear in stories written in the third person. In contrast to the standard detective persona, the black detective shares a sense of *Chandler* community and family that doesn't exist in the mainstream detective tradition. Black detectives are intimately connected to their surroundings, often involved in family relations, certainly deeply committed to exploring the meaning of blackness in the text and, in some cases, the nature of the text itself.

The blues detectives, like other standard detective types, use both ratiocination and violence to solve or, in some instances, further befuddle cases. What makes them different is that they apply African American consciousness in solving their cases. These detectives are complex, multitalented, and possessed of a social consciousness, even in the most extreme case of hardboiled characters like Himes's Coffin Ed Johnson and Grave Digger Jones. The blues detective first and foremost always delineates the color line as primary in any case or social relation. In this way a special environment is created within black detective novels that is often based on an exclusive set of priorities dealing with a community with its own cultural values. The blues detective creates a different set of priorities than either the classical or the hardboiled detective. Rather than focusing simply on the crime and capture of the suspect, blues detectives are interested in the social and political atmosphere, often to the exclusion of detection. This social and political atmosphere is inscribed by racial prejudice. The *Chandler* blues detective recognizes his or her own blackness as well as what blackness means to the characters in the text. The blues detective knows what it means to be an African American or, in the case of J. E. Bruce's *Black Sleuth*, learns what it means to become one. As in the traditional pattern of detection, there is often obfuscation as well as illumination in the process of discovery. However, the blues detective is a new creation in the detective literary landscape representing a complexity of African American cultural signs.

Pauline Hopkins and J. E. Bruce bring new personifications to the detective in the earliest stages of black detective writing. Their detectives, one a female and the other a male, function as part of a group detective identity in which their blackness becomes a specific factor in successful detection. Their connection with group activity and with the surrounding community suggests a different approach to the black detective persona at the very beginning of the tradition. Furthermore, the black detective in these texts is always conscious of racism and social injustice, and large sections of the text are devoted to exploring these issues.

This difference continues as we progress to Rudolph Fisher, who creates a text that shatters the traditional notion of the detective as all-powerful. Detective Dart of the Harlem homicide squad must *combine* his persona with that of Archer the physician to solve the case. In fact, the detectives in Fisher's *Conjure Man Dies* are multivoiced in that they actually break down into four characters, including the murdered man himself, who solves the mystery of his own murder.

Coffin Ed Johnson and Grave Digger Jones of Chester Himes's Harlem detective series are generally backgrounded to a plot of absurdist dimensions. Throughout the nine novels in which they appear their characterizations change. In the early novels they rule Harlem with an iron fist. From their signifyin(g) asides we know they have a well-developed sense of the injustices suffered by black people. But as they move from book to book their detective personas become more complicated. Despair, fatalism, and anger begin to take their toll, until in the last novels their viewpoint is essentially only as valid as that of any of the other characters. Consequently, we can trace a tragic disintegration in their ability to detect. Their connection to the community becomes more strained and more alienated as we progress to the end of the Harlem series. Finally, in the last novel, *Plan B,* the two detectives are set against each other, with fatal consequences.

The black detective PaPa LaBas in Ishmael Reed's *Mumbo Jumbo* appears and disappears in a text built of multiple mysteries that is itself in a continuous state of transformation. Detective LaBas represents a further development of African American consciousness in the black detective novel. LaBas's abilities are augmented by a spiritual connection and a revisionary interpretation of history leading to an enlarged African American consciousness. In Clarence Major's *Reflex and Bone Structure* the detective mingles with the narrator, eluding definition in this bewildering anti-detective, metafictional world. The experimentation in this novel forces a reexamination of accepted narrative conventions, deconstructs detective narrative and persona, and transfers much of the detective's work to the reader. A closer analysis of all these detective personas will show that they have much in common, sharing in part the black detective tradition of using their blackness to solve cases, working in groups with relation to community, and expressing a consistent African American worldview.

Double-Consciousness Detection

The use of double-conscious tropes in detective fiction is another area in which African American creativity has altered the traditional detective conventions. I see the use of double consciousness in black detective fiction in three areas: association of the trickster figure with the black detective and later with the very act of writing itself; the doubling aspects of masks, mistaken identities, and disguises revised by black consciousness; and amplification of the usual plot machinations of detective fiction by black themes. At times, for the sake of simplicity, I categorize the double-conscious trope as the "masking" trope.

Double consciousness as defined by W. E. B. Du Bois in *The Souls of Black Folk* (1903) recognizes a dynamic interaction between blacks and the world around them.

> [T]he Negro is a sort of seventh son, born with a veil, and gifted with second-sight in this American world,—a world which yields him no true self-consciousness, but only lets him see himself through the revelation of the other world. It is a peculiar sensation, this sense of always looking at one's self through the eyes of others, of measuring one's soul by the tape of a world that looks on in amused contempt and pity. One ever feels his twoness,—an American, a Negro; two souls, two thoughts, two unreconciled strivings; two warring ideals in one dark body, whose dogged strength alone keeps it from being torn asunder. (215)

Du Bois suggests that the nature of American racism, both de facto and de jure, forces black Americans to see the world filtered through two levels of consciousness. First and foremost, they are forced to see themselves as second-class citizens by reason of their African ancestry, both biological and cultural. Then and only then are they allowed the privilege of seeing themselves as American citizens. This double

consciousness comes into play consistently in white/black relationships. Specifically, it suggests that blacks share a sociopolitical consciousness or worldview that carries forth into their cultural
creations.

Though double consciousness in the pure Du Boisan sense suggests
a fractured worldview for black Americans, other critics such as Bell
have recognized a different aspect of the problem. Citing research in
anthropology, folklore, musicology, and linguistics among others,
Bell believes that "the conflicts between black culture and white society have resulted in creative as well as destructive tensions in black
people and their communities" (9). Bell is also convinced that this
double consciousness, when applied to literary texts, results in new
developments in the American novel.

> The uniqueness of the Afro-American novel, in short, derives from both
> the double-consciousness of its sociocultural and sociopsychological con-
> tent and the double vision immanent in the pattern of oral and literary
> conventions of Afro-American and Euro-American sign systems that struc-
> ture that content. (79)

Nathan Huggins in his book *Harlem Renaissance* (1971) continues
this line of argument when he recognizes another aspect of double
consciousness and its effect on African Americans:

> [T]his double consciousness opens to the Negro—through his own quest
> and passion—a unique insight into the vulnerable and unfulfilled soul of
> that other world; a possibility which once grasped, liberates one forever
> from the snarls of that other world's measuring tape. (244)

Similarly, I posit a positive creativity in my analysis of double consciousness in relation to black detective fiction. My emphasis here is
on the seventh son and the veil, two folk signs that signify a special
creation, a person with extraordinary powers. Whereas some critics,
such as Du Bois and Robert Stepto, see the veil as a negative force to
be overcome, I suggest the veil can be interpreted as a positive sign.
The veil or caul covering the newborn's face has long been considered
a powerful sign of a spiritual gift in black folk mythologies.

The use of masks, disguises, mistaken identities, and false identities
has been a staple of detective fiction from the very origin of the form.
The identity of the murderer in "The Murders in the Rue Morgue" is
a primary example of misidentification, given that all the witnesses

assume from different clues that the killer is human when it is not. Sherlock Holmes often assumed a disguise in solving his cases. There is, in fact, an almost endless list of masked and hidden detectives in the short history of the detective form. Finally, the very machine that makes detective fiction run is based on the mysterious identity of an unknown murderer, who usually is someone known to the reader but uncovered in his/her real identity only at the end of the novel. While this concept of duplicity is well known to detective fiction, black detective fiction carries it one step further through the application of double consciousness to the text. The masking aspect of detective fiction commonly had a classic function, as Hazel Carby points out in relation to Hopkins's *Hagar's Daughter*.

> Conventional use of disguise and double identities indicated a disruption of the natural order of events, whereas the revelations and resolutions of popular fiction signaled the reestablishment of order in the moral and social fabric of the characters' lives. (151)

We will see, however, that this masking aspect in black detective fiction takes on new meaning when appended to the perspective of double consciousness.

One way this is done is through emphasizing the trickster qualities of the detective character in our texts. Gates talks extensively about the transformation of the African trickster god Esu-Elegbara into African American forms in the first chapter of his book *The Signifying Monkey*. Esu-Elegbara is a mutable figure, both male and female, who possesses an almost endless list of characteristics: "satire, parody, irony, magic, . . . chance, uncertainty, disruption and reconciliation" (6). In fact, Gates sees Esu as the complex "classic figure of mediation and of the unity of opposed forces" (6). Gates recognizes Hermes, "messenger and interpreter for the gods" (8), as Esu's closest analogue in Western mythologies. By extension Gates sees a connection between Esu and the role of critic: "The various figures of Esu provide endless, fascinating references to the critic's role in interpretation and to the nature of interpretation itself" (29). Through the application of double consciousness to the detective persona, I further extend the connection between the trickster trope and black detection. All of the detectives in this study are black, and all of them are double-consciously aware of their blackness in relation to white society. By using the trickster qualities of masking, they make their detection work and in the process outwit their enemies in trickster fashion. Double consciousness in this sense gives black detectives a better understanding of the white and black criminal mind.

Houston Baker in *Modernism and the Harlem Renaissance* (1987) articulates some of the complexity of double-consciousness awareness when he discusses aspects of masks and renaming in relation to modernism and minstrelsy in America. Baker recognizes within the minstrel tradition an awareness of double-conscious trickster mentality so masterfully represented in Paul Laurence Dunbar's poem "We Wear the Mask": "And it is first and foremost, the mastery of the minstrel mask by blacks that constitutes a primary move in Afro-American discursive modernism" (*Modernism* 17). Working against the traditional notion of what he calls "minstrelsy's nonsensical stereotypes" (27), Baker stresses the double-conscious trickster qualities of this representational masking figure when he talks about "liberating manipulation of masks and a revolutionary *renaming*" in relation to "minstrelsy" acts by black leaders (25). Baker emphasizes the trickster qualities in African American writing at the turn of the century and in the Harlem Renaissance. Dunbar's poem, he says, "justifies the invocation of 'the mask' as an appropriate trope for turn-of-the-century Afro-American discourse" (39). Nathan Huggins tells us that "Negroes, accepting the pretense, wore the mask to move in and out of the white world with safety and profit" (261).

Speaking of the minstrel figure, Huggins perceives a sense of liberation and control coming from the masking tradition: "Thus, he becomes superior because his perspective allows him to judge himself and his people and because his pose places him above even those who had disdain for him to begin with" (259). By using what I term double-conscious techniques, black detectives can speak beyond the limits of their perceived position as female or male minstrels—that is, as detectives who are seen as inefficient in their assumed roles. For example, both the detectives in the first two black detective novels hide behind the mask and minstrelsy of the Negro servant. Himes's two detectives are seen by their chief officers as black strong-armers limited to the task of suppressing crime in the Harlem community. From behind this limiting mask, they take the opportunity to signify on Anderson, their white superior. Finally, the direct connection between double consciousness and the black detective texts can be seen in the ways that the text is constructed. African American detective writers are concerned with African American themes. Consequently, their double-conscious viewpoint colors the text, as the mishaps and coincidences of the typical detective text function not only for narrative movement and reader excitement but also to make an African American point. Thus the mistaken identities, the murders, and the kidnappings common to detective fiction are used to reveal hidden meanings. We shall see how this applies in the very first African American detective novel when masking becomes unmistakably associated with passing. My expanded notion of double consciousness in relation to the masking of detective fiction suggests the shaping of a worldview shared by black Americans that triumphs over prejudice. Bernard Bell emphasizes this triumph when he suggests that double consciousness is not psychotic or schizophrenic but a "healthful rather than a pathological adjustment by blacks to the New World" (6).

Much of African American creativity and reinterpretation, as Hurston puts it, is a positive outcome of double-conscious perceptions. Double-conscious perceptions applied to the detective novel confirm the ability of black Americans to reinterpret and revise existing Euro-American forms with heightened consciousness.

Vernaculars

Black vernaculars in detective fiction are major factors in differentiating black detective texts from other detective texts. By black vernaculars I mean specific expressive arts of black Americans that form part of their culture and are derived from the folk tradition. The vernaculars most common to detective fiction are music/dance, black language, and black cuisine. Ralph Ellison in *Shadow and Act* is one of the first modern black writers to recognize black cuisine as a distinctive African American creation, and Robert Elliot Fox in *Conscientious Sorcerers* makes note of "a proposal of Arthur Schomburg's to examine the 'ceremonial, symbolic, and African elements in black cooking' as one important index of the depth and significance of black culture" (88). Each of these vernaculars is a category of expression used to lesser or greater degree in each novel studied. References to music/dance, language, and food are laced into the detective text, forming what I call a *blackground*. This blackground is specific to black detective texts and is composed of all the aspects of African

American culture that help to define its uniqueness. For example, Chester Himes embroiders his descriptions of Harlem with black vernaculars such as blues and jazz, language use, food, and dance. Himes's description of the cityscape and portraits of characters from the streets typically command more attention than the crimes that motivated the plot. Vernaculars in this sense create their own subtext and extend the notion of the black detective tradition as they are repeated from novel to novel.

Zora Neale Hurston, one of the pioneers of the anthropological approach to black arts and black life, recognized the importance of black vernaculars. As Gates has mentioned in his afterword to Hurston's *Tell My Horse,* a collection of essays on voodoo practice in Haiti, "Hurston's ideas about language and craft undergird many of the most successful contributions to African-American literature that followed" (295). Hurston's fiction shows us how black vernaculars such as language, music, and dance express the uniqueness of black culture. She demonstrated how the repeated use of these African American creations forms what Gates calls "The traditional recurring canonical metaphors of black culture" (295).

Black detective authors use vernaculars to stress the importance of black culture in their texts. If detective fiction as a whole can be seen as a vernacular creation in the sense of its popular culture status, then African American authors transform vernacular fiction with the use of black vernaculars. For example, in black detective texts we find a repetitive use of blues and jazz references. The use of this black vernacular in literary works is not unique to detective texts. Houston Baker has made much of the blues in his examination of various texts in *Blues, Ideology, and Afro-American Literature.* In fact, for Baker, blues is the representative vernacular for all the special qualities of African American creations. His "guiding presupposition," he says, "is that Afro-American culture is a complex, reflexive enterprise which finds its proper figuration in blues conceived as a matrix" (3). Thus blues becomes a sign for Baker of the uniqueness and *particular* creativity of all African American peoples. Baker is not alone in recognizing blues as a primary creation in the African American repertoire of vernacular creations; for example, the works of Albert Murray, in both fiction and nonfiction, stress the importance of blues music to African American culture. The black detective tradition simply substantiates the blues tradition as an important vernacular trait.

The particularities of black language use are another vernacular trait that is extremely important to the black detective tradition. As Gates points out in *The Signifying Monkey* in relation to black texts,

> black formal repetition always repeats with a difference, a black difference that manifests itself in specific language use. And the repository that contains the language that is the source—and the reflection—of black difference is the black English vernacular tradition. (xxiii)

Whereas Baker elevates the blues and has it stand in for all black vernaculars, Gates elevates signifying as a metaphor for all black language skills. "I wish to argue that Signifyin(g) is the black trope of tropes, the figure for black rhetorical figures" (51). His list of language creations subsumed under signifying includes "marking, loud-talking, testifying, calling out (of one's name), sounding, rapping, playing the dozens, and so on" (52). Signifying can also be expressed through eye and hand motions. Signifying is a complex cultural act that carries a multitude of meanings, not all of which can be gone into in this study.[1] Suffice it to say that characters in black detective texts speak in specifically African American ways, using language traditions like signifying.

However, it must be noted, as Geneva Smitherman points out in *Talking and Testifying: The Language of Black America* (1986), that "Black Dialect consists of both language and style" (16). Some aspects of style, which Smitherman defines as "what you do with words" (16), are impossible to represent by the printed word alone. For example, tone is very important to black speech, carried over as it is from African tonal languages, but implied tone is next to impossible to differentiate in printed dialogue. Nonetheless, it is important to stress that black English (also called black dialect, black idiom, and ebonics) is a definitive cultural attribute used by black writers to help differentiate their detective texts from other detective texts. "Black Dialect," Smitherman writes, "is an Africanized form of English reflecting Black America's linguistic-cultural African heritage and the conditions of servitude, oppression and life·in America" (2). It cannot be looked at as simply as a corrupted version of standard English. As Smitherman indicates, "Black language is Euro-American speech with an Afro-American meaning, nuance, tone and gesture" (2). As such it has its own rules and regulations, many of them based on retentions from African languages. "Black English's main structural components are, of course, the adaptations based on African language rules" (9). An example of this is the use of the "zero copula" in black English, indicating syntactical patterns that have no form of the verb "to be." Black language use is further complicated by the way in which the grammatical components are incorporated into everyday speech patterns. Smitherman isolates four ways in which black language breaks down modes of discourse: "We may classify black modes of discourse into the following broad categories: call-response; signification (dozens); tonal semantics; narrative sequencing" (103). Representative examples of all these aspects of black language use are impossible for this study. I implement a few examples to suggest more extensive black language use in these detective texts.

There is another aspect of language use in detective fiction that must be considered: the contrast between language use in American hardboiled fiction and in black detective fiction. The distinct, direct style of hardboiled writing originated in pulp publications like *Black Mask* in the early 1920s, but its influence altered the face of detective fiction. In Chapter 3 I explore the contribution of magazine fiction to the detective tradition. Here I want to emphasize that the style of language used in the hardboiled school of writing differs from black detective fiction. The hardboiled school, as exemplified by Hammett and Chandler, has in itself become a type of detective formula. Critics have made much of what is commonly called the "objective" writing style of the hardboiled school. The pared-down prose of the hardboiled writer with its emphasis on understatement, physical description, and violence became a recognized convention. Although Hammett is generally credited with creating this "objective" style, acknowledgment must be given to others such as Carroll John Daly who developed its predominant characteristics. Whereas there are obvious connections between realism and the hardboiled detective novel, particularly in the later stages of the police procedural, the detective genre as a whole is more representative of a particular type of heroic fantasy than realism.[2] Primarily, detective fiction of the hardboiled school gives the illusion of realism while quite consciously constructing a romantic fantasy in which the detective possesses magical qualities of recuperation, insight, and stamina. Chandler, perhaps the greatest hardboiled stylist of all, was aware of this from the very beginning. F. R. Jameson in his article "On Raymond Chandler" writes that "In Chandler the presentation of social reality is involved immediately and directly with the problem of language. He thought of himself primarily as a stylist" (134). Initially, it was Dashiell Hammett who knowingly adapted the crude, escapist elements of detective fiction to more eloquent ends. The terse, colloquial approach of Hammett's first-person narrators set a standard for the craft. It was Chandler, however, who developed in Marlowe the sine qua non of the private investigator. Rick Lott in his article "A Matter of Style: Chandler's Hardboiled Disguise" writes: "The cynical, witty, ironical mind of Marlowe permeates the prose of Chandler, and is largely responsible for the distinctive quality of his style" (68). Thus the language with which the text is written becomes itself an integral ingredient of hardboiled fiction. Scott R. Christianson makes the important point that it is through language that "the best writers of this genre convey their complex sensibilities and attitudes towards modern experience, assert their and their protagonists' autonomy, and exercise language as power" (151).

African American writers diverge from this hardboiled tradition by writing in the third person rather than the first and by forgoing the typical hardboiled language patterns. The commanding white male prototype of Spade or Marlowe becomes ludicrous in black detective novels. For example, Chester Himes finds Coffin Ed Johnson's and Grave Digger Jones's immediate supervisor Lieutenant Anderson, who is modeled after the hardboiled hero, increasingly bizarre, corrupt, and anything but heroic. Even Himes's detective duo, who manifest some hardboiled attributes, begin to behave and sound like parodies of the form in the later novels. This hardboiled critique by Himes reaches vicious proportions in his portrayal of the New York detective Matt Walker in *Run, Man Run*. In Ishmael Reed's *Mumbo Jumbo* the "shadow sleuths" of "detective films" play an insidious background role as Reed weaves the language legacy of detective fiction into a parodic tapestry of critical attacks on the white detective model associated with hardboiled fiction. One example is Biff Musclewhite's demotion from police commissioner to curator of the Art Detention Center.

It is probably the inclusion of black language systems in the text that most noticeably differentiates black detective fiction from other detective fiction. For example, writers like Rudolph Fisher and Ishmael Reed interject African American wordplay into their narratives on a regular basis. These black word games help refocus attention on the contributions of the black language vernacular to black culture. As we move through the novels studied in this work, we can see a steady accumulation of black language acts, culminating in Reed's *Mumbo Jumbo*. Clarence Major then deconstructs this progressive history of language use back to its basic elements.

Hoodoo

The fourth and final major trope of black detection is the presence in the novels of hoodoo practice and hoodoo tradition. Hoodoo is a major trope of black detective novels because it delineates another distinctive way in which African Americans used the detective genre. Though hoodoo is primarily a folk tradition that is discredited by most of the white and *black* middle class and many educated Americans, it functions as an important aspect of the black vernacular tradition. I use the term "hoodoo" (as *voodoo* is commonly referred to in the United States) to represent indigenous, syncretic religions of African Americans in the New World, expanding the term to suggest that it also represents alternative worldviews of some black Americans.

To understand fully hoodoo's place in the black detective novel it is necessary to discuss some of the moral beliefs inherent in the Euro-American detective novel. Detective fiction, as we have seen, has always been associated with crime and murder. The murder in most classical detective fiction is neat, solitary, and confined to the upper classes. Hammett, as Chandler has said in "The Simple Art of Murder," put murder back into the alley. Crime and murder, in fact, reach epidemic proportions in hardboiled fiction. However, it was the hardboiled school that began to equate crime with corruption as a deeper social disease. George Grella in "The Hardboiled Detective Novel" writes "From the Op. through Archer, the detective's moral code develops from the simple notion of professionalism to the complex realization of human needs" (109). In fact, more than one critic has remarked on the corrupt ruling class at the heart of most hardboiled detective novels. More often than not, the original crime is found to have been spawned in a complicated web of internecine feuding among warring factions of a city's elite, including the local police force. Although Dennis Porter suggests that the mystery novel has from the beginning dealt with a "spreading stain," readers of *Red Harvest* and *The Big Sleep* are overwhelmed with corruption pervasive in all levels of society. The detective becomes a moral barometer surrounded by immoral characters that he must either kill or imprison. Even then, unlike the classical tradition, the hardboiled detective can be himself tainted—like the Op, who starts to enjoy his killing spree, or Sam Spade, who is morally ambiguous at best.

Stephen Knight in *Form and Ideology in Crime Fiction* (1980) deals specifically with the way the structural form of each author's detective work projects a certain ideology, whether conscious or not:

> This basic idea is embedded in the textual language, the presentation of incidents, characters and motives, and also in the overall structure. The text may not be simple or single in its meaning: it may well contain a conflict of world-view, which realizes perceived conflict in the world but which is artificially and consolingly resolved by the plotting and structure of the novel. (5)

It is just such a complacent and artificial worldview that African American detective fiction sets out to debunk. For example, Knight accurately pinpoints Marlowe's worldview as being particularly privileged and removed from African American consciousness:

> The elitism of the position proclaims itself; it basically resides in intellectual and emotional superiority, but the blank uninterest in poor and black citizens and the distrust of the rich indicate a strong underlying political attitude, that of the educated middle-class. (163)

Black detective fiction differs most dramatically from mainstream white detective fiction in the area of worldview, as exemplified in the religious and sociophilosophical beliefs of the characters. Mosley

One of the primary ways in which worldview is communicated in the detective text is through the use of hoodoo. Hoodoo as practiced by black Americans is a vernacular tradition in its own right. Evidence of its existence since the first blacks were brought to the New World is indisputable and has long been recognized. What has been neglected is the significance of hoodoo to black cultural identity and survival. The many references to hoodoo in black detective fiction attempt to address this neglect. The same important themes of empowerment and declaration of selfhood seen in the music and language vernaculars are inherent in hoodoo: Though the use of hoodoo by blacks in America has typically been maligned and categorized by members of the educated middle class as ignorant folk practice at best, it is an important aspect of African American cultural development expressed in oral as well as literary terms. Hoodoo is a folk tradition that complements other black American oral/performance arts such as tales, songs, and dances and helps to give expression to African American culture and self-awareness. As Lawrence Levine has noted in *Black Culture and Black Consciousness* (1977),

> Afro-American slaves following the practices of the African cultures they had been forced to leave behind them, assigned a central role to the spoken arts, . . . and utilized [them] to voice criticisms as well as to unfold traditional values and group cohesion. (6)

A reassessment of the importance of hoodoo to black cultural identity is now necessary in light of recent critical awareness of the variety and scope of African American cultural systems. Houston Baker and Henry Louis Gates have contributed greatly to this awareness by showing that multicultural African American creations are deeply rooted in the vernacular traditions of black Americans. Working in what Baker likes to call the Anthropology of Art, other critics such as John Roberts in *From Trickster to Badman: The Black Folk Hero in Slavery and Freedom* (1989) and Daryl Cumber Dance in *Shuckin' and Jivin': Folklore from Contemporary Black Americans* (1978) have illustrated the uniqueness and longevity of African American oral folk systems. The variety, meaning, and use of hoodoo practices make up an enormous area of folklore study. Hoodoo encompasses important oral traditions, religious practices, and performance spectacles that are integral aspects of black cultural identity. For example, Hurston's "Hoodoo in America," published in the *Journal of American Folklore* in 1931, outlines hoodoo practices passed down to individuals around New Orleans. From early on, these hoodoo principles and practices were instrumental in establishing community values among black members of the southern rural populace.

The term "voodoo" is generally recognized as a word of African origin derived from the Dahomean and Togo *vodou* or *vodoun*. Haiti proved to be voodoo's New World birthplace, and around 1724 many thousands of slaves were sold from Haiti to plantations around New Orleans. Hoodoo practice in the New World is an immensely diverse subject. As Hurston notes in *Tell My Horse,*

This work does not pretend to give a full account of either Voodoo or Voodoo gods. It would require several volumes to attempt to cover completely the gods and Voodoo practices of one vicinity alone. Voodoo in Haiti has gathered about itself more detail of gods and rites than the Catholic Church has in Rome. (131)

Hoodoo has been called "savage," "barbarous," and "frightful" by reporters in various magazine and newspaper articles from the late nineteenth and early twentieth centuries to the present. In 1926 Newbell Puckett defined voodoo as witchcraft, "a kind of perverted religion" (176). W. D. Weatherford in *Negro Life in the South* (1969) calls it a "murderous superstition" (124). This emphasis on superstition, witchcraft, and fetishism has diminished important worldview philosophies represented by hoodoo.

John W. Roberts, a professor of folklore at the University of Pennsylvania, in a chapter of *From Trickster to Badman* entitled "The Power Within: The Conjurer as Folk Hero," analyzes the affirmative cultural values of hoodoo. The retentive philosophical and religious constructs of African Americans are integral to Roberts's thesis. He writes: "In many ways, African enslavement created the need for rewriting the cultural policies that they already possessed, not wholesale reinvestment in the limited 'coverage' offered by Europeans" (11). Roberts suggests that black culture building in America "represents an extension of African culture-building and not European as it has so often been conceptualized" (4). He is particularly insightful concerning the relationship between the hoodoo tradition in the United States and ancient African religions. "Undoubtedly influenced by the presence of religious experts, from all available evidence, Africans enslaved in America attempted to reconstitute their religious institutions in America" (69), and these reconstituted religions often appeared as conjuration, obeah, and voodoo. Roberts makes reference to many African cultures, including parts of West Africa and the tribes of Trobriand, Zande, and Yoruba. He comments on the fact that a relatively minor number of slaves in the United States were of the Islamic religion, and he makes little reference to African Christian religions (105). In making this connection between various tribal religious beliefs and New World hoodoo, Roberts substantiates many other critics who recognize the source of hoodoo in African religions. For example, Joseph M. Murphy in *Working the Spirit: Ceremonies of the African Diaspora* (1994) discusses vodou, candomblé, santeria,

Revival Zion, and the Black Church as five important traditions of the African diaspora that share African, European, Native American, and other sources. Yet each one of these New World black religions is "like one another in that all recognize the special priority of their African roots" (1).

Roberts argues that hoodoo is in effect a New World transformation composed of religious elements from many African sources with their certain common denominators. While other folklorists and critics have focused on hoodoo ceremonial arts and the use of totems and fetishes, Roberts rightly recognizes the web of intercontinuity in hoodoo as being composed of important philosophical worldviews shared by African Americans. Some important constructs of this socioreligious world view are recognition of a higher power or "life force"; belief in ancestralism; belief in divination or prophecy; belief in animism; belief in a hierarchical chain of existence centered on the human being; and belief in the importance of full ontological being to happiness. Ontological being for the African, according to Roberts, depended on a harmonious connection among human beings, the natural world, and the higher plane of spiritual awareness. Human society was a microcosm of universal order, and as such, for Africans, "the cultural emphasis on harmony, cooperation, and solidarity was influenced directly and continuously by their religious worldview" (76).

A simple equation between conjure or hoodoo and witchcraft is fallacious, and the distinction must be made clear. The term "witchdoctor" is thus a misnomer when we consider that what are commonly referred to as witchcraft practices were not the only province of true African religious specialists, the term Roberts uses to include priests, conjurers, and others concerned with gods and spirits and the moral direction of their community. Roberts writes:

> To appreciate the function and meaning of the lore of conjuration to enslaved Africans and, more precisely, the conjurer as a folk hero in black culture, we must recognize that the role of religious specialists in African religious practice and worldview was not peripheral but central, especially as it related to the practice of magic. (70)

Because of this emphasis and the retention of socioreligious ideas in some areas of black America, hoodoo created new cultural heroes among many African Americans. Since whites refused to allow slaves their own freedom of religion, much of the original nature of their religious beliefs was transformed into hoodoo, among other new religions.

Hoodoo as a term represents for me an alternative to traditional Euro-American religions. Consequently, it stands for more than witchcraft to the authors of black detective fiction. Certainly, in the eyes of sensationalist outsiders, the witchcraft element in the Americas has subsumed the more priestly African function and preoccupied the press. But Fisher and Reed recognize, in what Reed calls Neo-HooDoo aesthetics, the importance of hoodoo in creating cohesive autonomous groups among black Americans as well as restoring pride in their origins. Reed gives a partial definition of hoodoo in his book *Shrovetide in Old New Orleans:* "In the Americas, it has come to mean the fusion of dance, drums, embroidery, herbal medicine, and cuisine of many African nations whose people were brought to Haiti during the slave trade" (9). Hoodoo is a residual African American syncretistic religion, borrowing freely from the Catholic catalogue of saints and substituting voodoo *loas* or gods. However, it would be a mistake to consider it a species of corrupted Christianity because hoodoo most commonly coexists with Christianity in a somewhat uneasy equilibrium.

The most important aspect of hoodoo, which has generally been ignored, is the pervasive influence of its combined beliefs in creating an alternate belief system. Roberts argues convincingly that black slaves in the United States worked against attempts by slaveholders to strip them of identities.

> The enslavers' behavior toward Africans, however, did not prevent the transformation of the common elements in the ritual and oral expressive traditions surrounding African religious specialists to create the conjure tradition in America. (70)

These alternative systems include all of the common African philosophies such as ancestralism, belief in a higher life force, and the concept of full ontological being, which can include aspects of divination, animism, and spiritual awareness through magic and conjure. Roberts argues that the role of the conjurer in African American communities, both slave and free, was influential and widespread (82–104). Joseph M. Murphy posits an even greater connection between African American religious practices and African American identity: "I believe what is distinctive about the spirituality of the religions of the African diaspora can be found in the way that the relationship between human beings and spirit is worked out in community ceremony" (6). Murphy sees this spirit as manifesting itself in a variety of cultural settings in the United States, but he notes specifically its African roots (1). Most importantly, "the spirit is a real and irreducible force uplifting communities throughout the African diaspora" (2).

In African American detective novels hoodoo comes to represent both this spirit and a unique worldview that is part of African American cultural identity. African American detective novelists rely heavily on their own folk traditions in constructing novels with black detectives. For example, the African trickster figure of Esu-Elegbara plays an important referential role in *Mumbo Jumbo* as we trace PaPa LaBas to the Haitian god Legba and his connection with Africa. PaPa LaBas maintains his own alternative detective agency behind the facade of the Mumbo Jumbo Kathedral, a hoodoo temple. LaBas and characters such as Frimbo in *The Conjure Man Dies,* who are in touch with a higher authority based on African beliefs, emphasize the importance of Afrocentrism to a healthy worldview. Their heroic status, reflected in part by their association with the time-honored independent detective hero, reflects an earlier hoodoo aesthetic. This earlier system, communicated orally for the most part, functioned as a remedial religion that developed its own language. In fact, Ishmael Reed, one of the primary literary priests and practitioners of hoodoo, writes in the preface to Hurston's *Tell My Horse* that hoodoo is "less a religion than the common language of slaves from different African tribes thrown together in the Americas for commercial reasons" (xiii).

Black Americans literally invested their *houngans* or hoodoo priests with folk-hero status. As the focal point for internal grievances in black communities, the conjurer could solve problems, aid in combatting evil, and even assume the role of seer. The oral tradition of conjure tales also provided a cultural forum for transmitting alternative moral messages. All of these functions are certainly consistent with the modern-day *houngans* Frimbo and LaBas, black heroes of detective novels who carry forth the mandate of black cultural hoodoo consciousness.

Among the common concerns of this consciousness is the presentation of alternative views of black culture corresponding to residual syncretic African American religious values and to a rewriting of history. The use of hoodoo in black detective fiction establishes an alternative socioreligious philosophical system that further supports the power of vernacular in reassessing the cultural heritage of blacks in America. The inclusion of African American worldviews in detective fiction shows blacks searching for a positive, open-ended system of self-definition and awareness. These worldviews are posited against the negative, closed, oppressive system of white-dominated worldviews in the typical detective novel.

In conclusion to this chapter I would like to discuss other ways that black writers appropriate detective conventions. A primary example of a pervasive structural detective convention involves the concept of suspense. Suspense in detective fiction is usually generated by the investigation, identification, capture, and punishment of the perpetrator of the crime. It also can be generated by the masking and masquerade features of the text. While this primary convention develops forward momentum, a secondary story fills in the background that led up to the murder, sketches the peculiarities of environment, and gives indications of the worldviews of the characters. Simultaneous movement in both directions is one of the peculiar attractions of detective fiction.[3] Dennis Porter writes:

> The initial crime on which the tale of detection is predicated is an end as well as a beginning. It concludes the 'hidden' story of the events leading up to itself at the same time it initiates the story of the process of detection. (29)

As Porter points out, this level of suspense is further complicated by suspension, that is, purposeful retardation of the plot. *Peripeteia* is a rhetorical device well known to the Greeks, and *Oedipus* would not be a tragedy without it. Porter's point, however, is that in detective fiction "the primacy of plot in such a conception of the art of plot composition is clear. Yet, the plot is not important for its own sake but for the emotions it enables an author to excite in a reader" (26). Retardation in detective fiction can involve the use of parallel story lines or the use of digressions.

In African American detective fiction the structural device of retardation is used with a difference. Though the search for a criminal still functions as a governing device in black detection, African American detective narratives become increasingly concerned with worldview themes outside the investigation. Often the blackground to the detective quest becomes primary instead of secondary. Plot retardation in Reed's *Mumbo Jumbo* and Fisher's *Conjure Man Dies* achieves monumental proportions, so that the digressions often in themselves become the story. *Bruce's Black Sleuth* uses monologues by black characters on social and political themes in the same way. Certainly, Arthur Conan Doyle in his first detective story, *A Study in Scarlet,* set a precedent for "a tale within a tale," or a lengthy digression that reorients the basic foundation of the criminal and the crime in the removed historical past. African American detective fiction borrows this convention and applies it to new purposes. Black detection redefines the past in terms of an Afrocentric orientation, suggesting African American continuity with an African past.

Another point that must be addressed concerns the emphasis on adventure rather than investigation in hardboiled detective fiction. The emphasis on danger, gunfights, murders, and kidnapping in hardboiled fiction made it a distinctively American product. Unlike classical detectives, the hardboiled detective got hurt and hurt others in return. His triumph over pain and violence often carried the plot. The American version of the detective story became an adventure as much as an intellectual feat of ratiocination. John Cawelti writes: "Most significantly, the creation of the hard-boiled pattern involved a shift in the underlying archetype of the detective story from the pattern of mystery to that of heroic adventure" (142). In Chapter 5 we will see how Chester Himes used the formula of violence to make an African American political statement. Before him, J. E. Bruce saturated his text with references to black nationalism and race pride, with an emphasis on the defensive use of violence by blacks. Black detective writers such as Pauline Hopkins and Ishmael Reed also altered the detective formulas of violence to fit black detective tropes. The issue of violence in detective fiction is particularly relevant in the case of Himes, who, perhaps more than any other black detective writer, was concerned with the mythical and metaphorical use of violence in his fiction. However, black detective writers such as Reed and Major also rework this convention in their postmodern, experimental texts.

In this chapter I have tried to show how African American authors signified on what many critics agree is a Euro-American form harking back to Poe's Dupin stories. Striving for a deeper understanding of black cultural identity, black writers transformed the formulas of detective fiction by substituting the tropes of black detective personas, double-conscious detection, black vernaculars, and hoodoo. Their texts utilize the conventions of retardation and violence to communicate a social message, and some black authors put a political spin on detective themes by addressing issues of nationalism, race pride, and Afrocentrism. The folk or vernacular traditions of black Americans as expressed in their music, language, and religion are integral aspects of black detective fiction and are used to help structure the narrative. In this capacity, they are grafted onto the usual romance conventions, producing a distinctive hybrid type of fiction. Generally, African American detective writers utilize all of the structural conventions of detective fiction without paying strict attention to either the order or the way in which they are used. In the following chapters I will show how the detective tradition as adapted by African Americans has created a unified body of work that uses a Euro-American popular culture form to express African American cultural identity.

3

Early African American Adaptations of Detective Conventions

It has been reported that black writer Charles W. Chesnutt said in 1926 that "a Pullman porter who performs wonderful feats in the detection of crime has great possibilities" (Bailey 119).[1] In fact, Chesnutt had already been proven correct. This type of detective trope, a black working-class character assuming a detective persona, had been utilized by African American authors publishing in periodical literature at the turn of the century. In this chapter I will look at the early use of detective conventions by African American authors publishing in magazines written for and published by black Americans. By contrasting the use of detective conventions by African American and white authors being published at the same time in mainstream pulp publications, I hope to show that African Americans were attempting from the very beginning to define a new approach to popular fiction that used detective conventions as a vehicle in which to express social critique of mainstream attitudes toward race, class, and gender. Detective writers such as Pauline Hopkins and J. E. Bruce initiated the use of distinctive African American cultural tropes in four areas: alteration of detective personas, double-conscious detection, black vernaculars, and hoodoo. Furthermore, these writers signify on the conventions of detective fiction by use of these tropes, establishing a tradition of black detection that extends over the twentieth century.

Recent critics of detective novels have been fascinated by the cultural, sociopolitical, and psychological questions posited by the vast popularity of detective stories. In particular, John Cawelti analyzes classical and hardboiled detective characters, settings, and themes and correlates these literary aspects to the cultural specifics of England and the United States in the early twentieth century when these

52

branches of detective fiction were most popular. In general, Cawelti finds that the classical detective story meets the needs of the English reading public in that it reflects the ascendancy of the family unit over religious and state authority and, in turn, the primacy of the individual within that family unit. We have also noted that the classical detective's objective, detached persona was a particular trademark of this particular formula (Cawelti, chap. 4). In addition, the classical detective was intuitive, almost poetic.

In America in the 1920s and 1930s Dashiell Hammett and Raymond Chandler created a new variation of the detective featuring a hardboiled hero who narrates his own story. The hardboiled story satisfied certain cultural imperatives by describing crime and urban living with a new realism while continuing to emphasize the individual (Cawelti, chap. 6). As we have seen, the hardboiled detective as developed by Hammett and Chandler, among others, devotes more attention to the criminal mentality while maintaining a subjective viewpoint through first-person narration. The detective also often becomes personally involved with the criminal, as Sam Spade does with Miss Wonderly in *The Maltese Falcon* (1930). The social patterns of the hardboiled story are different from those of the classical, demonstrated in part by the hardboiled detective's lower-class, democratic persona. In contrast to the classical detective, the hardboiled detective, as noted by Cawelti, Grella, and many others, was violent, saw himself outside of society, and consequently developed his own code of ethics.

Overall, it is interesting to assess the importance of these two detective tropes to the cultural needs of the readership of their respective periods. A brief summary of the common assumptions concerning class, gender, and race in mainstream detective fiction will allow a further exploration of the ways in which African American writers approached these issues in the pages of periodical literature. Ernest Mandel and other critics, such as Erik Routley in "The Case against the Detective Story," maintain a convincing argument that detective fiction as a whole supports a white, middle-class mentality that defends a traditional, conservative worldview in terms of race, class, and gender. According to Routley, "The detective story is the product and the weapon of a middle class puritan society whose morality makes claims that have no foundation" (163). Mandel, in *Delightful Murder: A Social History of the Crime Story,* is even more vehement.

He sees the mystery novel as a bourgeois creation intent on defusing real social unrest:

> But the mass of readers will not be led to seek to change the social status by reading crime stories, even though these stories portray conflicts between individuals and society. The criminalization of these conflicts makes them compatible with the defence of bourgeois law and order. (10)

Interestingly, much of his critique supports arguments presented by Stephen Knight in *Form and Ideology in Crime Fiction*. Knight is concerned with the form and style of crime fiction and how it represents certain worldviews through structural constructs: "The form validates, makes real and convincing, the ideology present in the selected material" (15).

Mandel sees a connection between Anglo-Saxon morality and a Euro-Americentric worldview in the polarization of class concepts in the crime novel. Mandel's thesis maintains that detective fiction is representative of a particular political worldview and in effect is handicapped by the very nature of its form. Therefore, a critique of the larger power structure of society is virtually impossible:

> Within such a formalized context, it is impossible to understand, or even to pose, the way the criminal and detective alike, along with crime and justice, prison and property, are products of the same society, of a specific stage of social development. . . . they are taken for granted, outside the specific social context and concrete historical development that have created them. (43)

Mandel is particularly concerned with the classical detective story in his analysis. However, his critique can also be applied to the hard-boiled school when we realize that the alienated detective, while politically aware of class, seldom acts in concert with any group in attempting to challenge political corruption. We will see how this contrasts with Pauline Hopkins's concerted effort to critique class institutions in a much more comprehensive fashion.

Also, the hardboiled detective formula seems particularly offensive in terms of gender. Whereas classical detective stories were often written by women and contained strong female characters, such as Agatha Christie's Miss Marple, hardboiled detective fiction paradoxically reduced females to objects of desire, fear, and loathing. The dominance of the white male viewpoint in early detective stories consequently presents the female as victim or as a threatening "black widow" character. The film-noir tradition, in particular, picked up on this motif.[2] This lamentable preoccupation with objectification reaches its most distressing level in Mickey Spillane's hardboiled executioner fantasies. Equally distressing is the fact that Spillane was one of the most-published authors of all time. According to Cawelti, "Spillane's books are an extreme embodiment of the fear, hostility, and ambiguity toward society and particularly toward women that are built into the hard-boiled detective formula" (187).

The popular arts in the United States during the eighteenth and nineteenth centuries, as well as reflecting political and gender bias, also projected racist attitudes. As pointed out in William Van Deburg's *Slavery and Race in American Popular Culture* (1984), the popular arts in the United States "record a great deal about the cultural underpinnings of American opinion on matters of race and slavery" (xi). During the years of the abolitionist movement and the Civil War, the popular arts provided a forum for debating the issues of slavery, but the primary images of blacks in popular culture were tainted from the beginning by the prejudices of white authors and publishers: "As outcasts in a white dominated society, blacks alternatively were portrayed as feeble-willed noble savages, comically musical minstrel figures and dehumanized brutes" (Van Deburg xi). Although many eighteenth-century American plays contained black characters, Van Deburg considers the appearance of Caesar Wharton in Cooper's novel *The Spy* (1821) to be the first "detailed portrait" of a slave. Among Wharton's personality traits were many that were to become clichés; excessive loyalty, comic appearance, and strong superstitions. The first appearance of a black in a detective story continued this pattern. Poe's Jupiter from "The Gold Bug" (1841) is stereotypically portrayed with malapropisms and exaggerated emotional behavior.[3]

These stereotypical portrayals, along with others such as the predominant desire of fictional blacks to imitate white behavior and appearance, led to a general list of traits that demeaned and falsely defined African Americans of the slave period. These biased attitudes continued in the white mainstream fiction of the late nineteenth and early twentieth centuries. One interesting exception to this pattern, which also indicates an early African American interest in the detective form, is a black musical comedy, *In Dahomey*, first produced in September 1902 in Boston, with lyrics by Paul Laurence Dunbar. In this musical the comedy/minstrel team of George Walker and Bert Williams portrayed two detectives—Shylock ("Shy") Homestead (Williams) and Rareback Pinkerton (Walker)—who travel to Africa to search for a treasure. An all-black production like this one did not represent the general approach to blacks in mainstream detective fiction, however. As Frankie Bailey notes, "[T]he depiction of black characters and even their presence in such works [crime and detective fiction] has been shaped by Eurocentric images of blacks" (xii). Bailey goes on to explain that the accepted "model for the detective hero has been a white male" (xi). The perpetuation of racial viewpoints was all but assured by this primary model and the various guises it took.

The narrow and restrictive persona of a white male or female detective remained unchallenged until Hopkins's novel. The perspective of the mainstream white author of detective texts is further explained by Bailey:

> Moreover, blacks as a group were unacceptable because the detective hero or heroine must be able to probe into the lives of the people involved in the criminal event. For an author to suggest that a black might be allowed to engage in this type of activity in a white community in which psychological and physical boundaries restricted black movement was ludicrous. (xii)

It is just this perspective that Hopkins, and those black writers who followed her, wished to challenge. The idea of a radically different detective possessing both a black skin *and* a black perspective, as indicated by double-conscious perception, initiates the unique path that black detection will take.

During the heyday of the pulp detective magazine explosion (roughly, from 1920 to 1940), all types of detective characters graced the pages of myriad magazines devoted exclusively to detective stories. Along with the many variations on the hardboiled detective, there were masked detectives, racetrack sleuths, blind detectives, and crippled detectives.[4] We can only suggest the immense range and diversity of detective stories and formulas developed in the popular publications of the time. This material has been discussed amply by Ron Goulart in *The Dime Detectives* (1988). In all of these publications, however, including the most popular *Black Mask*, there are no known black writers utilizing black detectives. In fact, Goulart notes that *Black Mask* publishers H. L. Mencken and George Nathan started the magazine after turning down an opportunity to do an all-

Negro pulp. Furthermore, any references to black characters in the typical genre fiction of the day are incidental and programmed by racist imagery based on what Bailey isolates as two primary conceptions of blacks in the United States: "the plantation slave/rural sharecropper" and "the urban slum dweller" (xii). Hazel Carby, in her introduction to *The Magazine Novels of Pauline Hopkins* (*MNPH*), mentions "Black Tom the Negro Detective" as representative of black characters used in dime novels around the turn of the century (xxxviii). And the white author Octavus Roy Cohen created a comic black detective called Florian Slappey, whose escapades were published in the *Saturday Evening Post* in the 1920s. His stories made fun of black characters and exaggerated their predicaments for the amusement of white audiences.

According to Van Deburg, African American writers attempted to combat stereotypes by using the popular arts as a forum for their own ideas. Writers such as William Wells Brown, Frank J. Webb, Martin Delany, and Harriet Jacobs "adopted an important and prophetic leadership role. While lashing out against false piety, misinformation, and racism, these individuals also spoke of intraracial solidarity and of rejection of white standards" (50). The themes of survival, sense of community, and self-definition that were established by these important black writers were carried forth after the Civil War into other publications. As noted by Van Deburg, black literary and library societies "provided much needed support and focus for black self-education efforts" (53). These autonomous and internal black community organizations for self-education were mirrored by another phenomenon of the post-Civil War period: independently published black local papers and magazines. Examples are the *Colored American Magazine* (1900–1909) in Boston and *McGirt's Magazine* (1903–1909) in Philadelphia. From the very start these popular culture compendiums of poetry, fiction, and essays, written by African American writers for African American audiences, showed a fascination with detective mystery formats and conventions.

African American use of detective conventions in periodical literature established a precedent for the development of new ideas about class, gender, and race. The authors of periodical literature experimented with the form to comment on the social history of pre-and post-Civil War society in America. As Van Deburg notes, "Black and white creative expression might have appeared similar in style, but in terms of content and spirit they often stood in quarrelsome contrast" (51).

What did African Americans writing in America during the early part of this century do with detective formulas in their own fiction? As Cawelti has suggested, a culture's attitudes are reflected in its popular acceptance and support of literary formulas. "What cultural values or beliefs do these patterns affirm, what tensions do they seek to resolve, what underlying or latent feelings seek expression in this particular formula?" (98). I will address these questions as they relate to the use of detective conventions by black writers in two African American periodical literature publications from the beginning of this century. These serialized novels establish that detective formulas were already being used as a tool of cultural expression and social critique in the earliest black detective fiction.[5]

The proliferation of magazines for a general reading public has been recognized as a major influence on the detective story. The pulp publication *Black Mask* fostered and fed the growing demand for hardboiled detective fiction. Goulart states that during the period 1926–36 "the hard-boiled detective story had grown up and been perfected in the pages of *Black Mask*" (21). African Americans writing fiction during this same time period—late nineteenth and early twentieth century—did not have access to these pulp publications, just as they had difficulty in publishing in mainstream magazines and publications. As Henry Louis Gates notes in the *Chronicle of Higher Education* (*CHE*), "White publishing houses did not offer many opportunities to black people to publish" (8). Charles Chesnutt, who published consistently in the *Atlantic Monthly,* was an exception to this rule, but his identity as a black writer was hidden for many years, even from his editor and publisher.[6] However, recent research by, among others, the Black Periodical Project under Henry Louis Gates, Jr., and the Black Fiction Project under Maryemma Graham at Northeastern University has uncovered a vast amount of material by black Americans in publications written for and sold to African Americans. Gates notes in relation to the Black Periodical Project that "few if any scholars suspected the number of black periodicals that existed during the 19th century and early 20th century, or the amount of literature they contained" (*CHE* 7). These magazines published novels serially, as well as poetry and short stories written for a local and more general African American audience. Evidence from the black periodical literature indicates that African Americans were quick to pick up on the popular art form of detective fiction.

Two representative serial novels from this period are Pauline Hopkins's *Hagar's Daughter* (1901–2) published in the *Colored American Magazine* and J. E. Bruce's *Black Sleuth* (1907–9) published in *McGirt's Magazine*. Both of these novels use detective devices and demonstrate a fascination with sensational mystery and detective story formats. They also show, contrary to Mandel's claim, that detective fiction can be used as a vehicle for social criticism, and we shall see that black writers will continue to use the detective format for cultural statements as well as moral critiques. Black periodical literature did not hesitate to deal with overt and covert discrimination in pre-and post-Civil War society or to indict the social conditions of the period in which they were written. Much of the periodical literature published for African Americans is lost or lying in libraries uncollated, and there may well be even earlier examples of black detective novels yet to be discovered.

Hagar's Daughter by Pauline Hopkins (1859–1930), a noted African American woman of letters, social activist, and editor of *Colored American Magazine,* has been recently reissued in totality by the Schomburg Library of Nineteenth-Century Black Women Writers in *The Magazine Novels of Pauline Hopkins* (1988). As Hazel Carby notes in the introduction, "These magazine novels . . . represent a sustained attempt to develop an Afro-American popular fiction" (*MNPH* xxix). Carby feels, in fact, that Hopkins's novels form a bridge between the earlier popular periodical literature of William Wells Brown and Victoria Earle Matthews and the detective fiction of Chester Himes published in the 1950s.

The full novella written by J. E. Bruce has not been reprinted, but the New York Public Library's Schomburg Center for Research into Black Culture contains microfiche copies of *McGirt's Magazine,* from which I obtained a copy of *The Black Sleuth*. Bruce is a decidedly confident author utilizing an altered detective persona and double-conscious detection in an unusual narrative with an interesting African American perspective on an African-born detective. A number of critics, including John McCluskey, Jr., in *The City of Refuge* (1987), have referred to Bruce's *Black Sleuth* as the first detective novel written by an African American. Henry Louis Gates says that it is "the earliest known black detective novel, a genre that includes Ishmael

Reed's *Mumbo Jumbo* of 1972" (*CHE* 8). The discovery of *Hagar's Daughter* and *The Black Sleuth* proves that African American writers have written detective fiction since the beginning of the twentieth century.

As I have noted, *Hagar's Daughter* was published in serial form several years before *The Black Sleuth* appeared. (Hopkins's earlier story "The Mystery within Us," which appeared in the inaugural edition of *Colored American Magazine*, 1900, is not a detective story.) Hopkins's novel contains two black detectives, one a female, and establishes itself through the use of African American detective tropes as the first African American detective novel. *Hagar's Daughter* also alters elements of the classical detective tradition and anticipates to some degree hardboiled detective fiction. Combining components of the classical tradition with innovative alteration of the detective persona and the detection process, Hopkins uses the detective form to critique class institutions in a much more comprehensive fashion than was the case with white mainstream detective fiction. She was the first African American writer to utilize detective fiction for a social and political attack on racial discrimination in the United States. Interestingly, Hopkins regarded detective fiction as a powerful tool that could be used to celebrate African American cultural values and critique white racist ideology, and she does this by using the detective form to question the moral and cultural foundation that typical detective fiction supports through the reestablishment of the natural order.

The first half of the novel is plotted around a purported murder and a suicide; the last half of the novel contains a murder and a kidnapping. As is the case in *The Black Sleuth*, the detective characters truly enter the narrative only in the last third of the novel. Even though the first part of *Hagar's Daughter* does not follow the standard format, it contains many of the elements common to detective fiction, such as disguise and coincidence. Furthermore, the novel's plot machinations revolve around what the reader believes is the murder of white aristocrat Ellis Enson by his brother St. Clair and the apparent suicide of the mulatto Hagar and death of her young daughter by drowning. Though Hopkins uses explicit detective conventions only in the last half of the novel, there are many implicit references to romance conventions in the work.

Hopkins's primary metaphor for the evil of slave society and racial prejudice is *passing,* both conscious and unconscious, and the passing theme underlies the explicit use of detective conventions in the novel. For example, the use of the mysterious-birth theme, a typical detective convention ploy, structures the whole of the novel. Untypically, the mysterious birthright turns out to be black blood, which is revealed in the recognition scene at the end of the novel, another convention of detective writing. Throughout the novel the hidden and mistaken identities are part of a detective tradition altered to reflect Hopkins's critique of the color line. The second half of the narrative closely follows the detectives in their pursuit of the criminals and validates the uniqueness of Venus, the black maid, as a detective persona.

In this author's opinion *Hagar's Daughter* represents the earliest known use of African American detective tropes in a work written by a black American containing a black detective. If this novel remains the earliest known use of a black detective in African American fiction, it will have broken ground by illustrating how detective conventions could be signified on by African American writers. Most importantly, *Hagar's Daughter* refutes the assumption that the popular arts cannot be used to discuss issues of class, gender, and race in meaningful ways.

Certainly, the early date of both of these novels brings up an interesting point in regard to the use of detective conventions by African Americans. Even though Poe invented the detective formula in the 1840s, there were not that many literary detective narratives until the creation of Sherlock Holmes late in the nineteenth century (Goulart 6). Poe's brilliant amateur detective Dupin was the model for what has proven to be an extremely popular genre, and he established many of the conventions of the detective novel, including a story narrated by a close associate of the detective, a bumbling police force, an eccentric detective, a locked-room mystery, and the use of clues leading to the discovery of the criminal. Evidence from the black periodical literature shows that early African American authors were quick to pick up on what soon became an extremely popular art form. As Goulart tells us,

> Detective short stories were very popular from the 1890s onward, due initially to the impact of Sherlock Holmes, and were also staples of the slick-paper magazines. A misconception about the genre is that this type of material was shunned by the more respectable, family-oriented periodicals. (9)

The proud use of black detectives in both *Hagar's Daughter* and *The Black Sleuth* demonstrates that African American authors were aware of the potential of detective characters and plots for attracting readers at a very early date. We can assume that other authors, as yet undiscovered, used detective fiction in black periodical literature. However, what is impressive about the two novels we do have is the fact that Hopkins and Bruce recognized that detective fiction could be used to dramatize black political and social concerns.

The political agenda of Pauline Hopkins and her activism in social causes influenced the direction of the *Colored American Magazine*.[7] The dynamics of her political concerns are evident in *Hagar's Daughter,* and they are partially effected through the utilization of detective conventions. Carby says that "Hopkins both utilizes the strategies and formulas of nineteenth-century dime novels and story papers and reveals the limits of these popular American narrative forms for black characterization" (*MNPH* xxix). Hopkins reveals the limits of the detective forms by showing how these forms can be transformed to more positive ends through the use of detective tropes demonstrating black cultural strengths and African American worldviews.

Hopkins's use of popular formulas is markedly different from any detective writing of the time because she ties detective conventions to social and critical values. The larger moral message of her attack on racism and slavery is evident in the first pages of the novel. The first chapter is essentially a polemic against slavery, recounting the social conditions that led up to the Civil War. The novel is about greed, corruption, and prejudice in pre-and post-Civil War southern aristocratic society. The evils of slavery and racial prejudice are indicted through the passing theme, which stains the fabric of the novel in all its interwoven aspects. Unconscious passing in the case of Hagar and her daughter Jewel destroys the Enson family in part 1 of the novel and the Sumner and Bowen families in part 2. These families are shattered because of their inability to accept any person of black blood into their heritage:

> But the one drop of black blood neutralized all her [Hagar's] virtues, and she became, from the moment of exposure, an unclean thing. Can anything more unjust be imagined in a republican form of government whose excuse for existence is the upbuilding of mankind! (Hopkins 62)

In fact, all of the tragic elements of the novel can be attributed to the unjust social system of racial prejudice that resulted from slavery. The love of Ellis for Hagar cannot withstand the blow to Ellis's aristocratic propriety when he finds out Hagar is part black and legally still a slave. Ellis cannot stay married to a black slave in the United States and chooses exile to Europe instead. Before he can leave with Hagar and his daughter, he is apparently killed. The myth of racial purity condemns the members of the Enson family (and later the Bowen family) to unhappiness and disaster.

The first half of the novel outlines the plantation environment of the Enson estate around the year 1860. Ellis and St. Clair Enson are the sons of a rich Maryland slave owner. When St. Clair is disowned for behavior unfitting a gentlemen, Ellis becomes the sole heir of the Enson estate, including ownership of the slave family of Aunt Henny and her daughter Marthy. A conservative bachelor, Ellis remains unmarried until his fortieth year when he falls in love with Hagar Sargeant, the daughter of a neighbor, just returned from private school. Hagar and Ellis marry and have one daughter. Upon notification of his niece's birth, St. Clair decides to return home in the company of the slave dealer Walker, sending his personal servant, Isaac, before him. Aunt Henny, who was born under a veil, predicts that St. Clair's return will bring no good because St. Clair was born under a hoodoo curse instigated by a slave conjurer, Unc' Ned. Indeed, Walker has retained papers on Hagar Sargeant that prove she is actually the daughter of a slave who was adopted by the Sargeants. Ellis is informed of the fact that he is married to a slave by St. Clair and Walker and in turn informs Hagar of her birthright. After much difficulty Ellis decides to remain married and go to Europe to live, but before he can put the plan into effect, he disappears. Some time later a man with Ellis's wallet and gun is found with his head blown off at the edge of the plantation. Suicide is ruled, and St. Clair throws Hagar out of the house into the arms of Walker, who decides to sell her on the market with her young daughter, also a slave by law. Before Hagar and her daughter can be sold, she escapes from the slave compound and jumps into the Potomac, apparently drowning both herself and her daughter.

The second half of the book takes place twenty years later in Washington, where Sen. Zenas Bowen, his wife Estelle (Hagar), and his foundling daughter Jewel have arrived from California. General Benson (St. Clair), Major Madison (Walker), and Madison's daughter Aurelia (daughter of a slave passing as white) are also in Washington. Cuthbert Sumner, scion of an old New England family, works for General Benson, as does Elsie Bradford, Benson's former mistress. Aunt Henny, along with Marthy and her two children by Isaac, Oliver and Venus, also now live in Washington as free blacks. Aunt Henny works as a washerwoman for the U. S. Treasury, Oliver goes to school, and Venus works as a maid for Jewel. Isaac is a shiftless schemer employed by Benson to do his dirty work. Cuthbert Sumner, Aurelia's former lover, falls in love with Jewel, and they plan to marry. Envious of Senator Bowen's wealth, Benson and Madison formulate a plan: Aurelia will befriend Jewel and steal back Cuthbert Sumner, leaving the way open for General Benson to woo and marry Jewel and become heir to her fortune. Elsie Bradford has an illegitimate son by Benson. When she tries to talk him into supporting the child, he kills her, but not before she reveals to Cuthbert the devious plans afoot.

Jewel rejects Benson but despairs over Sumner's apparent return to Aurelia. Sumner, who was the last person seen with Elsie, is accused of her murder. Jewel then realizes her mistake, and marries Sumner while he is in jail. She goes to see Detective Henson, head of a federal detective agency, who is actually Ellis Enson. Henson takes on the case, which is further complicated when Senator Bowen is poisoned by Benson, who writes a fake will in his name. Aunt Henny, who witnessed Elsie's murder, and Jewel are kidnapped by Isaac and hidden at the remote Enson plantation. Sumner is put on trial, and Detective Henson is at a loss to prove his innocence. Venus uses her inherited hoodoo powers to figure out where Aunt Henny and Jewel are being held. She volunteers to help Henson, and he employs her along with a black detective named Henry Smith to spy on the old Enson estate. When Venus frees Aunt Henny and Jewel, Aunt Henny becomes the surprise witness at the trial, Sumner is freed, and General Benson (St. Clair) and Major Madison (Walker) are convicted of murder and conspiracy to defraud Senator Bowen of his millions. It is also discovered that St. Clair was part of a conspiracy to shoot President Lincoln. He is shot while trying to escape, and Walker dies in jail. Ellis and Hagar are reunited, and a hidden locket reveals that Jewel is actually their daughter. That, however, makes Jewel part black, and Sumner cannot accept the fact that he is married to a Negro. He leaves for Europe, but returns a year later to look for Jewel and declare his love. Instead, he finds Jewel's grave on the Enson property. In despair, he finally understands that his sin of racial prejudice is the nation's sin.

Pauline Hopkins's *Hagar's Daughter* demonstrates a familiarity with classical detective conventions while foreshadowing some elements of hardboiled detection. The novel was published more than twenty years before the first hardboiled detective story, Carroll John Daly's "Knights of the Open Palm" (1923). Though *Hagar's Daughter* does not share the excessive violence, first-person narration, or male viewpoint of much of hardboiled fiction, its use of vernacular language and the attention paid to the everyday lifestyle of black Americans certainly foreshadow some of hardboiled fiction's common-man viewpoints. Also, Venus's status as concerned participant predates the hardboiled convention of involving the detective in the action. Certainly, Venus's lower-class status suggests the democratic man-of-the-streets aspect of Hammett's and Chandler's detectives. These positive contributions to a new style of detective fiction occurred years before the rise of the hardboiled style, which did little to improve the image of females or blacks.

Hopkins's alteration of the detective persona immediately breaks the pattern of the isolated eccentric detective of both the classical and hardboiled varieties. *Hagar's Daughter* shows white and black detectives working as a team to solve the crime. Also, unlike most classical and hardboiled detectives, the detectives in this story are closely associated with their families, who are important aspects of their identities. As noted, *Hagar's Daughter* has one white and two black detectives, the servant girl Venus Johnson and Henry Smith, a Civil War veteran in the employ of Chief Detective Henson.

It is in the last third of the novel that Hopkins begins systematically adapting detective conventions. One example is her portrayal of Detective Henson. As "chief of the secret service," Henson has an office with his name on it—"J. Henson Detective"—and official status in a government agency that allows him to take no outside cases (186). As the leader of a group of detectives he functions much like an FBI director and seems to be modeled on a Pinkerton agent. In the way Henson works, we can see suggestions of a relatively recent form of detective novel, the police procedural. George N. Dove, in *The Police*

Procedural, 1945 lists three criteria that differentiate the police procedural from other detective fiction: (1) employing police procedures and following police routines; (2) introducing the reader to the police mind; and (3) using police technology (10–11). Although *Hagar's Daughter* does not strictly fulfill these criteria, it does emphasize the official police procedures and the workings of the detective mind. The use of a team of detectives also foreshadows a type of police procedural as well as underlying an important facet of black detective fiction: the use of detective groups rather than individual detectives, with each detective contributing a particular investigative skill to the group.

Henson adheres to another convention of the classical detective, the use of disguise. Holmes, for example, often uses disguise to solve his cases. Henson, however, is masquerading as a detective under an assumed name and identity. In the tradition of the classical detective, Henson ignores Jewel's offer of money, but he does profess belief in her intuitive suspicions, even though he represents the classical detective's professed analytical abilities. The detectives in *Hagar's Daughter* reflect the rational/irrational split seen in the classical detective, a duality manifested by an ability to juggle the factual world against an almost mystical interiority. Dupin uses both ratiocination and intuitive creativity to solve his cases, and everyone is familiar with Holmes's bizarre introverted episodes when he becomes lost to the world in a strange meditative trance, only to emerge with a seemingly unfounded solution. The balance between deductive/inductive and intuitive/analytical creates some of the attractive tension in both classical and hardboiled detective fiction. This tension is further complicated in *Hagar's Daughter* when the double-conscious detective abilities of the black detective Venus are stressed in the closing part of the novel. Venus possesses an intuition that gives her insight into the case, and she guesses correctly where the kidnapped Jewel is hidden. Her double-conscious detective abilities seem directly related to Aunt Henny's hoodoo second sight, which may have been passed down to Venus.

In contrast to the classical detective's famous detached attitude and unattached social status, Detective Henson is intimately connected with all members of the cast of characters. Jewel is his long-lost daughter, Mrs. Bowen (Hagar) is his wife, and General Benson is his brother St. Clair. These intimate relations will eventually destroy his mask as Detective Henson, prove him ineffectual in the last stages of the novel, and return him to the ranks of the common man. However, Henson's real failure as a detective is illustrated by Venus's success. Henson cannot solve the case because he lacks access to both the black community and the double-conscious deductive ability that Venus possesses, part of which includes her blackness, which allows her entry to places the white Henson cannot access.

As I have suggested, *Hagar's Daughter* is a novel about the evils of a social system that corrupts individuals and families through greed and discrimination. The complicated plot concerns female characters whose lives are ruined because a fraction of black blood alienates them from the white social system. The ultimate irony is predicated on the fact that *only* a black female maid disguised as a black male can rescue Hagar's daughter Jewel. Venus Johnson is able to do this because she uses her black skin, her double consciousness, and her knowledge of the black community to figure out where the kidnapped Jewel is being held. When Venus volunteers to join Detective Henson in his search for the murderer of Elsie Bradford and for the kidnapped Jewel, she is transformed by the white detective Henson (the "murdered" Ellis Enson of the first half of the novel) into a detective disguised as a black male, enabling her to infiltrate the black community around the ruined Enson estate where Aunt Henny and Jewel are being held against their will.

As the first female black detective in African American fiction, Venus Johnson shares attributes with other strong female characters in the novel thought to be white who are later revealed to be black. Aurelia Madison, Jewel's rival for Cuthbert Sumner's affection, is a quadroon who breaks the bonds of convention. As General Benson comments, she is "a woman who can join a man in a social glass, have a cigar with him, or hold her own in winning or losing a game with no Sunday-school nonsense about her" (Hopkins 78). Besides being unconventional and manipulative, Aurelia possesses a strength of spirit that elicits respect even from those who hate her: "There was something, too, that compelled admiration in this resolute standing to her guns with the determination to face the worst that fate might have in store for her" (238). Venus too possesses strong individual qualities. She is aware of her own abilities and her importance—so much so that she willingly defies the social strictures imposed on her position, color, and sex. As a detective, she works in close connection with the black detective Henry Smith, a veteran of the Civil War who left a leg at the Battle of Honey Hill. Smith was a member of the famous black regiment, the fifty-fourth of Massachusetts, and he talks about the Battle of Fort Wagner and the death of Colonel Robert Shaw, the white commander. Hopkins's sketch of Smith's background is indicative of her conscious use of affirmative black history, generally omitted, in this and other works.

Venus Johnson is also drawn with affirmative strokes. It is her double-conscious detective status, her conscious use of her blackness and hoodoo vision, combined with personal courage that solves the case. Henson follows up her suspicions concerning Benson (St. Clair) and his use of the old Enson estate for a hiding place for Jewel. But he can only go so far, restricted as he is by his color from infiltrating the black community surrounding the hiding place. Venus volunteers her efforts after Detective Henson comes up empty: "I'll see if this one little black girl can't get the best of as mean a set of villains as was ever born" (221). Venus, the uneducated black maid, proves instrumental in solving the case because she possesses intimate knowledge of her community. Her blackness also allows her to be privy to information in the local store, a gathering spot for blacks. With this information, her double-conscious intuitive powers, and her natural wit and intellect, she is a formidable character who earns the praise of the chief detective. "Chief Henson was particularly pleased with the ability shown by his colored detectives" (239). In this case the detective persona assumed by Venus helps establish her identity as a strong, independent black female.

Hopkins's combination of double consciousness and detection is an important contribution to the black detective tradition. In black detective novels this double consciousness becomes a tool of detection, allowing characters to assume identities and masks and giving them special insight into the criminal mind. Hopkins shows particular skill in her use in the novel of the passing theme. Passing as a narrative strategy emphasizes suspense and conditions coincidence and surprise throughout the novel. Almost all of the major white female characters are actually black by virtue of some distant ancestor's blood. The contrast between their appearance and behavior and the "expected" appearance and behavior of blacks predicates much of the novel's tragedy and suspense, and the revelation of their "condition" leads to betrayal, disillusionment, and death. This theme is common in melodramatic novels of this and earlier periods, but Hopkins uses passing in other ways. As Hazel Carby notes in her introduction,

> Hopkins does not offer her readers narratives of "passing." The "whiteness" of her major female figures is constructed in response to the formal prerequisites of popular fictional formulas of disguises and double identities. (*MNPH* xxxix)

Hopkins's ability to take these prerequisites and use them for social critique is what makes the novel so important. Certainly, *Hagar's Daughter* uses passing to structure a critique of unjust racial laws and pervasive racial attitudes while altering typical detective conventions. Passing in this sense is closely related to the motif of masking or minstrelsy in African American detective fiction. However, I also see passing as a telling metaphor for the African American detective principle of double consciousness as illustrated in the novel. In the detective novels this double consciousness becomes a tool of detection, allowing characters to assume identities and masks in the trickster tradition, hide their detective personas behind their blackness, and use hoodoo powers in their detective work. Passing, whether conscious or unconscious, establishes this motif of masking or minstrelsy as an attribute of African American detective fiction.

Hopkins sets up a duality of black and white consciousness early in the novel by breaking the narrative down into sections that describe consciousness from a white, aristocratic perspective and from a black, working-class perspective. This upstairs/downstairs motif structures the novel and also shows how intertwined the lives of blacks and whites are. Desire for wealth and commodities, including slaves, is the primary motivation of the evil white characters. Desire to survive with dignity and foster community values is the primary motivation of the good black characters. The heritage and patriarchal line of the white aristocracy contrasts with the marginality of the black characters, whose families are matriarchal and dispersed. By playing the negative white value systems against the positive black worldviews, Hopkins allows for an assertive presentation of African American cultural values. These values—close family ties (about to be torn apart), sense of community and place, and faith in religion and moral righteousness—are underlined in the novel. The crossover occurs in the cases of unconscious passing, which causes the disintegration of the white aristocracy due to its inflexible racial attitudes. In the final analysis, however, it is the black characters who rescue the white characters from ultimate destruction. Even so, the novel ends on a disastrous note.

The two halves of the novel mirror one another. In the last half of the narrative many of the characters from the first half appear again twenty years later, hiding behind masks of false identity. My contention is that masking or hiding one's identity from oneself as well as the outside world is a primary theme of this first black detective novel. This is further illustrated as detection in the novel shows passing to be the one social ill that Detective Henson cannot "solve" for his son-in-law, Cuthbert Sumner. To know that you are black in a white society based on prejudice requires double consciousness. To *not* know you are black in the same society and then to find out is double consciousness with a vengeance.

In the last third of the novel, the passing motif connects explicitly to the mask or masquerading aspect of detection commonly seen in many detective novels. The black detectives in this novel use dual awareness of their blackness in positive ways to solve the mystery. When Venus costumes herself as a black male named "Billy" to rescue her white mistress, who is actually black, the ironies of the text demonstrate Hopkins's creative use of detective conventions. But even before this, Venus has clairvoyantly pierced the evil workings of St. Clair's mind because of the special hoodoo gifts inherited from her grandmother. Her gift of divination, part of what I call double-conscious detection, enables her to get into the mind of the devil-criminal St. Clair and intuitively divine his machinations. Double-consciousness detection in this sense is a specific perception that stresses the positive qualities of racial and cultural differences amplified by the mystical abilities of hoodoo. Not only does this perception enable black detectives to get into the criminal mind and solve crimes, but it also, in some ways, signifies on the detective doubling so often seen in classical detective fiction in the use of the narrator/detective, such as Watson/Holmes. Double-conscious detection is a powerful combination of these detective conventions melded into an individual persona that combines intuitive hoodoo and trickster qualities. In *Hagar's Daughter* the double-conscious strength of Venus the black maid is pitted against the injustice of racial prejudice. The interwoven irony of the passing theme demonstrates clearly the duplicity of the prevailing social system. Hopkins's plot structure of hidden identities,

misinterpreted conversations, compromising situations, and disguise
—all stock elements of detective fiction—begin to take on further
meaning as they illustrate the immorality of a system based on racial
prejudice and segregation.

Hopkins's use of black vernaculars in positive ways is also revolutionary. Large sections of the novel are written from the viewpoint of
slaves and free blacks, and the language of these characters is often
used to authenticate black speech patterns. In times of stress or con-
viviality the veneer of white speech patterns falls away: "Venus forgot
her education in her earnestness, and fell into the Negro vernacular,
talking and crying at the same time" (224). But black characters such
as Aunt Henny, Isaac, Marthy, Oliver, and Venus are not buffoonish,
maudlin, or ignorant, and they are not presented simply in humorous
contrast to whites. Their occupations run the gamut from slave to
college student, and they bring dignity to all levels of work.

The larger theme of the novel contrasts a white, divisive, aristocratic, commodity culture with a black, integrated, caring community.
Hopkins expresses community values by showing the cohesiveness
of the black family even when threatened by slavery. During the
slave auction at the beginning of the novel, Hopkins has Walker, the
evil slave dealer, say to a young man:

> "Get out on that plank and dance. I want to see how supple you are."
> "I don't like to dance, mass; I'se got religion." (11)

Here, as throughout the novel, Hopkins works against stereotypes
to dignify blacks, even in a demeaning situation. Aunt Henny, the
grandmother of Oliver and Venus, in her capacity as washerwoman
at the U. S. Treasury once discovered a large sum of money that had
been inadvertently left outside a safe. Without informing her family,
she sat up all night at her job to protect the money and return it to
its rightful place in the morning. The virtues of honesty, industri-
ousness, and hard work are shown to be important African American
values, in contrast to the typical depictions of blacks as lazy and
dishonest. Marthy, who helps pay her son Oliver's college tuition by
doing washing, argues with her son about the dignity of her labor:

> Does you think money's jes' a growing on bushes ready to shuck into your
> hand when you gits through college? Pears lak to me, Oliver, you'd better
> make up yer min' to hussle aroun' fer awhile. I don't want ter feel that a
> chile o'/min's too biggotty to do anything hones' fer a living. (171)

Other examples of black vernaculars in the novel include the singing of black spirituals and a concentration on food. Hopkins presents
meals as healing communal events several times in the work, stressing
the specialness of black cuisine.

> When the meal was on the table, smoking hot,—corn pone, gumbo soup,
> chicken and rice and coffee of an amber hue,—the children ate with
> gusto. . . .
>   "Have some mo' this gumbo soup, my baby. I reckon you don' git
> nothin' like it up yonder with all the fixin's you has there." (218)

This attention to black vernaculars is a key aspect of Hopkins's text
that is duplicated in future black detective texts. Through the presence of such black vernaculars in *Hagar's Daughter,* Hopkins cele-
brates black culture and emphasizes African Americans' fidelity to
community and family values against tremendous odds.

Another Hopkins innovation is her use of hoodoo, which she depicts in a positive light as a black religious system of self-empowerment. In this novel, some blacks are shown to possess the occult
ability to alter the power structures at times and affect the fates of
characters who cross them. The tragic result of Hagar's passing comes
about because of an earlier hoodoo curse. St. Clair, the unscrupulous
Enson brother, is revealed by Aunt Henny to have been born under
the sign of the devil.

> Jes' 'fore Marse St. Cla'r was born, ole Missee Enson was settin' in there
> an' a turrible thunder storm came up an' jes' raised Jeemes Henry with
> houses an' trees, an' tored up eberythin'. Ol' Miss so dar 'feared to move
> even one teeny bit her li'l' finger. While she sot dar all white an' trimbly de
> debbil jes' showed he face to her an' grinned. (63)

We learn that this visit from the devil was actually instigated by "Unc'
Ned conjure man," who had been threatened by the master with a
whipping (64). According to Henny, Unc' Ned positioned himself
with the devil and petitioned thusly: "I's had de power, continer de
power; make me strong in your cause, make me faithful to you, an'
help me to conquer my enemies, an' I will try to deserve a seat at
your right han'!" (64).

In *Hagar's Daughter* hoodoo power strengthens the identity of the
black community. Unlike traditional Christianity, which blacks also
adopted to less subversive ends, hoodoo provides immediate power
over the elements and one's enemies. However, once this power is

unleashed, as in the creation of St. Clair, it can have disastrous effects not foreseen by the original conjurer—witness the effect of St. Clair's scheming on the mulatto Hagar and her daughter Jewel. The African origins of hoodoo, by way of Haiti, suggest that it takes a person with integrity to control its powers.

Aunt Henny possesses such integrity and proves instrumental in the eventual outcome of the novel. She is at the scene of the murder of Elsie Bradford because of her job as washerwoman, but she also senses or "sees" in a dream (as does her daughter Marthy) that something bad is going to happen. Early in the novel Henny brags about her abilities: "Dat's jes' what I thought. No use yer lyin' ter me, Isaac, yer Aunt Henny *was born wif veil.* I knows a heap o' things by seein' 'em fo' dey happens. I don' tell all I sees, but I keeps up a steddyin' 'bout it" (43). This connection between occult powers and being born with a caul over one's face is a traditional motif in hoodoo symbology.

Hagar's Daughter, as the first novel in the detective tradition, asserts a positive role for hoodoo and suggests that hoodoo and detection are strongly connected. Prophecy and conjure are powerful tools for the blacks in this novel, aligning them with a cosmic universe outside the influence of white control and giving them detective resources of a mystical kind. Uncle Ned can conjure the elements to do his bidding, and Aunt Henny can change the course of events by her ability to see into the future. Hoodoo reinforces the sense of black distinctiveness and ability to stand up to a powerful master. Henny's belief in hoodoo is given validity as part of a larger worldview system. The community values that blacks maintain and express throughout the novel are in the end the saviors of not only themselves but the whites whom they serve. By instituting a separate system of worldview beliefs, African Americans work to keep their communities intact and escape oppression. *Hagar's Daughter* establishes a precedent by emphasizing the separate spiritual world that exists for blacks.

Afrocentrism is another element of African American culture touched upon in *Hagar's Daughter.* Although the novel does not fully explore all the aspects of Afrocentrism, it does make note of Hagar's awakening realization of her African heritage. She refers to the biblical source of her name and to her African past after she finds out she is a slave, and she recalls lines of verse that give her comfort.

> Farewell! I go, but Egypt's mighty gods
> Will go with me, and my avengers be.
> And in whatever distant land your god,
> Your cruel god of Israel, is known,
> There, too, the wrongs that you have done this day
> To Hagar and your first-born,
> Shall waken and uncoil themselves, and hiss
> Like adders at the name of Abraham. (58)

Rejection of the Judeo-Christian tradition in favor of African or Egyptian gods is an important aspect of Hagar's growing disdain for Euro-Americentric values. In the remaining chapters of this work we will see how hoodoo and Afrocentrism continue to reflect African American belief systems in other important detective novels.

Hagar's Daughter not only uses detective conventions to subvert stereotypes but signifies on the accepted use of detective conventions by breaking the formulas. One of the ways it does this is by contrasting the use of black detective double consciousness with accepted uses of double identities in crime fiction. "Conventional popular fictional use of disguise and double identities indicates a disruption of natural order of events in a society or community" (Carby, *MNPH* xli). As I have suggested, this disruption of natural order is further complicated in the novel by the illustration of racial injustice through the passing theme. Double consciousness in this sense suggests that no moral rectitude is possible in this detective novel. Carby and others have correctly pointed out that traditional detective fiction commonly restores moral order, but as she notes, *Hagar's Daughter* purposely rejects the social order as imposed by white values:

> [T]he resolutions to *Hagar's Daughter* reveal the contradictions inherent in Hopkins's attempt to use popular and easily accessible narrative forms to question the morality of, rather than to restore faith in, the social formation. (xli)

What Carby sees as contradictions, I see as early contributions to the black detective tradition.

I find Hopkins particularly successful in demonstrating the bankruptcy of white society through her alterations of standard detective conventions. This is supported in the last section of the novel by the ultimate failure of Cuthbert Sumner to accept Jewel as his wife after he learns of her mixed blood. One obvious reflection of the upstairs/downstairs theme is that at the end of the novel Venus and her family are reunited, but the white aristocracy, rife with prejudice, falls apart. Intraracial solidarity confirms the power of blacks working together. Whites lack this solidarity and cannot function outside the social conventions of white supremacy. One of the ultimate ironies of the novel is that the chief detective, the primary motivating consciousness in most detective novels, reverses roles and gives up being a detective to become husband to Hagar and father to Jewel. Henson demonstrates that he is a changed man when he compares his earlier life as Enson to Sumner's immediate predicament over his love for Jewel: "My dear boy, I know just where you are. I went all through the old arguments from your point of view twenty years ago. I wavered and wavered, but nature was stronger than prejudice" (Hopkins 270). Sumner, who in fact comes from a liberal Yankee family, cannot be persuaded to accept Jewel as his wife. The tragic ending of the novel and Jewel's death are directly related to this fact. The myth of racial purity has inevitably led to unhappiness and disaster.

Hopkins's bold stroke in making a black female maid a detective launches the black detective tradition and points the way to further adaptation of the detective persona by black writers. The powerful white male detective succumbs, while the powerless black female detective succeeds. This reversal of roles is the chief one in a novel full of reversals. Jewel, the "white" heroine, is rescued by her black maid from a dungeon where she is keeping company with Venus's black grandmother, Aunt Henny. In contrast to the accepted stereotypes of blacks and females of this period, it is black female ingenuity and individuality that rescues the kidnapped Jewel. This adaptation of detective conventions in *Hagar's Daughter* works on a number of different levels, showing Hopkins's familiarity with the genre. As Carby notes, Hopkins created "narratives of the relations between the races that challenged racist ideologies" (*MNPH* xxxi). Venus is valuable in solving the case *just because she is black and female.*

I have tried to show how in the earliest known African American detective novel the conventions of class, race, and gender are obviously challenged. *Hagar's Daughter* subverts many of the accepted conventions of the classic detective formula and adumbrates some of the hardboiled techniques. Venus, the black maid, is the ultimate foil to the white male aristocratic model as represented by Sherlock Holmes. As a primary work in the detective tradition, *Hagar's Daughter* reverses pervasive stereotypes while creating new avenues of expression for black Americans in the areas of detective personas, double consciousness, black vernaculars, and hoodoo. Considering the early date of the work, Hopkins's strategies are particularly fascinating. Hopkins's conscious use of African American tropes in a novel of social and political critique will be followed by other black writers using the detective formula. One case in point is the novel *The Black Sleuth* written by John E. Bruce (1856–1924) in the first decade of the twentieth century.

The model of *Hagar's Daughter* is particularly interesting when compared to *The Black Sleuth,* which was published in serial form in *McGirt's Magazine* beginning in September 1907.[8] John Edward Bruce was born a slave in Maryland but rose to be a respected author and political activist who wrote and published exclusively for a black press and audience. Because of this exclusivity and his refusal to join any organizations with white members, Bruce has been ignored by both black and white historians. Peter Gilbert, who edited *The Selected Writings of John Edward Bruce, Militant Black Journalist* (1971), considers Bruce an important link between pre-Civil War black writers and antebellum writers as well as a precursor of the New Negro movement (1):

> Though overlooked by black and white historians alike, John Edward Bruce was a uniquely qualified and popular voice that spoke to and for America's black masses. His philosophy showed that vigorous protest and agitation could be successfully merged with ideas of radical unity and black separatism. (9)

Furthermore, his association with Alexander Crummell and with Marcus Garvey and his Universal Negro Improvement Association (UNIA) substantiated Bruce's reputation as a radical black nationalist as well as an advocate of the common black people.

Bruce wrote and published articles throughout his life and was associated with many different periodicals. Under the pseudonym of "Bruce Grit" he published articles, essays, poems, and short sketches in publications such as the *Colored American* of Washington, D.C. He established the *Sunday Item* in 1880, the first black Sunday newspaper, and he was the author of a published novel entitled *The Awakening of Hezekiah Jones* (1916).

Bruce was also a member and founder of several African American organizations while working for Marcus Garvey. A firm defender of black history, Bruce organized, with A. A. Schomburg, the Negro Society for Historical Research in 1911. Gilbert writes that "as early as the 1880's Bruce emphasized black history, the beauty of black and the particular cultural aesthetic of the Negro" (9). Bruce was a prescient pioneer of the Black Power movement in the United States; the issues he dealt with in his fiction and articles prophesied Black Power concerns in the areas of race pride and solidarity, black history, and black separatist organizations. Bruce was a unique voice in his support of the use of force and violence in obtaining black rights, and, like Garvey, he urged the creation of a free black nation in Africa. The radical nature of these political and social programs stands in sharp contrast to Booker T. Washington's contemporaneous assimilationist philosophy and W. E. B. Du Bois's theory of the talented tenth. Bruce helped found the Afro-American League and the Afro-American Council, black militant organizations that counseled black people to pursue through agitation and civil disobedience their just and deserved rights. Bruce's ideas were radical in conception and a forerunner of many twentieth-century African American issues. He brought these ideas to the only known example of detective fiction that he wrote, justifying my claim that black detective fiction provided a vehicle for African American political and social issues. Interestingly, all of Bruce's political ideas are developed in the later detective fiction of Chester Himes and Ishmael Reed, which I will be examining in Chapters 5 and 6.

Bruce's use of detective conventions in *The Black Sleuth* supports Hopkins's innovations while extending the black detective tradition in new directions. Comparisons between these two early novels illustrate a number of interesting intersecting points in methods and intent. Once again, detective personas are altered and double-conscious detection tropes are brought into play. However, black vernaculars and hoodoo play a lesser role in the narrative, giving way to Bruce's interest in black pride and black history, Afrocentrism, and African culture.

The Black Sleuth is written in the third person in a direct style that is suitably unadorned for a popular audience. Bruce cleverly alters conventional detective plots by insinuating extended ideological monologues and dialogues that attempt to reverse the stereotypes concerning black intelligence, black civilization, and black history. These powerful personal arguments as executed by the African Okukenu family dramatize the signifyin(g) power of black characters in confronting white misconceptions about the black race. In particular, Bruce must be recognized as one of the early African Americans who saw the importance of a positive reassessment of Africa and the African past. As Marion Berghahn in *Images of Africa in Black American Literature* (1977) writes,

> The great importance of ethnicty was recognized by a number of Afro-Americans quite early on. They tried to bring about a reorientation of their group and to give Africa a positive meaning in Afro-American consciousness. (32)

Specifically, Bruce's reassessment of Africa was an attempt to defeat the widespread assumption by whites that Africans were savages, brutes, and primitive intellectually and morally. Berghahn sums up the general opinion of Africa held by white and black Americans at the time of Bruce's novel: "This picture of a barbaric continent inhabited by spiritually, morally and intellectually backward and inferior peoples met with little opposition until the end of the nineteenth century" (12). Bruce's sense of nationalism was derived without the benefit of a visit to the mother country. However, it is quite obvious from the text of the novel that Bruce was mainly interested in reconstructing the intellectual reputation of the African male. John Gruesser makes the interesting point that Sadipe's brother Mojola was most likely based on a real African minister named Majola Agbebi, whom Bruce met in 1903 and who was highly influential in Bruce's development of African nationalist ideas.[9]

Regardless of Bruce's models, his choice of a detective format for African intellectual revisionism makes absolute sense considering the classical detective model of ratiocination developed by Poe and handed down to detective figures ever afterward. As Berghahn points out, "Logical thinking and rationality . . . were believed to be . . . proof of a general intellectual superiority" (11). Bruce's master stroke was in taking popular culture's most accepted model of intellectual superiority—the detective—and turning him into a black African who was more rational than and hence superior to any white in the book. In fact, Bruce uses not only one black detective, Sadipe Okukenu, to prove his point but also Sadipe's father and Sadipe's brother Mojola.

Bruce's detective vision is also expanded by his use of an international setting, an African-born detective, and a fresh perspective on American white supremacy, imperialism, and racial prejudice. The detective persona is altered and magnified in the novel for both dramatic and didactic purposes. Unlike the classical or hardboiled detective. Sadipe's background and family are extremely important to understanding his success as a detective. Like *Hagar's Daughter*, the novel is a study in conflicting cultures and a severe indictment of racial bigotry and prejudice. However, where as Hopkins pits African American perceptions against southern white prejudice in a novel about passing, Bruce contrasts African perceptions with southern white and international white prejudice in a novel about raised black consciousness. Of the four main episodes in the novel, two take place in Africa, one in America, and one in England. *The Black Sleuth* uses the detective convention of a crime and pursuit of the criminals to structure a sophisticated social critique of Euro-American value systems and civilization.

There is no clear evidence that Bruce read detective stories. However, his knowledgeable use of detective conventions in his text suggests a familiarity with the form. Remaining true to Hopkins's initial use of the detective agency as opposed to the individual detective, Bruce places his black detective, Sadipe Okukenu, among a group of detectives. Sadipe is an agent of the private International Detective Agency, "which had branch offices in all the great capitals of Europe, and . . . employed hundreds of trained thief catchers—men of every civilized race" (Bruce 1). Sadipe, like Venus, works under a white supervisor, in this case named Samuel Hunter, and is part of a team of detectives, including blacks. This team approach to detective fiction suggests to me a conscious attempt by black detective writers to show the strength of solidarity, and in *The Black Sleuth* Bruce expands on this theme by supporting the detective persona with other manifestations of black superiority in the persons of close relatives. The team approach also reinforces the foreshadowing of the police procedural discussed earlier in this chapter. Finally, the gargantuan size of Bruce's detective agency, which spans the Western Hemisphere, seems to suggest an international organization of law and morality that rises above common restrictions of borders and governments. This organization is paid to work for the common good and hires individuals of exceptional merit. Apparently chief among the personal qualifications of the employees is lack of racial prejudice, as exemplified by Sadipe's immediate supervisor, Samuel Hunter. The breadth and purity of this International Detective Agency carry an aura of science fiction and a powerful element of wish fulfillment. Given Bruce's predilection for black political organizations, the International Detective Agency with its agents from every civilized race seems to be a futuristic projection of a political magnitude not represented in the reality of the world Bruce depicts in *The Black Sleuth*. With its connotations of world order, the agency suggests international cooperative organizations such as the yet unheard of League of Nations and United Nations. Bruce uses this umbrella of an all-powerful detective agency as a tool to discuss issues such as the color line and to bring an interesting perspective to African American race relations.

Bruce pulls no punches in notifying his readers of the altered detective persona in this novel and the moral use to which he will apply detective fiction. In fact, he makes an issue of it by starting his novel with the sentence, "Do you mean to tell me that nigger is a detective, and that you are going to put him on this case, Mr. Hunter?" (1). This incredulous query by the southern white, American-born Capt. George De Forrest, whose African diamond (given to him by Mojola Okukenu, brother of Sadipe) has been stolen by a band of white impostors, acts as a challenge to readers and to Sadipe, who overhears the remark. De Forrest is American by birth but English by adoption and full of "the foolish American antipathy and prejudice to people of darker hue" (2). His verbal challenge sets the tone of the novel and provides an overt structure for the white/black dynamics of the plot. Every episode of this narrative has one basic theme: to prove the superiority of the black race over the white. The ignorance, hypocrisy, and outright prejudice of the white characters in *The Black Sleuth* are manifested at every turn of the plot and are effectively undercut by the contrasting virtues of the black characters. Finally, this outrageous first sentence is obviously a structural device to engage attention, since the detective aspect of the story does not reappear until the last third of the novel.

The Black Sleuth is not a finished novel. The sixty-four pages that have been published in *McGirt's* end on a minor note before the inevitable capture and arrest of the culprits. Since it is written in installments and there is no indication that this is the last installment, I see no reason to consider this anticlimactic ending part of the author's intent. Furthermore, the challenge that launches the narrative has not been answered in totality as the text suggests it will be. Sadipe has overheard the remark and "registered a vow that he would make that particular captain own the force of his genius and feel very much ashamed of himself by showing him how cleverly a 'nigger' can do his work" (2). Although the novel is unfinished, there is enough evidence to place it firmly within the black detective tradition.

The Black Sleuth concerns the separation and journeys of the male members of an African family. In fact, the novel remains a text exclusively in the male domain. Unlike *Hagar's Daughter,* the novel does not confront or refigure gender stereotypes. The patriarchal line is the most important in the novel, and Bruce's characterizations of women break no new ground in gender relations. The Okukenu family consists of the father and two sons, Mojola and Sadipe. At the urging of the sagacious father, the two brothers part company and leave their homeland at the beginning of the novel. Mojola travels to England with an English teacher, and Sadipe sails to the United States with an American captain in the sailing vessel *Water Witch.* After the first short chapter, which takes place in the detective bureau in England, the novel breaks down into flashback digressions. The first relates Mojola's journey to England where he confronts racial prejudice and the naive impressions of the English about blacks. When Mojola is questioned by Captain De Forrest as to whether he felt fear at his first sight of a railroad steam engine, Mojola answers disdainfully:

> I do not think, sir, that I ever was afraid or "scared," as you call it, of anybody or anything except when I first saw a man of your race [whom] we Africans . . . associate with the prince of evil and all that is wicked and bad. (5)

Mojola is soon disgusted with England's "sham and hypocrisy" and the "hollowness of [its] pretensions of brotherhood" (6). He tells Captain De Forrest:

> Before your race had a civilization or a religion, mine was, and from it your race has borrowed or stolen all that was best and most useful in art, science, religion, letters, politics, and government, from which you have evolved what you proudly term Anglo-Saxon civilization. Intelligent Africans laugh at your complacent egotism. (6)

Returning to Africa, he meets Captain De Forrest and attempts to *give* him an extremely large and valuable diamond, in part to show up the greed of the white man. "The accumulation and hoarding of wealth is an invention of the white man, and Africa is just now the centre of this activity. He is plundering Africa like a buccaneer in quest of gold and diamonds and ivory" (9). Mojola responds to De Forrest's greed and prejudice by offering him a lecture on the true nature of black consciousness: "Opportunity and environment are the standard by which all men should be judged, not color" (10). Inevitably, the African nation will triumph over the white intrusion, and Mojola predicts the future in which Ethiopia will triumph: "Africans will absorb and assimilate your learning . . . and then construct her own code of morals and ethics for use against the time when 'Ethiopia shall suddenly stretch out her hands to God' " (9). At the end of this section Mojola departs from De Forrest's ship and disappears from the narrative. Chapter 5 then takes up Sadipe's story.

The Okukenu family is from Ekiti County in Terubaland on the west coast of Africa. Also known as the Yorubas, this tribe numbers among its members "the best scholars in Africa" (3). Mojola Okukenu speaks and writes the Yoruba language as well as French, German, Arabic, Italian, and English (3). Sadipe is also well educated, "having graduated from Eton College, in England, with high honors, a fine linguist, an expert in chess, and as perfectly developed physically as an Apollo Belvidere" (2). The family speaks Arabic as well as native dialects. They read the Koran and are followers of Mohammed. At the beginning of chapter 5 Sadipe is about to embark on his voyage to America on the *Water Witch,* captained by an American down-easterner named Barnard. Barnard voices the same ignorant presuppositions about the black race that De Forrest manifests in the first section.

The Black Sleuth features an international setting with a cast of characters from South Africa, West Africa, England, and the United States. However, it is the African past of Sadipe Okukenu that proves most interesting in this detective novel. It brings to mind the memories of an African past that made the first quarter of *The Life of Olaudah Equiano* (1789) so fascinating. In this novel Sadipe Okukenu's African past is a significant aspect of the narrative. Before Sadipe leaves for the United States, his father engages in a heated exchange with Captain Barnard of the *Water Witch,* the ship that will take him away. The nature of this exchange concerns race relations in the United States. The elder Okukenu is a man who has studied the white race closely, and he muses that "this white man actually believes that his race can teach me something" (11). Barnard tells him that Sadipe will benefit from education by Americans because "We have a very kind feeling in our hearts for the black people and we are helping them through our churches and schools in learning to become self-respecting and useful citizens" (12). Incisive questioning by Sadipe's father confirms his knowledge of the color-line prejudice inherent in American society:

> Why do you have Negro colleges if all men have the same rights in your country and are all equal? Why do you thus separate the races? . . . I have heard that you Americans have stolen thousands of my people from their homes here in Africa to make them slaves, and that since freedom came to them you kill them by burning them at the stake and lynching them, as you call it. Are these white men superior to black men? (12)

The captain's reaction to these pointed questions is puzzlement, confusion, and embarrassment: "Here in the very heart of Africa he was standing face to face with one of her [sable?] sons, who was discussing with him a question of ethics that made him blush for shame for the 'most Christian nation on earth' " (12). In this unusual chapter we find clues to Sadipe's detective character in his African heritage. The description of Sadipe's father by Captain Barnard is particularly telling when contrasted with Sadipe's future role as a detective disguised as a black servant named Randolph. Sadipe's father is a "shrewd old African" who is described as "A man whose appearance concealed more than it revealed: a deep, cool headed old Negro with a logical mind, who was putting questions to him that stung his pride and made him ashamed to own the name 'American' " (12). The double-consciousness theme as applied to black detective novels suggests the trickster qualities of appearance versus reality.

We have already discussed how passing in *Hagar's Daughter* combines with the detective tropes of disguise and masking. In *The Black Sleuth* this masking tradition is continued but emphasizes black pride instead of passing. Sadipe's eventual role as a detective is a function, in part, of inherited traits generated by his father and his African heritage:

> Sadipe was a boy of uncommon native and acquired abilities for one of his age. He was of a lively temperament, high-spirited and manly in bearing, quick-witted and apt. He was passionately fond of books, and, young as

he was—he was just turning nineteen—he spoke two native dialects and was quite familiar with Arabic. (13)

Unlike most African journeys to America, Sadipe's is blessed by his father, who reminds him of his proud heritage. He tells Captain Barnard:

> I have no fear about his not returning to his home here in Africa. The Okukenus will not submit to oppression or injustice in any form, no matter where they are, and if Sadipe is not treated well in your country he will find a way to get back to the land of his fathers. (13)

This strong emphasis on African roots establishes a foundation of Afrocentric pride that will be built upon in other black detective novels. It also gives us a very different picture of African culture than is found in conventional Euro-Americentric viewpoints. For example, the emphasis on education, community values, and importance of family in a long tradition refutes common stereotypes of native black Africans as ignorant, superstitious, and displaced. In this way and others *The Black Sleuth,* as Henry Louis Gates suggests, "undermines the convention of the noble savage" and prepares the way for further use of Afrocentric worldviews in detective fiction (*CHE* 8).

Outdone at every turn, Barnard admits defeat, but he has answered Sadipe's father honestly. The elder Okukenu allows his son to go to America for important reasons that have little to do with Barnard's avowed Christian sentiment: "I wish him to go that he may see for himself how the white man in America lives" (13). Sadipe's experiences in America demonstrate his father's wisdom, as Sadipe's understanding of white behavior proves useful to him later on in his detective career. Sadipe's disillusionment with America begins on his journey south from Maine where he has studied for eighteen months. He has received a scholarship to Eckington College for Colored Youth in a faraway southern state. His problems begin in Washington, "where equality of citizenship is proclaimed in the National Congress" and where from the top of the Capitol the "goddess of Liberty stood in mock seriousness keeping guard (?) over the liberties and rights of the people" (16). First, he is accosted at the gate of the train station by a coarse Irishman who demands his ticket and then slaps Sadipe condescendingly on the back. Sadipe is outraged at this affront and with the aid of another gentleman finds the superintendent of the railroad and lodges a complaint, which results in the upbraiding of the ticket taker.

Sadipe's troubles are not over. As he proceeds south in the first-class car he is informed by the conductor that "you belong in the kyar for Nigras. This heah kyar is for white folks only" (19). Confronted with the Jim Crow restrictions on train travel in the South, Sadipe "could not believe his senses. He was nonplussed, stupefied, and he was angry" (19). The conductor threatens him with force. Sadipe resists, and the conductor calls in two black porters to throw him into "Nigger heaven," both of whom refuse to obey his orders. Sadipe refuses to leave his seat and is supported by a white gentleman named R. M. De Mortie, commander of a crack Negro regiment in the West. De Mortie slips him a revolver and tells him to shoot the "first scoundrel that lays hands on you. I will take care of the others" (21). Sadipe responds, "I assure you that I am not afraid to die, if need be, in defense of my honor and my manhood" (21). The conductor is forced to retreat. Sadipe's unflinching acceptance of his right to defend his black honor stands in sharp contrast to the subservient blacks he meets in the South. In addition, it demonstrates Bruce's early Black Power sentiments and his commitment to use any means necessary to defend the rights of his people.

Upon arrival at his destination, Sadipe is met by Professor Swift, principal of Eckington College, who explains to him that "Prejudice to color is a wicked thing, but we in this section have to suffer a great many inconveniences on account of our black faces" (24). Sadipe finds this quite unbelievable: "I had no idea that human beings could be so intolerant of the rights of others, and all this in free America" (24). Things go from bad to worse as Sadipe and Swift are insulted by whites at every turn in their journey around the town. In less than twenty-four hours Sadipe writes a letter to General De Mortie informing him that he cannot stay at the college: "Where freedom is throttled and manacled it cannot survive" (26). He also finds the curriculum at the all-Negro college inadequate and is repelled by the principal's fawning attitude in front of whites and his petitioning them for money. Ready to return north, Sadipe reminds De Mortie that he mentioned a friend "who is establishing an International Detective Bureau" and says that he believes he has "some talent for this kind of work" (26).

Before Sadipe can leave, however, he has a final confrontation with

white southern mentality in the form of Skinner, a returned missionary from western Africa, who addresses the assembled student body.
His speech, which Sadipe attends, was of "the stereotyped kind,"
stressing the "all-powerful white race" whom almighty God had com-
missioned to deliver the Negro in Africa from darkness and "give him
civilization, teach him morality, educate his head, heart and hand,
and thus make him useful to his kind" (29). Sadipe rushes to the
front of the auditorium and refutes the missionary's speech, paying
particular attention to the religious hypocrisy of the speaker's sentiments:

> I am at a loss to understand why the white Christians of America, with all
> their prejudices to race and color, persist in sending missionaries to Africa
> . . . to civilize and christianize the "heathen" . . . when there are so many
> heathen at their own doors. (30)

Sadipe also confronts Skinner on the important issue of black pride
in a Pan-African context. He is outraged at the cavalier attitude of
Skinner, who characterizes races that are "red, black, brown or
yellow" as weaker and inferior. Sadipe tells him that the "weak-
nesses" of

> all the so-called weaker races, whose weakness consists in being unlike the
> Anglo in that they do not covet their neighbors goods and are not engaged
> in cruel warfare to extend their power . . . will prove the sources of their
> greatest strength when the awakening of the nations, which is fast ap-
> proaching, takes place. (30)

The sentiments expressed here foreshadow the international Black
Power movements of the last half of the twentieth century as well as
the Pan-African revolutionary rhetoric of Marcus Garvey and the rise
of Third World consciousness.

The missionary leaves the auditorium ashamed, and word spreads
through town about an educated Negro, "uppish and impudent,"
who dared confront his superiors. Sadipe finds a letter from De Mortie in his room telling him that he has been appointed "a special
representative" of the detective bureau and that he should leave immediately for New York to meet the chief of the bureau. Sadipe leaves
on the train that evening just as an enraged horde of whites bent on
lynching him storms the principal's house.

The final section of *The Black Sleuth* takes place in London three years later. Sadipe's "career as a sleuth had been an Iliad of successes" (37), and the reader picks up the story of Captain De Forrest and the huge diamond he has brought back from Africa. At this point the detective conventions of the narrative become dominant. This last section follows Sadipe closely as, outfitted in many disguises, he follows the trail of a band of four crooks. The preceding sections concerning both Mojola's and Sadipe's journeys are, to my mind, extended *blackgrounds* that help to define the particular double-conscious identity of the black detective Sadipe. As we have seen, the foregoing narrative emphasizes the Afrocentric nature of Sadipe's personal history: his proud, angry, and brave personality; and the superior qualities of his heritage, his intellect, and his deductive rationality. Sadipe's black consciousness, nurtured carefully in his African homeland, has blossomed in his travels, stimulated by contact with American abuse of civil liberties. Like his father and brother before him, Sadipe detects white hypocrisy and prejudice with unflinching accuracy. Because of his outsider status in white society he is acutely aware of masks and masking, as well as being capable, in the trickster tradition, of assuming disguise to outwit his opponents. His black detective skills will prove to be instrumental in tracking down the jewel thieves, Colonel Bradshawe, Miss Crenshawe, and their two accomplices.

The heightened black consciousness of Sadipe and his brother Mojola is both an inherited and a learned skill. Mojola functions in the text primarily as a reinforcement of Sadipe's personality; they are like twins or mirror images of each other. Their father's insightful wisdom into white behavior provides an example for the sons, and Bruce strongly implies that African blood provides inherited characteristics that give the black race special talents. These talents will be demonstrated through black vernaculars and hoodoo in other black detective novels, but here they relate more to superior rational and intellectual qualities and innate observational skills. One talent that has been demonstrated by the father and both brothers is the ability to manipulate language. In every confrontation with whites the Africans prove to be superb debaters, expounding with clarity and ingenuity a fresh perspective on black identity. As Captain De Forrest says to Mojola, "You have converted me . . . while you were talking so earnestly and eloquently a few moments ago" (10). The elder Okukenu outwits Captain Barnard with incisive questions, and

Sadipe signifies so effectively on Skinner that he is almost lynched for his words.

Mojola and Sadipe part with Africa and their family at the request of their father, who wants them to "learn more about the white man in his native land" (4). This voluntary separation of family based on a parental decision to study the white man in his natural environment provides an interesting contrast to the forced separation of families instituted in the slavery model. In fact, *The Black Sleuth* reverses stereotypes at every turn. Common stereotypes of blacks as ignorant, lazy, and superstitious are replaced by the Okukenus' model of high intelligence, education, and love of community. The mystical aspects of other black detective characters are replaced by ratiocination and psychological observational skills highly prized in detective personas of both classical and hardboiled varieties. For example, Sadipe immediately suspects Bradshawe of being a criminal by listening closely to his language. Inconsistency and confusion are the clues Sadipe picks up on, quickly unraveling Bradshawe's story by deconstructing his conversation.

It is in this final section that Sadipe shows off his deductive detective abilities and his trickster qualities. As the invisible black among a group of unsuspecting whites foiled by their own prejudices, Sadipe infiltrates the robber band. Although much better educated and more sophisticated than Venus the black maid, Sadipe, like her, assumes a disguise. Sadipe's masquerade as Randolph, a waiter in a restaurant, proves to be instrumental in solving the case, as does the color of the man's skin, which allows him to be privy to conversations by the culprits.

> And we must not forget Randolph, the black, whose role in this little drama, about to be enacted, was, to say the least, as difficult as it was delicate and dangerous, yet for which he was admirably fitted in view of the fact that his black face [disarmed] all suspicion as to his true character. (43–44)

In fact, Randolph plays his part so well that he is described as "quiet, unobtrusive, obsequious, a model servant" (44). This initial disguise allows him close contact with the band of thieves led by the evil Colonel Bradshawe and the duplicitous Miss Crenshawe. Sadipe is described by the manager of the detective bureau as "versatile and resourceful" and as "one of the most valuable men in the service of the agency" (2), and his success is evidently directly attributable to his African race and his color. Sadipe proves this in the text by expanding the servant role into a dizzying array of disguises, all of which use his skin color as a positive power in the course of his detection.

Sadipe recognizes Bradshawe as a fraud from the first moment he meets him, even though others such as Captain De Forrest are fooled by his glib charades. When Sadipe follows Bradshawe to his hideout, Hunter praises him for his "marked skill as a sleuth in that you successfully located the rendezvous of these shrewd swindlers, who have thus far eluded the vigilance of the best detectives in Scotland Yard" (62). However, it is not only Sadipe's skin color or his chameleonlike ability to change his appearance that eminently suits him to the detective role. He has certain innate and learned qualities that make him a particularly good representative of double-conscious detection. His display of detective trickster abilities and his heightened perception of the criminal mentality can be attributed to two well-developed areas of his past, his African birthright and his experience in the prejudiced South of the United States. Sadipe has an observational acuity normally associated with the detective but in this case further heightened by his double-conscious abilities. When his supervisor compliments him on his versatility and resourcefulness (44), Sadipe proudly tells him that an African and a North American Indian never forget a face (48) and says he considers himself "vain enough to believe that I have some talent for this kind of work" (26). Disguised as an African student, Sadipe catches a glimpse of Colonel Bradshawe in a crowded auditorium and says to himself, "No matter how he dresses or disguises himself, I can never forget that face. Where I see it I will know it" (50). This is in sharp contrast to Miss Crenshawe, who must sketch Captain De Forrest to be sure she will not forget his appearance.

Certainly these talents are shared by other detectives of both classical and hardboiled schools, but in Sadipe's case Bruce gives particular reasons to explain why his detective is so skillful. Much of Sadipe's detective skill is based on his African birthright. Double-conscious detection in fact plays a large role in the narrative by filtering the black detective tropes through an African perspective. Mr. Hunter acknowledges this when he tells Sadipe:

I have every confidence in your ability and in your judgement. You Africans have many advantages over us Europeans, and there are some things you can do better than we when you try. Your black face will be an important aid in the capture of Mandeville [Bradshawe] and your knowledge of French will come in handy . . . he will never suspect that you understand that tongue. (49)

The irony of the text is based in part on the typical bigotry of whites who cannot see beyond the color of a man's face. Race prejudice is turned to advantage by Sadipe, who can hide his true identity behind the mask of his black face. The fact that Bradshawe and his cronies see only a black face underlines all the white preconceptions that Bruce has attacked throughout the novel. Race prejudice is shown to contaminate all levels of white society, since Bradshawe is the dispossessed son of an English nobleman.

This double-conscious detective deception is only one of many tricks Sadipe pulls on the criminals. He masquerades as an African student (49), a rich African merchant (62), and a native African hoo-doo fortuneteller (54) who in a hoodoo session with the evil Miss Crenshawe is asked, "What are your charges . . . for lifting the veil and giving us a peep into the future" (56). Sadipe obliges, predicting "trouble and bloodshed" for whoever possesses the diamond, and then goes on to assure the criminals that they will be caught and imprisoned. The text ends here, but the implications of Sadipe's power as a detective, succeeding against the tremendous odds of inter-national white supremacy and prejudice, suggest a context for larger speculations. Sadipe's father has predicted his return "to the land of his fathers" (13). Both Mojola and Sadipe have highly developed black consciousnesses that would logically be put to best use in sup-porting the rise of Black Power and a new African, if not Pan-African, nationalism, and this is hinted at in the text with both brothers ex-pressing their undivided commitment to African history, black pride, and the rejection of white prejudice and imperialism wherever it is encountered. This native manifestation of Afrocentrism provides an interesting model of comparison for later black detective novels.

The novel ends on an abrupt note, but its sixty-four pages have established without a doubt the continuity of black detective tropes, particularly the altered detective persona and use of double-conscious detection. It has replaced an emphasis on black vernaculars and hoodoo with early manifestations of race pride, Pan-African nationalism, and Afrocentric revisionist history while indicating an early Black Power motif in the acceptance of the use of violence to defend black rights. These issues will be taken up by successive African American detective writers.

As we have seen, *The Black Sleuth* uses the black servant as a detective trope. It uses as well the elements of group detection, disguise, and blackness to determine the double-conscious nature of the detective persona. Common attributes of both the novels studied in this chapter establish important African American detective tropes which will be seen in successive works. These tropes are the African American detective writer's way of signifying on the Euro-American detective form. In the earlier part of this chapter we discussed how detective fiction can reflect cultural values, resolve tensions, and express latent feelings common to the needs of a particular culture. African American detective writers utilized detective conventions for their own ends and presented to the African American community, through popular black periodical literature, a revised interpretation of black consciousness. They did this by recognizing that blackness, the knowledge of African American folk customs, and a recognition of Afrocentrism are integral to the detective stories and personas presented. The key to solving these cases is always determined by the *blackness* of the detectives, and the text further illustrates the positive attributes of African American worldviews and communities and Afrocentric awareness. Finally, these texts show that from the very beginning black detective fiction has been written primarily as a vehicle for political and social critique of Euro-Americentric value systems. The insistent moral message inherent in African American popular fiction contrasts remarkably with much of the detective fiction published in the classical and hardboiled tradition. It is this tension that provides a continuing dynamic in the novels of black detection written in this century.

African American detective fiction deals with the issues of slavery, repression, and prejudice and refutes the common assumption that the popular arts cannot be used to discuss issues of class, gender, and race in meaningful ways. The political and social legacy left by Pauline Hopkins and J. E. Bruce set a precedent for later black detective writers. We know that detective fiction was of interest to and had an influence on other major black writers such as Richard Wright and Toni Morrison. However, black writers like Rudolph Fisher, Chester Himes, Ishmael Reed, and Clarence Major demonstrate a much more conscious experimentation with the form in their detective novels, producing a rich black detective tradition that extends to the present day.

4

Detective of the Harlem Renaissance: Rudolph Fisher

Rudolph Fisher is responsible for two works of detective fiction, a novel entitled *The Conjure Man Dies* (1932) and a short story entitled "John Archer's Nose" (1935). Both texts deal with a team of detectives working together to solve a murder case. Perry Dart is an official detective of the New York police force, and John Archer is a physician turned amateur detective. Although many critics have considered *The Conjure Man Dies* to be the first detective novel written by a black American, we have seen that this novel is preceded by two serialized novels in the African American detective tradition. The black detective themes presented in *The Conjure Man Dies* have much in common with these two previous novels in the areas of altered detective personas, double-conscious detection, black vernaculars, and hoodoo. However, Fisher brings a new understanding of African American culture to the black detective tradition by setting his novel in Harlem during the Jazz Age. *The Conjure Man Dies* is the first black detective novel to assert proudly its detective themes in a completely black environment with an all-black cast of characters. Furthermore, Fisher executes a startling revision of standard detective personas by introducing four black detectives into the novel.

The Conjure Man Dies has not received any extended critical analysis until recently. Both Robert Bone's *Negro Novel in America* (1958) and Addison Gayle's *Way of the New World* (1975) fail to mention *The Conjure Man Dies*, and other critics treat it superficially. However, Bernard Bell in *The Afro-American Novel and Its Tradition* includes an incisive analysis of the novel, emphasizing the important detective tropes. John McCluskey, Jr., in *The City of Refuge: The Collected Stories of Rudolph Fisher* (1987), also redresses this issue by analyzing the novel astutely and praising it as "intellectually . . .

93

the most engaging of Fisher's fiction" (xxxvi). I believe *The Conjure Man Dies* demonstrates how urban African American culture and Harlem Renaissance themes (1919–29) can be incorporated into a detective story format.

Rudolph Fisher, as a Harlem Renaissance writer, recognized that Harlem was a "city within a city," with its own African American value systems and culture. His short story "City of Refuge" (1925) features King Solomon Gillis, a black migrant from the South, who experiences the freedom and the dangers of an all-black Harlem for the first time. Fisher recognized that Harlem provided African Americans with a unique environment, full of the joys and problems that changed the African American concept of self in the modern era. Fisher's novel dramatizes the conflicts within the Harlem community while trying to define African American identity as it moved into the twentieth century. He developed the use of such black vernaculars as language and music by creating a more complete blackground than either Hopkins or Bruce. Fisher also elaborated on the theme of double-conscious detection through the clever characterization of N'Gana Frimbo, the conjure man of the title, who possesses dual nationality and eventually becomes one of the four detectives used in the novel. As both an African and an American citizen, N'Gana Frimbo develops the theme of black nationalism and Afrocentrism first touched on in *Bruce's Black Sleuth*. At the same time Fisher connected double-conscious detection to typical detective tropes of disguise and masquerade and made hoodoo a significant aspect of the trickster elements displayed in the novel.

Fisher's novel is a testing ground for important issues in African American culture in the 1920s and 1930s. Fisher was concerned with how rural and urban characters with vernacular beliefs came into conflict with modern scientific and philosophical attitudes and black urban problems. One example of this is the tradition-bearing mother in "John Archer's Nose" who kills her son because of his drug habit. Another example is Bubber Brown who, as one of the detectives in *The Conjure Man Dies,* represents the folk vernacular tradition. N'gana Frimbo, the conjure man, juggles two cultures at once. As a graduate of Harvard he combines scientific rationalism with his traditional African belief in and practice of mysticism and hoodoo. Fisher is also concerned with the importance of African American themes such as ancestralism and primitivism and how they connect with the African past.[1] The conflicts between old and new, rural and urban, and science and religion in Harlem's black community provide an introduction to Harlem Renaissance themes in the context of detective fiction. Fisher understood how these conflicts evolved out of the changing cityscape of Harlem as it expanded under southern black migration.

The son of a Baptist minister, Rudolph Fisher (1897–1934) was born in Washington, D.C., and brought up in Providence, Rhode Island. Fisher earned bachelor's and master's degrees from Brown University and a degree in medicine at Howard, with a specialty in roentgenology, a branch of radiology that deals with the use of X rays for diagnosis or treatment of disease. He worked as a physician in New York City while writing his stories, plays, and novels, and his medical background is apparent in *The Conjure Man Dies,* where much of the evidence in the investigation concerns forensic clues such as blood type and bridgework. Fisher is best known as the author of *The Walls of Jericho* (1928), a novel of class conflict in Harlem which contains two working-class characters, Bubber and Jinx, who also appear in *The Conjure Man Dies.* Arna Bontemps speaks of Fisher as a Harlem Renaissance writer who in his short life "gave us pictures of ordinary work-a-day blacks who were largely neglected by other Renaissance writers" (45). This is true in the sense that Fisher was careful to present a range of characters in his novels, including criminals, working-class people, and upper-class blacks. More importantly, Fisher was one of the few black writers to place his stories and novels entirely in Harlem.

The first publication of *The Conjure Man Dies* in 1932 was followed by a reissue in 1971 and another in 1992 by the University of Michigan Press. In the preface to the Arno Press edition of 1971, Stanley Ellin claims that "there had been no Negro writer who utilized this technique [detective fiction] as a means of literary expression until Fisher came along." With the recent discoveries of serialized novels published in African American periodical literature, Fisher can no longer be considered the first black writer to use the detective form. Nonetheless, *The Conjure Man Dies* is an extremely important novel in the African American detective tradition precisely because it sets new standards for applying detective story conventions to African American concerns.

The Conjure Man Dies must be considered in relation to Harlem

Renaissance themes. The Harlem Renaissance gave birth to what Alain Locke in 1925 called the "New Negro" in post-World War I culture and fiction.[2] "New Negro" was a term applied to a movement that engaged young blacks in a social and political reassessment of their race. As a movement it had its roots in turn-of-the-century changes in black attitudes about themselves as more and more blacks fought for education, economic advancement, and class recognition. A growing sense of self-pride, race nationalism, and self-determination spurred blacks toward demanding the equal rights due them under the democratic system. Enforced segregation, the race riots after World War I, and growing economic deprivations forced blacks to unite to fight for survival in the early twentieth century. The emerging New Negro of the 1920s emphasized black pride, celebrated the African American vernacular tradition, and revised black history with a recognition of a positive African heritage. Early advocates for black self-determination, such as Alexander Crummell (1819–98), generated economic and social empowerment ideas in the 1870s and 1880s that laid the groundwork for the New Negro movement. In the last chapter I discussed J. E. Bruce's contribution to other early manifestations of black separatist and Afrocentric concepts that were also part of the New Negro mentality. The publication and widespread popularity of Jean Toomer's *Cane* (1923) also helped develop a growing awareness of an emerging African American consciousness. Though the New Negro movement was widespread and not limited by class participation, it tended to speak to the artists and intellectuals of the period.

In some ways W. E. B. Du Bois influenced the New Negro movement with his black militancy and his theory of the "talented tenth," his term for blacks with college educations, humanitarian values, and upper-class aspirations. In Du Bois's view it was the talented tenth, or top 10 percent of the black population, who would be responsible for leading the race into the future. However, the New Negro movement and, more particularly, the Harlem Renaissance writers and artists were heavily criticized by Du Bois for celebrating the primitive qualities of lower-and working-class blacks which he believed reinforced negative stereotypes of African Americans. Conversely, for the Harlem Renaissance writers, primitivism was an elemental connection with primal life forces that was more positive than negative.

Primitivism was often depicted through the black vernaculars of speech, dance, music, and food found in the vibrant and sensual interiors of bars and clubs. Robert A. Coles and Diane Isaacs in their essay "Primitivism as Therapeutic Pursuit" make the distinction between exoticism, which "exploits primitivism," and true primitivism, which they find became a healthy alternative for Harlem Renaissance writers: "Contrary to the negative connotations that often surround the concept of primitivism, it functioned as an affirmative force in many ways during the Harlem Renaissance years" (11). Primitivism is closely connected to ancestralism, which Bell describes as the "celebration of race consciousness" in Harlem Renaissance literature (114). Primitivism and ancestralism forge a link between Africa and African Americans and redefine Africa as the homeland of racial purity and positive creative energies.

While the earthy and sensual aspects of Harlem were important to Harlem Renaissance writers, they were also quick to include other characters who represented the mental and spiritual achievements of blacks. In *The Conjure Man Dies* Fisher cleverly layers one character with a complex range of traits and turns out N'Gana Frimbo, one of the more brilliant and confused blacks in modern detective literature. N'Gana Frimbo, as the conjure man, represents a cultural struggle among African Americans, as the book ambitiously confronts black identity issues within its own detective boundaries. From street hustler to doctor to African hoodoo priest, Fisher documents a range of African American types while presenting a unique Harlem cityscape.

The literary and artistic ferment created by black artists and intellectuals during the Harlem Renaissance launched an unprecedented reappraisal of African American contributions to society. Critics like Alain Locke, publishers and collectors like James L. Coady and Albert C. Barnes, and organizations such as the Harmon Foundation stressed the positive attributes of African Americans. The first major exhibition of art by black Americans was held at the International House in New York City in 1928. A sense of self-reliance, self-respect, and pride in African ancestry fostered an art movement that included Aaron Douglas, Palmer Hayden, and Archibald Motley, Jr., among others. White music critic, photographer, and novelist Carl Van Vechten helped popularize Harlem, and black photographers such as James Van Derzee, Morgan and Marvin Smith, and Gordon Parks recorded the lively scene. Black entertainers and dancers like Bill Robinson and Josephine Baker created a new audience for black arts. The popularity of African American cultural expression in music, dance, and fashion led to an international awareness of black American creativity during the Jazz Age.

Rudolph Fisher was a major intellectual light of the Harlem Renaissance, which Cary D. Wintz in his book *Black Culture and the Harlem Renaissance* (1988) characterizes as "primarily a literary and intellectual movement" (1). Witty, highly educated, and conversant with all the intense debates about black pride, assimilation, and nationalism, Fisher also enjoyed and studiously observed the dance halls, cabarets, and street life of Harlem (McCluskey xxxii-xxxiii). The community of Harlem encapsulated aspects of black society and presented questions about black cultural development in United States. Was the black American? African? Neither? Or a combination of both? Should blacks move into white society and accept Euro-American value systems? Or should blacks remain separate? These are the kinds of questions that *The Conjure Man Dies* dramatizes as it unravels the mystery of N'Gana Frimbo's murder. Fisher's contribution to the philosophical ferment of that period can be explored in Margaret Perry's *Silence to the Drums,* Bernard Bell's chapter, "The Harlem Renaissance and the Search for New Modes of Narrative" in his *Afro-American Novel,* and Nathan Irvin Huggins's *Harlem Renaissance.*

The writers, poets, and artists of the Harlem Renaissance struggled to present a new African American cultural identity while deriving their inspiration from what was going on around them. Harlem reflected both the best and the worst of African American hopes and dreams. In a community alive with the black vernaculars and folk customs of rural migrants and the sophisticated urban creations of educated blacks, Harlem Renaissance writers embraced a new black consciousness. The bedrock of this consciousness was a celebration of the inherent beauty and genius of black Americans connected to an African past. One of the primary themes of the Harlem Renaissance was a resurgence of race pride and a reassessment of African American history by tracing African American roots to Africa. In 1926 Langston Hughes wrote his seminal essay "The Negro Artist and the Racial Mountain," in which he urged the black artist to reject "the desire to pour racial individuality into the mold of American standardization, and to be as little Negro and as much American as possible."[3] In this sense Hughes was calling for the recognition of an African American culture. His rejection of assimilation and implicit call for African American self-definition are issues that Fisher confronts in *The Conjure Man Dies*. Margaret Perry in her survey of the literature of the Harlem Renaissance states that "thematically Fisher was concerned with the idea of black unity and discovery of self" (66). She goes on to say that *Conjure Man* was "an important addition to the literature of the Harlem Renaissance because it exhibited again Fisher's abiding interest in his race and the formulation of ties with the African homeland" (67). *The Conjure Man Dies* shows that Fisher was aware of renewed African American hopes for self-determination and self-definition and conscious of the importance of Harlem to achieving further emancipation for blacks. Fisher was instrumental in creating what James De Jongh in *Vicious Modernism: Black Harlem and the Literary Imagination* calls the "topos" of the city:

> Black Harlem in literature is an original twentieth-century topos, a modern motif created by African-American writers inspired by the fervor of the racial transformation of the Manhattan neighborhood north of Central Park. (209)

De Jongh examines the many manifestations of Harlem in African American literature inspired by this island of black citizens in the midst of a larger city.

Harlem in the 1920s was a relatively new phenomenon. According to Wintz, southern black migrants began relocating to Harlem in earnest around 1903. By 1920 Harlem had become, by virtue of the sheer number of black residents, the chief social and cultural African American community in the United States (Wintz 18–20). Fisher gave Harlem a popular name, "city of refuge," taken from his short story of the same title published in the *New Negro*. With its complexity and blend of citizens from throughout the United States and the African diaspora, Harlem came to represent a new stage of high hopes and harsh realities for African Americans. Black citizens living in poverty were denied the essential rights of white citizens in nearby boroughs. Yet more and more people poured into the community.

Fisher recognized the detective novel's usefulness in presenting important African American cultural statements on issues of race, class, and identity. In a radio interview from January 1933, Fisher states:

> Darkness and mystery go together, don't they? The children of the night—and I say this in all seriousness—are children of mystery. The very setting is mystery—outsiders know nothing of Harlem life as it really is . . . what goes on behind the scenes and beneath the dark skins of Harlem folk—fiction has not found much of that yet. And much of it is perfectly in tune with the best of mystery tradition—variety, color, mysticism, superstition, malice and violence. (Quoted in Perry 67)

Fisher's familiarity with detective novels is evident from this passage, in which he isolates some of the chief psychological aspects of the detective tradition. Furthermore, he reveals that one of the primary aims of his detective fiction is to describe the community and its people in intimate ways. In his only detective novel, Fisher laid the groundwork for sequels. McCluskey says that Fisher planned two and that at the time of his death he was writing one called "Thus Spake the Prophet" (xxxvi). However, "John Archer's Nose" is the only other published story containing John Archer the physician-turned-sleuth and Perry Dart the black police detective.

The Conjure Man Dies is about the murder of the hoodoo visionary N'Gana Frimbo in his house in Harlem. The novel opens at night in the middle of winter. The wind howls down the streets of Harlem, but on Seventh Avenue in the center of Harlem the mood is anything but frigid. The night is alive with gaiety as men in camel hair coats and women in rabbit fur and muskrat weave in and out of clubs and dance halls. On the remote side street of 130th it is dark, quiet, and mysterious. On the third floor of a brownstone, which harbors the undertaker Samuel Crouch in the basement, N'Gana Frimbo is holding conjure office hours in a shadowy room. The single bright lamp is focused on a black man named Jinx Jenkins. Suddenly, Frimbo is killed in midsentence, struck soundlessly from behind with a human thigh bone—one of a pair that decorated the waiting room mantlepiece—and then suffocated with a balled-up handkerchief. Among the suspects are Jinx and six people who are in the waiting room: Martha Crouch, wife of the undertaker who owns the building; Mrs. Aramintha Snead, a religious lady whose husband has a drinking problem; Spider Webb, a numbers runner; Easley Jones, a railroad porter; Doty Hicks, a drug addict; and Bubber Brown, companion to Jinx Jenkins. There is one other suspect, N'Gana Frimbo's personal attendant, N'Ogo Frimbo, who has mysteriously disappeared from the scene.

The murder opens up an investigation of an individual's past (N'Gana Frimbo) that reflects the collective past of African Americans in general and gives the reader an inside view of Harlem society. Doctor Archer, a neighbor who lives across the street, pronounces N'Gana Frimbo dead and teams up with Perry Dart, a black detective on the Manhattan police force, to investigate the crime. The story takes place over one long night and the following day and night and includes a long series of interviews with all the people who were present in the building on the night of Frimbo's supposed murder. The novel uses many tricks from the classical tradition, including analytical deductions in the mode of Sherlock Holmes, bumbling assistants, and ineffectual policemen. Clever twists in plot motivations suggest Agatha Christie's puzzles. For example, the body of the murdered man disappears, and Bubber Brown stumbles upon a hidden corpse in the basement, which proves to be not N'Gana Frimbo but his servant and close kinsman N'Ogo Frimbo, who looks very much like him. The reader discovers that N'Gana Frimbo had been masquerading as his servant in an attempt to find the killer who planned to murder him. N'Gana Frimbo's mysterious resurrection from the dead halfway through the novel makes him, oddly enough, a suspect in his own "murder." At this point N'Gana Frimbo takes over the investigation. Even his psychic ability cannot prevent the murderer from trying again, however, and Frimbo is killed in the end. It turns out that Easley Jones is an impostor; the undertaker Crouch has been masquerading as the railroad porter and planning to kill N'Gana Frimbo, who has been having an affair with his wife, Martha.

The novel follows the classical detective format in structure and plot development. The opening crescendo of a murder is followed by the developing theme of the investigation of the suspects. The book mimics the classical tradition and the English country-house mystery made famous by Agatha Christie but alters the landscape to cityscape and changes the characters from English gentry to a range of African American personalities. As in the country-house murders, the suspects are confined to one locale. In this case there are seven suspects, from which number the murderer must be found. An outside detective is brought in to investigate, and red herrings are scattered through the text. The novel also suggests the locked-room mystery first set up as a detective problem in Poe's "Murders in the Rue Morgue." Though the novel follows all the prerequisites, as discussed in Chapter 1, of the classical elements of detection, it also signifies on the classical model by experimenting with black detective tropes. The closed atmosphere and method of investigation of *The Conjure Man Dies* reflect the classical tradition, yet Fisher uses this basic structure to expand upon Harlem Renaissance themes and introduce hardboiled attributes in his use of vernacular language, social commentary, and police procedural methods. Even though *The Conjure Man Dies* meets many requirements of the classical detective tale supplanted to Harlem, there are issues of class and language that show other influences, such as Dashiell Hammett and other *Black Mask* writers, as Stanley Ellin notes in the preface to *Conjure Man:*

> Fisher's extremely complex plotting and his occasionally too-pedantic writing of descriptive and expository passages is in the classical mode. But the characters, their broad range of background, and the handling of dialogue are wholly of Hammett's realistic school.

Ellin goes on to suggest that Fisher's "adherence to the new realism . . . invests [the novel] with qualities of a social document recording a time and place without seeming to." What Ellin fails to discuss is the significance of this social document in terms of African American cultural attributes and Fisher's use of the four black detective tropes.

As I have suggested, the first two black detective novels studied questioned the identity of the detective hero in terms of class, race, and gender. *Conjure Man* continues the African American reassessment of the detective persona by questioning the reality of the detective himself. Clarence Major will carry this exploration to its postmodern conclusion in his novel, *Reflex and Bone Structure* (1975). Typically, in terms of African American creativity, Fisher is not content to accept any Euro-American literary formula whole hog. To begin with, there are actually four detectives in the novel, and all contribute to the solving of the case. Archer and Dart are the primary detectives, with Bubber Brown and N'Gana Frimbo contributing to a group investigation. In fact, Bubber, the least organized and intellectual of the four, is responsible for the big breakthrough in the case when he stumbles on the hidden corpse in the cellar. The fourth detective, Frimbo himself, actually becomes a detective *and* a criminal in the final stages of the novel as he destroys the evidence of his servant's death and tricks both Archer and Dart in his attempts to solve his own murder. This community of detectives continues a pattern established with our first two novels in which a group works better than a single individual, strongly signifying on both the classical and the hardboiled tradition of the alienated, lone detective.

Black detective persona elements enter the text early. The team of Doctor Archer and Detective Dart can be seen as an extension of the Dupin/nameless-narrator and Holmes/Watson dualities. The names themselves are obviously symbolic as Archer often directs Dart in the investigation. They are on a more equal footing than Sherlock Holmes and Watson but share some of the same personal characteristics. While Archer ruminates and philosophizes much in the tradition of the brilliant amateur detective Holmes, Dart strong-arms, intimidates, and uses all the powers of the official police force. Archer's quick mind leads to complexities of conjecture that Dart cannot follow, but Dart is more pragmatic and is in control of the apparatus of detection. This includes the typical cast of police procedural figures such as the forensic expert who takes fingerprints and the police medical examiner. In this way, *The Conjure Man Dies* prefigures advancements in the detective form that will enter the field in 1945. As in other detective teams, there is a symbiosis of character that makes the two function better together than separately. The dual function of the Archer/Dart team is commented on in "John Archer's Nose": "Spiritually the two bachelors were as opposite as the two halves of a circle—and as complementary" (McCluskey 158).

The two detectives alter the persona in other ways. Both of them are black, although Archer is lighter in color. Dart is described as having grown up in Manhattan and as knowing "Harlem from the lowest dive to loftiest temple" (*Conjure Man* 14). The importance of this double-conscious knowledge of Harlem becomes clearer as the case progresses and Dart uses street personalities to ferret out information. His color is also instrumental in his position. Dart is the first of ten Harlem policemen to be promoted to detective and is given that honor so as "to leave no doubt in the public mind as to [the city administration's] intention in the matter" (*Conjure Man* 14). Apparently, the black community of Harlem demanded a black detective, and Dart makes clear that his chief goal is service to the black community. Nothing else of Dart's background is given, but Archer's background suggests the struggle for achievement that lies behind the black detective persona. Social problems not generally presented in white detective personas are clearly part of Archer's development. In part, Archer's past has involved a constant battle against racial and economic discrimination: "the summers of menial work as a bell boy or waiter or porter somewhere, constantly taking orders from your inferiors, both black and white" (*Conjure Man* 224). Together, these two detectives indicate the importance of blackness to the success of the investigation as well as underlining the struggle for economic survival in the Harlem community.

We have looked at the first two detectives, Archer and Dart, as reflections of both a traditional detective pairing and manifestations of the scientific and pragmatic duality inherent in the novel. Dr. John Archer is an educated black man with an extremely light complexion who owns his own house. As part of the primary detective team, Archer represents education and high intelligence. On the other hand, Bubber Brown is dark, uneducated, and superstitious but street-wise. In this way, Fisher composes a spectrum of African American types inhabiting the special environment of Harlem. Bubber Brown is a rotund black man with a comic's approach to life. When he is searched at the behest of Detective Dart, a business card is found on him which reads:

BUBBER BROWN INC.
(formerly with the City of New York)
Evidence obtained in the affairs of the heart etc.
Special attention to cheaters and backbiters

Bubber has come to N'Gana Frimbo for help in solving a case he is in the process of investigating. As a self-employed detective working for hire, Bubber reminds the reader of the hardboiled private eye brought to the Harlem milieu. Archer and Dart are detectives of the mind, but Bubber is a detective of the heart. The character of N'Gana Frimbo includes all of these detective attributes while emphasizing double-conscious detective themes. Frimbo also crosses classes, having elements of the primitive and the intellectual classes in his background. As we have seen in our discussion of *Hagar's Daughter,* the issue of class is closely connected to skin color.

Though "passing" is not a theme in *The Conjure Man Dies,* the idea of class in relation to language use and folk beliefs does enter the text. Archer represents the educated class of black Americans. His practice and belief in modern medicine, his introduction of the scientific method to the case, and his skepticism concerning folk superstitions are upper-class traits we see in both the novel and the short story. In fact, "John Archer's Nose" is essentially about the conflict of modern medicine and superstition, and Archer's upper-class prejudice is much more apparent in the short story. In the novel, Archer is slowly convinced of N'Gana Frimbo's mystical abilities. He is impressed by Frimbo's intelligence and education, but in the end it is Frimbo the hoodoo priest who gets Archer's respect. Fisher sees humor in all levels of black society, and we sense that he sees Harlem's range of class and color as a positive aspect, reflecting a dynamic social environment in which all class elements intermingle to the benefit of the community. But it is Fisher's fidelity to double-conscious detection, black vernaculars, hoodoo, and the blackground atmosphere of Harlem that makes his work so distinctive.

Fisher's innovative strength continues to manifest itself in the second area of African American detective tradition, double-conscious detection. As we have discussed in Chapter 2 and seen in *Hagar's Daughter* and *The Black Sleuth,* double-conscious detection signifies on detective conventions by using elements of the trickster tradition, including masking, to develop African American themes. Double consciousness redefines black characters in relation to other black characters as well as the white world. Double-conscious detectives are noted for their *blackness* as well as their sleuthing abilities. Their blackness is an advantage that they take into account when assessing their chances of solving the case. In effect, black detectives use their blackness as a specialty that gives them insight into a variety of problems. The doubling aspects of masks and disguises play an extremely important role in *The Conjure Man Dies.* In the tradition of double-conscious detection as we have outlined it, *The Conjure Man Dies* covers a number of different double-consciousness motifs. There is no question that the condition of blackness and an assessment of its place within a white world of Euro-Americentric values are concerns of the novel. The geography of Harlem reflects these concerns, as does Frimbo's double-conscious awareness of self, a theme that lies at the heart of the novel.

Conjure Man carries the dynamic conceits of split characters and multiple personalities to interesting levels. So much is devoted to this theme, in fact, that it becomes clear early in the narrative that the book is concerned with the issue of double-conscious detection in a world of masquerades and identities hidden behind veils. For example, as we have seen, the original murder victim is actually N'Gana Frimbo's assistant N'Ogo Frimbo. The two are from the same African tribe, and this tribal bond will prove important in the Afrocentric worldview that Frimbo elaborates on near the end of the novel. Much like the novel *Hagar's Daughter,* in which characters struggle with the issue of identity under various disguises of "passing," *Conjure Man* debates the issues of African heritage and community and how they relate to the urban world of modern man and to the complexity of the African American worldview.

In Chapter 2 we suggested that double-conscious detection serves to amplify the usual plot machinations of the conventional detective story by allowing it to critique racial discrimination. *Hagar's Daughter* and *The Black Sleuth,* as the first two novels in the African American detective tradition, applied detective conventions such as mysterious disappearances, assumed identities, misinterpreted messages, murder, and kidnapping to the larger mission of expressing African American themes. We have shown how double-conscious detection doubled the masking aspect of detective fiction by introducing elements of the trickster tradition and hoodoo to the text. In *The Conjure Man Dies* double-conscious detection includes other aspects of disguise and masquerade. The primary example of this is N'Gana Frimbo's multiple role as hoodoo priest, detective, and murder victim, a paradox probably unique to detective fiction. This doubling on the common use of masking in detective fiction is further complicated by N'Gana Frimbo's dual role as scientific philosopher and hoodoo priest. Consequently, these doubling aspects of Frimbo's character, coupled with his trickster qualities, provide one of the more interesting triumphs of character complexity in black detective fiction. Double-conscious techniques provide much of the tension in the novel, as the reader struggles with the facets of the murder investigation while investigating Frimbo's identity dilemma.

N'Gana Frimbo continually speculates on the duality of the life force—the rational and irrational, determinism and free will, cause and effect. He attempts to combine scientific determinism and hoodoo into one philosophical construct and thereby control the future. His death and ultimate failure to reconcile African and Euro-Americentric worldviews dramatize the double-conscious conflict within the African American community itself. Confronting the problem of black/white segregation and discrimination, he questions why skin color should determine a person's position in society. One of his reasons for becoming a conjure man in Harlem is to use his powers to help members of his own race break the color-line prejudice so evident in the United States. N'Gana Frimbo's African past is an essential ingredient in his understanding of self and the universe. It is with his hoodoo powers that he hopes to unravel the mysteries of the universe. He says to Doctor Archer: "The profoundest mysteries are those things which we blandly accept without question. See you are almost white. I almost black. Find out why and you've solved a mystery" (230). This elemental double-conscious division is reflected in the structure of the novel.

By transferring the English manor-house mystery to a Harlem brownstone, Fisher metaphorically represents African American double-conscious themes. The novel is about parts searching for a whole and about characters creating identities out of a fragmented past. This temporal and epistemological theme is reflected in the double-conscious and hoodoo aspects of Frimbo's character. The house in which most of the mystery takes place reflects the dualities of the novel. At the front of the house, there is a swinging black and white sign that advertises both an undertaker and a spiritualist. The house stands for the divided African American people torn in two directions, one leading to their black roots in the African past and the other toward the Euro-Americentric values manifested by the culture in which they live. This war of cultural identity is best seen in N'Gana Frimbo, but it is also mirrored by other Harlem characters such as Bubber, who represents the rural folk tradition, and Doctor Archer, the educated light-skinned black man who can move relatively freely in white society.

The black and white sign represents warring dualities on a number of levels. For example, the undertaker and the spiritualist represent two thematic poles of this ambitious novel: blatant murder for purely physical and emotional reasons opposed to a redefinition of an African past by way of a highly spiritualized consciousness. This duality is further extended in the layout of the house, with the undertaker (death) in the basement and the spiritualist (mind and soul) on the top floor. In between the cellar and roof, the building is a cluttered storehouse of African American social signs. The descriptions of N'Gana Frimbo's rooms suggest a trickster's den. Frimbo is a bizarre amalgamation of dualities, including advanced intellect coupled with primitive characteristics, and his waiting room is stockpiled with authentic African artifacts: masks, clubs, shields, human bones in the shape of war clubs, and numerous jars of preserved male sex organs. He is the curator of his own African ancestral museum. These objects are more than decorations for his waiting room; they are integral items from Frimbo's past that reflect his African origins, suggesting the importance of African heritage to black Americans. This early acknowledgment by Fisher of the importance of African heritage continues a pattern established by The Black Sleuth. N'Gana Frimbo's intellect also reminds the reader of Bruce's Okukenu family, and provides further evidence of the African's inherent mental superiority. Furthermore, Fisher's use of African artifacts illustrates his Afrocentric orientation, in accordance with other Harlem Renaissance authors, in searching for a usable past connected to African American life through primitivism and ancestralism. In this sense it is interesting to see how Fisher demonstrates that Afrocentric totems are living testaments rather than simple relics of an almost forgotten and irrelevant past. This visual display of African art objects suggests the beauty of these ancestral items as well as their importance to African American images of Africa.

There is also a trickster quality to N'Gana Frimbo's method. His "other" African life, mostly hidden from view, is contrasted with his Harlem existence. Throughout the novel N'Gana Frimbo is a master of disguise. Dart accuses him: "To avert suspicion, you masqueraded as your servant by a trick of your eyes" (303). An example of N'Gana Frimbo's many trickster qualities is shown in the way he hid the identity of his servant and the fact that the man looked exactly like him, even possessing the same surname, until his hand was forced by the investigation. In a chilling scene, Frimbo burns his servant's body in a furnace. The scene foreshadows Richard Wright and Bigger's burning of Mary, but it also serves a ritual purpose within the text. N'Gana Frimbo's African tribe, the Buwongo, have to burn their dead ancestors to purify them and assure their entry into the spiritual world.

Frimbo is a man of many personas, demonstrated by the secret rooms he keeps in his house which reflect different aspects of his personality. Throughout the novel Frimbo's identity is so fluid that by his own testament he is "able to escape the set pattern of cause and effect" (268), a boast proved hollow, however, when he is killed by a jealous husband. His bedroom is sparsely furnished, its walls described as stark naked, without pictures or ornamentation. His clothes are neatly arranged in closets, half of them containing African costumes and half given to Western garb. Next to the bedroom is a study with a magnificent desk and walls lined with fictitious tomes on esoteric Euro-Americentric philosophies such as "Tankard's *Determinism and Fatalism: A Critical Contrast*" and "Bostwick's *The Concept of Inevitability*." Also on the wall is a bachelor of arts degree from Harvard in the name of N'Gana Frimbo. Here we have a native African, a Harvard graduate, a student of Euro-Americentric philosophies, a sorcerer, a dead man who is not dead—the list of identities doubles on itself. The many facets of Frimbo's identity represent the epic mythological African trickster brought to Harlem. But there is danger here also in that the trickster might trick himself. Frimbo illustrates his dilemma when he talks on many esoteric subjects with Doctor Archer. The conversation amazes Archer, not so much for its brilliance (Archer himself is brilliant) but because of the weight and depth of N'Gana Frimbo's concerns. Frimbo has assumed the task of singlehandedly attempting to right the racial injustices of world. He reveals the real intent behind the "murder mystery" when he says to Archer, "But what on earth does it really matter who killed Frimbo —except to Frimbo. The rest of the world would do better to concern itself with why Frimbo was black" (230). Frimbo's obsession with black identity permeates the novel. At one point or another each character makes reference to his blackness, reinforcing the self-reflexive aspect of double consciousness. The many facets of blackness illustrated in the novel might be seen as a partial answer to the question that Frimbo poses. By emphasizing the positive aspects of black cultural identity, Fisher essentially provides the groundwork for a new African American identity.

As we noted earlier, Houston Baker indicates that minstrelsy was coopted and transformed at the beginning of the modern period by African Americans. Using trickster techniques, African Americans mastered a form of ridicule and turned it into a modern vehicle for social critique. Huggins confirms this when he suggests that minstrelsy "often cuts both ways, making comment on the higher as well as the lower order" (269). In *Conjure Man* Fisher confirms that black writers have always been concerned with the self-creating aspect of African American consciousness. Through double-conscious detection, minstrelsy becomes an African American tool of control as long as the authentic social identity is not displaced. The masks of Frimbo's changing identities reflect both the minstrelsy of appearance versus reality and the trickster's use of disguise. Frimbo is modern and ancient, African and American, primitive and sophisticated, mystic and rationalist. He is, in effect, Alain Locke's New Negro. Houston Baker writes: "Locke's *New Negro* is . . . I believe a broadening and enlargement of the field of traditional Afro-American discursive possibilities. . . . [the work summons concerns] of a newly emergent 'race' or 'nation'—a *national culture*" (*Modernism* 73). The heady mixture of Frimbo's interests, combining aspects of folk culture with scientific rationalism, places him in a new category of consciousness. Frimbo amazes Doctor Archer, who recognizes their "similarly reflective minds":

> the nature of matter and mind and the possible relations between them;
> the current researchers of physics, in which matter apparently vanished
> into energy, and Frimbo's own hypothesis that probably mind did likewise.
> (*Conjure Man* 214)

Through the nature of their conversation, Archer realizes that he is dealing with an exceptional individual who represents something new. Frimbo is a perfect combination of the rational and irrational, the religious and the scientific; and this impresses Archer the most. Archer compliments Frimbo by saying, "You certainly have the gift of harmonizing apparently opposite concepts. You should be king—there'd be no conflicting parties under your regime" (215). Frimbo answers that he is a king, a continuation of an ancient African line of royalty. This revelation leads to the long digression into the African past that constitutes a portion of the final third of the novel.

N'Gana Frimbo's ultimate use of double-conscious detection occurs in the final recognition scene when he sets up a meeting of all the suspects in the case and subjects them to a psychic examination in the presence of Archer and Dart. By booby-trapping the room with electrical current, he tricks the murderer into revealing himself. But his last trick backfires as Crouch the undertaker, masquerading as Easley Jones the railroad porter, manages to shoot Frimbo before he trips the light switch and electrocutes himself.

N'Gana Frimbo is the most complex double-conscious character in black detective fiction that we have seen so far. His use of double-conscious detective techniques in a variety of guises mirrors Fisher's own double-conscious alteration of the detective text in writing a novel containing four detectives. However, in the final stages of the investigation a cautionary note is sounded concerning the difficulty of Frimbo's balancing act. Both Doctor Archer and Detective Dart are convinced that N'Gana Frimbo is a confused paranoiac whose mental instability will eventually lead to his demise, and the ending certainly suggests a tragic flaw in Frimbo's character. His weakness for a married woman seems an unlikely trait to bring down such a lofty intellect. Perhaps Fisher's message implies that the burden of the African American double-conscious dilemma can result in self-destruction due to the sheer difficulty of achieving equilibrium.

Fisher was an active player in helping to define black cultural attributes in the vernacular tradition. Some of these vernacular forms, such as blues music and black dances like the Charleston, are taken for granted today, but during the 1920s and 1930s black racial pride was stimulated by the worldwide recognition achieved by these black vernaculars. African American creations were given long overdue attention by both white and black intellectuals, artists, and the general public. Fisher included in his work many representations of black vernaculars, acknowledging such culturally specific traits as language, music, and black rituals, both sacred and secular. From the opening page of the novel we are immersed in a world that valorizes "doing the dozens" and blues songs as common social functions. The extensive use of black vernaculars in *The Conjure Man Dies* extends and cements an important trope in African American detective fiction.

Fisher is a master at weaving vernacular references into detective story atmospherics. Bubber and Jinx constantly signify and use black dialect in their conversations. They function in *Conjure Man* much as they do in Fisher's *Walls of Jericho*, providing the humor and representing the worldview of the urban black working class. They love to play the dozens, a word game of one-upmanship and comical insult, and use exaggerated mimicry. As we discussed in Chapter 2, the dozens is part of the signifyin(g) tradition and takes the form of a verbal duel based on family and heritage insults. A characteristic passage reads:

> "Don't worry, son. Nobody'll ever know how ugly you is. Yo' ugliness is shrouded in mystery."
> "Well yo' dumbness ain't. It's right there for all the world to see. You ought to be back in Africa with the other dumb boogies."
> "African boogies ain't dumb," explained Jinx. "They' jes' dark. "You ain't been away from there long, is you?"
> "My folks," returned Bubber crushingly, "left Africa ten generations ago."
> "Yo' folks? Shuh. Ten generations ago, you-all wasn't folks. You-all hadn't qualified as apes." (*Conjure Man* 33)

This passage contains all the elements of vernacular language dueling that sociolinguist Geneva Smitherman recognizes as "a verbal game based on negative talk about somebody's mother." As such, this verbal game is part of the tradition of signifyin(g) which, she says, "refers to the act of talking negatively about somebody through stunning and clever verbal putdowns" (82). Characteristically, the dozens is played by young black males in ritual language confrontations that are meant to be humorous and provocative without proceeding to physical violence. We also have to note the "mock" genealogy of this text. The reference to ancestors as "apes" strikes two chords and suggests a third. Apes and monkeys by context suggest the antecedent trickster figure of the "signifying monkey," the archetypal folk character of African Americans, while also signifying on white racist imagery of blacks as beasts. The third meaning suggests blacks' pure thirst for their African heritage, which has been degraded, distorted, or erased by white control of their history. Bubber's and Jinx's access to a more rewarding interpretation of their African past is limited by their own understanding of their history and the history of Africa. In *The Black Sleuth* the Okukenu family refigures the typical portrait of Africans as wild beasts. In this novel a similar reworking of African identity is accomplished through characters such as Archer, Dart, and N'Gana Frimbo.

Black language use, or, as Geneva Smitherman variously calls it, black idiom or black dialect, is a complicated subject that has many components. Examples given here are meant to suggest there are many others in the text. The above exchange between Bubber and

Jinx is useful in that it demonstrates some of the characteristic manipulation of tenses and dropping of consonants mentioned by Smitherman, Labov, Dillard, Ives, and Gates.[4]

Other aspects of vernacular contribution are established in this early detective novel by the use of music. *Conjure Man* joins almost every Harlem Renaissance novel from Carl Van Vechten's *Nigger Heaven* (1926) to Claude McKay's *Home to Harlem* (1928) in containing passages from popular blues tunes and references to jazz clubs.[5] P. L. Dunbar's *Sport of the Gods* (1902) and James W. Johnson's *Autobiography of an Ex-Colored Man* (1912) antedate and foreshadow the central use of blues music to establish setting, theme, and character of Harlem life. Chester Himes further elaborates on this vernacular tradition in his series of Harlem detective novels. In fact, the jazz club is described in detail in Fisher's only other novel, *The Walls of Jericho*. McCluskey makes the point that *Conjure Man* differs from that novel and much of Fisher's other work in that the jazz club, although referred to, is noticeable by its absence. McCluskey believes that Fisher substituted the description of the African feast of procreation called Malindo for the important "unifying effect of myth and performance" (xxxv). Although myth and performance are certainly sustained by N'Gana Frimbo's recollection of this important initiation rite, there are other examples in the text of blues and gospel music. One scene takes place in the cellar of the house, when Bubber, who has stumbled over the hidden body of the servant N'Ogo Frimbo, hears a chorus of voices singing gospel hymns. It turns out there is a church service going on in the adjoining room. While the music and the chorus—"Oh, am I born to die / To lay this body down?"—have a chilling effect on Bubber, the scene also shares a similarity with Wright's surrealistic church scene in his story "The Man Who Lived Underground."

Though Fisher does not use the jazz club in any major scene in the novel, he does use other aspects of secular Harlem's urban folk rituals, including trading wisecracks with other males while strolling down the street, eating at a soul food restaurant, and playing blackjack at a local poolroom/bar. For example, after attending a "mystery movie" to pass the time, Bubber Brown stops at "Nappy Shank's Cafe for supper," where he eats "pigtails and hoppin'-john" (231). Afterward, he enters "Henry Patmore's Pool Room," proceeds to the rear room, and joins a blackjack game in which he wins forty dollars from Spider Webb. Spider is playing with "numbers" money that does not belong to him and later tries to set Bubber up for a roll. Earlier in the novel, as he wanders the streets, Bubber witnesses a knife fight in which one of the adversaries is shot with a pistol and left on the sidewalk. There are many other examples of urban-black folk atmosphere in the novel. In fact, *The Conjure Man Dies,* is framed by specific references to vernacular music. The then popular jive hit "You Rascal You" blares from every street corner. A transcription of its verses appears on the first and last pages of the novel and reflects the primary motivation for the murder of N'Gana Frimbo:

> I'll be glad when you're dead, you rascal you.
> I'll be glad when you're dead, you rascal you.
> What is it that you've got
> Makes my wife think you so hot?
> Oh you dog—I'll be glad when you're gone! (3, 316)

The sum total of these urban vernacular aspects, in my estimation, makes up for the lack of the specific jazz club scenario common to Fisher's other work, such as in *The Walls of Jericho* and his short story, "Common Meter" (1930).

From the examples I have chosen, we can see that Fisher obviously understands and appreciates the atmosphere of Harlem. He continues to lace the novel with vernacular references, to the extent that they assume a life of their own in providing an interconnected blackground against which the murder mystery is played. This blackground expands upon the initial premisés presented in Hopkins's and Bruce's work, but Fisher's blackground presents a more variegated aspect of the black cultural experience in the sense of community expressions, use of black vernaculars, and description of urban-black folk customs. Harlem's importance in defining these areas in the modern period cannot be underestimated. As Cary Wintz writes, "Harlem played an important role in the Renaissance because Harlem itself symbolized the central experience of American blacks in the early twentieth century—the urbanization of black America" (3). Fisher's insistence on this blackgrounding of his work makes him the first black detective writer to celebrate consistently the power of black vernaculars. We know from our discussion in Chapter 1 that Hammett, Daly, and other white detective writers were at this time forging new work in the area of vernacular language in the pages of *Black Mask*. Four out of five of Hammett's novels had been published at the time of *The Conjure Man Dies*. Fisher's interest in the detective format at this early stage in the hardboiled tradition would suggest that he was aware that detective novels could be written about common people.

Finally, the novel demonstrates how hoodoo had grown from its folk roots in New Orleans and the rural South as it moved with migration into the northern cities. Black detective writers use it as an alternative to both orthodox white and black Christian worldviews. The common conception of hoodoo as the superstitious use of charms and the casting of spells held by many whites and middle-class blacks has been argued against by John Roberts, in particular, who sees hoodoo as a synthesis of Christian and non-Christian principles and practices that helped forge an alternative black worldview. An important aspect of detective fiction is that its open-ended form allows for much experimentation. Exploration of religious values and worldviews is rare in early mainstream Euro-American detective fiction, but *The Conjure Man Dies* explores the spiritual heritage of African Americans by using hoodoo as a dynamic central metaphor. This is a challenging attempt to show how detective novels could be used to discuss important African and African American worldviews.

One of the great conventions of detective fiction as a whole is the recognition scene in the last chapter in which the untidy ends of the mystery are tied together by the detective.[6] Sometimes this is accomplished solely through statements by the detective himself or herself. In other instances, the detective is the instrument that makes the guilty parties talk, or reveal themselves through another attempt at murder, as in the case of *The Conjure Man Dies*. In this perfect world of circular cause and effect, the past is explored as providing meaning to the present, and the murder is solved. This is one of the crucial aspects of the detective novel that Porter recognizes as integral:

> In the process of telling one tale a classic detective story uncovers another. It purports to narrate the course of an investigation, but the "open" story of the investigation gradually unravels the "hidden" story of the crime. (29)

The Conjure Man Dies contains a similar scene in which N'Gana Frimbo, the conjure man, explains the strange circumstances of his "murder." The unusual aspect of this recognition scene lies in the nature of the past he reveals and how it affects his present.

Frimbo's African past becomes the most important element of the narrative because of the tribal bonds manifested through his ethnic fidelity to his fellow tribal member, the servant who dies in his place. The bond between N'Gana Frimbo and his manservant N'Ogo Frimbo, like the bond between N'Gana Frimbo and a heritage that reaches far into the past, is a central issue in the novel. This direct link is one more affirmation of the importance of ancestralism to the modern African American Renaissance. This sense of heritage and responsibility is reflected in Frimbo's desire to help American blacks combat the effects of racism and discrimination. Frimbo sees himself as the maker of community and the controller of dualities. As Smitherman notes, "the traditional African world view emphasizes the synthesis of dualities to achieve balance and harmony in the universe and in the community of men and women" (113).

As we have suggested, the novel is an examination of N'Gana Frimbo's or *the conjurer's* identity.[7] What begins as a search for a murderer changes as the book progresses to a search for the meaning of Frimbo's past. Frimbo's illumination of his past includes by extension all African American pasts in the sense that all African Americans share Africa as their continent of ancestral origin.[8]

Frimbo is an educated black African struggling with the meaning of his existence and his past in relation to the Euro-American tradition. As McCluskey has pointed out, this conflict is at the very center of Fisher's concerns. Frimbo is trying to balance an intuitive Afrocentric worldview with a scientific Euro-Americentric one. Archer calls him "the most remarkable person I have ever met in my life" (*Conjure Man* 267). Frimbo's positive role in solving the mystery and Archer's unreserved admiration of the man both suggest that a meld of Afrocentric and Euro-Americentric views might be possible. However, the *real* murder of N'Gana Frimbo in the last pages of the novel counters this speculation with cold, negative reality.

Frimbo's African worldview places spirituality and religion based on hoodoo principles at the forefront of experience. By extension, through the use of this primary theme in the novel, Fisher indicates that hoodoo also can function as a new African American worldview.

Frimbo's spiritual African heritage extends to the predawn of history. The hoodoo element of Frimbo's worldview manifests itself as a central image in the novel in a number of ways. The extended digression on N'Gana Frimbo's past informs us that Frimbo was born in Africa, not surprisingly the son of a king. It was there that his extraordinary talents for spiritualism were recognized and fostered. He relates in detail early tribal religious ceremonies in which the themes of animism and hoodoo played a predominant role. In these early African religious practices humans and animals were conjured into natural objects, and traces of these native practices are included in the novel. For example, Bubber Brown reads an early prophecy of doom in the three clouds that obscure the full moon on the first page of novel. However, his superstitious folk beliefs are purposefully contrasted with Frimbo's elevated spirituality, which draws upon the cultural resources of his ancient race through a ceremony called the "rite of the gonad":

> Yes, Frimbo said, a distant look creeping into his deepset eyes. The germ-plasm, of which the gonad is the only existing sample, is the unbroken heritage of the past. . . . It is the epitome of the past. He who can learn its use can be master of his past. And he who can master his past—that man is free. (267)

Through the use of "gonad power," Frimbo connects to a higher spiritual world not available to the scientific Euro-Americentric world. He is not determined by scientific rationality. He is a mystic who shapes the lives of others. He is a prophet. He is someone who knows how to escape the predetermined order of this universe. His self-ordained mission is to help the other members of his race. All of this is demonstrated through his seances and his selfless determination to alter reality to change racial prejudice:

> Here in a world of rigidly determined causes and effects, Frimbo is free—as free as a being of another order. . . . It is thus I am able to be of service to those who come to me. I act upon their lives. . . . I am a catalyst. I accelerate or retard a reaction without entering into it. This changes the cross currents, so that the coincidences are different from what they would otherwise be. (228)

Frimbo draws his strength from African spirituality and the "germ-plasm" of generations of heritage. His loyalty to N'Ogo Frimbo, the manservant who shares his tribal name, is beyond question. "I would sooner kill myself than one of my clan" (305), he says. Frimbo is willing to put himself in jeopardy to find the killer. "My concern is not for my own protection but the discharge of my obligation as king" (305).

As Niara Sudarkasa (Gloria A. Marshall) points out in her essay "African and Afro-American Family Structure," there are a number of principles governing African family relations.

> I have elsewhere suggested that four principles—namely, *respect, restraint, responsibility,* and *reciprocity*—underlie and undergird interpersonal behavior in the family and the wider community in most indigenous African societies. (147)

Frimbo is the bridge between Africa and America. He emphasizes the need for a religious basis to African American life, and his hoodoo activity is his attempt to change society. By making hoodoo a central part of his story, Fisher defined new areas of African American expression in the detective novel. It must be noted, however, that Fisher's comic sensibilities prevent him from advocating hoodoo wholeheartedly. His tongue-in-cheek portrayal of Frimbo's "rite of the gonad" suggests a good measure of buffoonery. However, it is important to note that this ironic tone does not alter the importance of this trope to the novel and to the detective tradition.

As we have seen, conjuring or hoodoo is not new to African American fiction. Charles W. Chesnutt's use of conjuring in his Uncle Julius tales published in 1899 created a precedent for interweaving its themes and rituals into plots—in which their use enabled slaves to triumph over their oppressors. What is new in Rudolph Fisher's novel, and in the Harlem Renaissance movement as a whole, is the validation of hoodoo as a viable article of African American identity in the modern urban environment. Hoodoo expands the breadth of African American achievement of cultural independence. Frimbo connects with generations of ancestors when he goes into a trance. Houston Baker suggests that modernism in African American culture is connected with recognition of the actual and literary potential of this alternative spiritual network:

> In mediumistic trance, the medium is possessed by a benign spirit that transmits socially beneficial prophecy, advice, knowledge, healing, and precognition. . . . "to trance" is to make contact with the numinous ele-

ment of the universe [which can] be coded as the history of the Afro-American soul in its tortuous striving to convert a possessed state of slavery into the liberated beauty of a freeing and, I think, deeply Afro-American religious song. (*Workings* 100)

Hoodoo, then, is not just religious practice; it is a cultural sign implying a link with an African past. It becomes part of a new language or, as Baker suggests, a new *sound*. Fisher was at the forefront of a new movement in African American culture that recognized the importance of folk religion and ritual to forging African American identity.

By combining all four black detective tropes Fisher created a balanced novel that amply illustrates African American creative reinterpretation of detective conventions. *The Conjure Man Dies* brought the black detective novel into the modern period. It demonstrated convincingly that black detective fiction would be measurably different from white mainstream detective fiction by steadfastly addressing issues of African American culture. The inclusion of new black detective personas that signify on both classical and hardboiled models abruptly challenged typical detective formulas. Double-conscious detection once again structures the novel's approach, and black vernaculars and hoodoo motifs are now seen to be integral aspects of African American culture. In this sense, Fisher opened the way for other black writers such as Himes, Reed, and Major, who would take the detective form to new heights of black expression.

The short story "John Archer's Nose" shares many motifs with the novel, in particular the conflict between modern medicine and hoodoo religious beliefs. However, even though the publication date of this story is three years later than the novel, its thematic material seems less developed. Again, we have the two friends acting as joint detectives. Detective Dart is visiting Doctor Archer in his apartment when the story opens. Over whiskey and cigars they are discussing the recent tragedy of a young child who died because the father, Solomon Bright, refused to approve an X-ray examination. Instead, he chose to use a conjure charm of fried human hair, and Archer says that the child died as a result of "superstition." During this conversation Archer is called to visit the scene of a crime, and Dart accompanies him. A young man named Sonny Dewey has been stabbed to death in his own bedroom while members of his family were present in adjoining rooms. Dart and Archer then proceed with an investigation that includes the members of the family and a close friend who lives in the same apartment.

There are similarities to *The Conjure Man Dies* in the closed-room and isolated-house aspects of the crime. The question of how the murder could have been accomplished so close to potential witnesses is also a component of the mystery. However, the story's essential conflict is the one between superstition and science. After having suffered through the death of a child that day due to the superstitious use of a hoodoo charm when X rays were called for, Archer is in no mood for further "ignorant" manifestations of Harlem mentality. Given Fisher's own medical background, it may be safe to say that Archer's reactions and disdain may to some degree reflect Fisher's own thinking. However, what is interesting—especially in relation to the novel—is Fisher's less judgmental appreciation of the hoodoo characteristics of African American folk culture. In the short story these folk aspects of black Harlem are treated with less enthusiasm than in the novel. We have little in the way of vernacular atmosphere, except for differences in dialect, since the story takes place in the cramped locale of one apartment. Other than the typical Harlem tenement descriptions, the story contains no real exploration of Harlem venues. Consequently, the tone of the story lacks the humor and lightness of the novel. Dart and Archer argue affectionately but without the charm of the earlier novel. Archer is once again the pedant undercut by the more down-to-earth Dart:

> "I am of course in error. A single graphic example, while impressive, does not warrant a general conclusion. Such reasoning, as pointed out by no less an authority than the great Bacon—"
> "I prefer ham," cut in Dart as the phone rang. (McCluskey 160)

The eventual solution to the crime of Sonny's murder is forced out in a recognition scene in the tenement's living room. Suspicion has fallen on all members of the family, including Sonny's sister, Petal, brother Ben, and Ben's wife. A boarder named Red, who sleeps in Sonny's bed in the daytime, is also under suspicion. A subtle undercurrent of possible adultery, homosexuality, and even incest taints the air of this grimy working-class apartment. The most likely suspect is the mother, an old southern black lady. When Dart pretends that the knife used to kill Sonny has incriminating fingerprints, Ma Dewey breaks down and confesses that she murdered her son to save him: "You don' know what it means to a mother to see a child goin' down and down. Sonny was my youngest child, my baby. He was sick, body and soul" (189). However, Archer is one step ahead of the game. Because of his acute sense of smell, he has ascertained that Sonny and his mother have the same "charm" smell as the one found on the dead infant earlier in the day. He has Solomon Bright, the child's father, arrested, and Bright admits committing the crime. It turns out that the charm had been made by Ma Dewey, and Solomon Bright had vowed to kill all of the family in revenge. Doctor Archer ends the story with the weighty observation that "Superstition killed Sonny."

This somber assessment of hoodoo folk beliefs strongly supports modern medicine as much as it condemns ignorant superstition. "But I suppose every religion is a confusion of superstitions" (193). This unequivocal judgment by John Archer of Afrocentric religions seems harsh, negative, and out of character when compared to his enthusiasm for Frimbo in the novel. It must be noted, though, that Fisher seems to condemn ignorance—that is, the *unsophisticated* use of hoodoo—rather than hoodoo itself. An indication of this is the weak depiction of the character of the mother, who hardly says a word. She has no distinctive physical description or emotional depth. Her somewhat maudlin attachment to her dissolute son, who is dying of tuberculosis, is the central motivation for the story. As a conjure woman with connections to an ancient heritage, she seems particularly drab and unenthusiastic.

Overall, the short story lacks the wit, the descriptive talent, and the use of extended metaphor that make the novel so fascinating. Perhaps the short detective form was inadequate for Fisher's talents. Then again, Fisher may have been arguing for a position he intellectually understood but emotionally questioned. With its undertone of sexual deviance and its depressing denouement, "John Archer's Nose" is a weak short story with no ambience or character development. The "puzzle" aspects of the plot are not enough to carry the wooden presentation.

Fisher was a groundbreaker in many ways in his use of African American cultural themes, but gender was not one of them. His depictions of females and their relationship with males remain mundane. Archer and Dart, for example, expecting a visit from the beautiful Petal, talk about hiding the murder knife. Dart suggests that they hide it under Archer's bed.

> "No. The girl might come for it."
> "That's just why I'll be nearby. Leave you alone and she'll get it."
> "Shouldn't be at all surprised. Lovely little thing."
> "But not too little."
> "Nor too lovely."
> "Aren't you ashamed of yourself?"
> "Not at all. You see—"
> "Yea, I see. Never mind the long explanation. Adam saw, too."
> (McCluskey 175–76)

This bantering reduces the innocent Petal to an object of desire and is uncharacteristic of Archer and Dart's usual gentlemanly behavior. Frimbo also has little respect for females. At one point, when Frimbo is talking to Archer in his laboratory, which includes jars of pickled penises, he mentions sexual relations: "this is my real pleasure [science]. The other is necessary to comfort, like blowing one's nose" (*Conjure Man* 268). For an individual who expresses the loftiest sentiments concerning humankind, this kind of remark seems inappropriate. Also, its dramatic verity is undercut by eventual revelations of Frimbo's sexual obsession with a married female. Overall, neither the novel nor the short story has strong female character rendered on her own terms. This is perhaps Fisher's closest connection to the hard-boiled school of writing. In fact, the denouement of *Conjure Man* is most disappointing because of its banality, particularly when contrasted to Frimbo's quest to perfect the world. He is killed by a jealous husband—Samuel Crouch, the undertaker, who has been masquerading as a railroad worker. Frimbo, it turns out, has committed that most common of sins—sleeping with another man's wife. The jealousy motive is hackneyed and not well developed. Martha Crouch's love for Frimbo seems contrived, and Frimbo's manifest disregard for women makes his part in this love affair less than sympathetic. The background hints about this sexual relationship are sketchy at best, and overall, the love triangle appears pedestrian when compared to the more developed and ambitious themes in the book.

I have tried to show that *The Conjure Man Dies* rewrites the detective story with black characters in a black environment, something totally new in the detective tradition. Furthermore, Fisher combined this elementary transformation with themes associated with the Harlem Renaissance and the emerging definition of the New Negro. Fisher's creativity with the form indicates that he knew the conventions of the detective novel well. *The Conjure Man Dies* is an improvisation on the locked-room mystery and the country-manor convention so common in the classical detective tradition. It also plays with the convention of the private detective versus the public detective and in some ways foreshadows the urban police procedural, particularly in its use of forensic medicine. Moreover, by having Frimbo, the victim, become part of the detective apparatus, Fisher comments on the inadequacy of the brilliant-supersleuth detective trope. The novel also contains many plot devices familiar to detective novels, including the disappearing body, the haunted house, mistaken identities, masquerades, and coincidences. Therefore, in many ways *The Conjure Man Dies* is an ambitious undertaking. The variety of tensions it manages to juggle is enough to set it apart from detective novels common to the period, but *The Conjure Man Dies* does even more than this. My main thesis suggests that much of the detective novel apparatus is used by Fisher consciously to present African American themes of changing detective persona, double-conscious detection, black vernaculars, and hoodoo. In this way he moves beyond the technical contributions of the previous two authors, Hopkins and Bruce. Specifically, he understood how an aware artist or storyteller could graft African American worldviews onto a white popular form.

McCluskey and Frankie Bailey both note that Fisher prepared the way for Chester Himes and Ishmael Reed in the detective novel tradition. Himes picked up on the "city within a city" theme when he wrote a series of novels set in Harlem. He shares with Fisher an affinity for absurd plots, topsy-turvy coincidences, bizarre characters, and incidental violence. Reed, in *Mumbo Jumbo,* returns to the 1920s in Harlem for a novel that shares many of Fisher's concerns. His detective, PaPa LaBas, is a curious combination of both scientific and religious values. Like Frimbo, he has a revisionary view of history that traces the African American experience back to Africa. In Reed's *Mumbo Jumbo,* as in *The Conjure Man Dies,* the hoodoo-related components of ancestralism and primitivism are considered important elements of African American culture. None of this could have been accomplished without the groundbreaking elements of *The Conjure Man Dies*. Fisher was a pioneer in recognizing the potential for making political and social statements in what was generally considered a low form of popular culture. In the following chapters I will try to show how Fisher's modern consciousness was developed and revised in twentieth-century black detective fiction.

5

City within a City: The Detective Fiction of Chester Himes

With the publication of his first detective novel, *For Love of Imabelle* (1957), Chester Himes initiated a unique contribution to the African American detective tradition. Originally published in France as *La Reine des Pommes* (or *The Five-Cornered Square*), the novel won the Grand Prix de Littérature Policière for 1958 and was followed by nine other novels in what is generally called Himes's Harlem domestic series. The critical and public reception of his detective novels was much more positive in France, where they were published first, than in Himes's own country.

> Perhaps some critics in America would consider Himes's Harlem detective novels, published in France and in the United States between 1957–1969, as minor works of questionable value, especially in view of his early fame in this country as a traditional writer of serious novels. Apparently it is not so in France. (Smith 18)

These ten novels substantiate an achievement in detective fiction unmatched by any other African American writer. Himes took the hardboiled detective novel and transformed it with African American sensibilities, extending the use of detective personas, double-conscious detection, black vernaculars, and hoodoo as previously presented in the works of Hopkins, Bruce, and Fisher.

Himes also elevated the depiction of violence, one of the primary tropes of detective fiction, to a new plane of expression. The evolution of the use of violence in Himes's detective novels reflects both an increased aesthetic awareness of this common hardboiled trope and a thematic statement. Of all the black detective writers studied so far, Himes's work is foremost in presenting a social critique that unequivocally demonstrates the effects of racism and poverty in Harlem. The violence in Himes's novels develops throughout the works as he portrays a community in turmoil, tilting toward chaos and then erupting into anarchy. Finally, in the last works, violence becomes a tool of revolt as well as an expression of despair.

The detective story plot, melded with the social, religious, and political background of Harlem, provided the perfect marriage of imagination and reality, well suited to Himes's episodic style, racial consciousness, and satiric sensibilities. The Harlem series makes important commentary on race and class in both white and black worlds, while thrilling and delighting the reader with chases, fights, and outlandish scams. Himes transforms traditional detective fiction by using its conventions in a number of experimental ways. Once again, we see creative reinterpretations of the detective formulas by alterations of the classical and hardboiled traditions. Himes also restructures the narrative, introducing simultaneous time frames while creating a mythical Harlem landscape that offered what he often referred to as an absurdist vision of African American existence. At the same time, Himes's cityscape further enlarged on what has been discussed as the topos of Harlem in the literary imagination. This absurd vision depicted so well in the detective novels harbors within it the seed of a bitter truth. The extreme behavior of Himes's black characters, while outrageous in a slapstick fashion, is predicated on the simple but serious fact that racism completely controls their lives.

The first page of the second volume of his autobiography, entitled *My Life of Absurdity* (*MLA*), reflects a sentiment repeated again and again in his autobiography and in interviews:

> Albert Camus once said that racism is absurd. Racism introduces absurdity into the human condition. Not only does racism express the absurdity of the racists, but it generates absurdity in the victims. And the absurdity of the victims intensifies the absurdity of the racists, ad infinitum. If one lives in a country where racism is held valid and practiced in all ways of life, eventually, no matter whether one is a racist or a victim, one comes to feel the absurdity of life. (*MLA* 1)

This vision of absurdity as a direct result of racism figures prominently in Himes's Harlem detective novels.[1] Harlem as a "city within a city" becomes a microcosmic testing ground for his portrayal of African American existence. Himes's two detectives, Coffin Ed Johnson and Grave Digger Jones, fully understand the social injustice and poverty that lie at the root of Harlem's problems.

In some ways, Harlem itself becomes as important as plot and character in the detective novels since it represents all the isolated and segregated black communities throughout the United States. In powerfully descriptive prose, Himes uses a combination of African American detective tropes to create the blackground of Harlem. As mentioned earlier, the term "blackground" suggests to me the particular black urban atmosphere of African American folk culture as it is depicted in America's largest black community.

Himes had been searching for a new method of expression after his arrival in France in 1953. He writes:

> I had the creative urge, but the old, used forms for the black American writer did not fit my creations. I wanted to break through the barrier that labeled me as a "protest writer." I knew the life of an American black needed another image than just the victim of racism. We were unique individuals, funny but not clowns, solemn but not serious, hurt but not suffering, sexualists but not whores in the usual sense of the word; we had a tremendous love of life, a love of sex, a love of ourselves. We were absurd. (*MLA* 36)

The primary result of this experimentation was the series of ten detective novels. Various critics have tried to define these novels as manifestos of black rage, as modernist black-humor vehicles, or as antigenre grotesques. James Lundquist writes that "the effectiveness of Himes's protest and his art in his detective novels derives from the interplay of character and setting" (106). Stephen F. Milliken adds that, "in the final analysis, the concessions made to popular taste, and to the traditions of the subgenre, are never so extensive that they blunt the impact of the basic message of protest and outrage" (251). Robert E. Skinner says that "Himes . . . displays the unique character of Black humor that has helped this race of people survive in the modern world" (22). Gilbert H. Muller says that, "by means of his grotesque art, Himes aligns himself with a tradition of absurdist fiction that has both European and American antecedents" (118). I would agree that Himes's novels can indeed be analyzed in these ways.

It is also necessary to recognize the importance of the novels as a unit expressing a definitive achievement in black detective fiction both in the use of the four tropes and in a radical new approach to the traditional use of violence in detective fiction. Himes's contribution of ten novels forms an essential bridge in detective fiction connecting the work of Hopkins, Bruce, and Fisher with that of Reed and Major. As vehicles of African American cultural expression with a political and social message, Himes's detective novels present midcentury problems of African American identity in the predominantly black cityscape of Harlem. Because these novels deal with both white and black forms of prejudice and injustice, they suggest a new awareness in African American consciousness of race and class, though not necessarily gender, in black culture. Therefore, I would disagree with Milliken, who sees Himes as "turning aside from the high ambitions" of his earlier work "to limit himself almost entirely to describing black criminals, black crime, black poverty, and black violence" (211).

Himes's work is not limited in this sense but is instead an important progression in detective technique and content. His work connects with an established black tradition in detective writing. We know, for example, that he was familiar with Fisher's work and had met him personally (Williams 315). Himes also has Jimmy, the hero of his *Run, Man Run,* look into a store window where Fisher's *Conjure Man Dies* is displayed. Jimmy's thoughts at that moment are revealing.

> Suddenly he felt safe. There, in the heart of the Negro community, he was lulled into a sense of absolute security. He was surrounded by black people who talked his language and thought his thoughts . . . he was presented with the literature of black people. (*Run* 152)

Himes is not an isolated, eccentric manipulator of detective fiction conventions. The ten detective novels establish a continuity that firmly locates Himes as the keystone in the arch of black detective fiction. The overall effect of these ten novels communicates an appreciation and understanding of the complexities of African American cultural life and expression. To understand fully Himes's contribution, it is necessary to examine three areas: his autobiography, his earlier and later short stories, and the ten novels themselves. The ten novels of the Harlem domestic series with American publication dates are: *For Love of Imabelle* (1957); *The Real Cool Killers* (1959); *The Crazy Kill* (1959); *The Big Gold Dream* (1960); *All Shot Up* (1960); *Cotton Comes to Harlem* (1965); *Run, Man Run* (1966); *The Heat's On* (1966); *Blind Man with a Pistol* (1969); and the posthumously published *Plan B* (1993).

In the following pages I hope to make a connection between Himes's life and his detective writing while showing the progressive stages of the development of his aesthetic. Perhaps the most important element in this assessment concerns Himes's violent personal history and how that contributed to his vision and his writing of detective novels. The following quotation indicates to me the validity of this connection.

> I was awakened by a gurgling scream to see a fountain of blood spurting from the cut throat onto the bottom of the mattress of the bunk over-head. . . . A convict had slipped up on another while he was sleeping and cut his throat to the bone. (*Quality of Hurt* [*QH*] 63)

This is not a passage from one of Chester Himes's Harlem detective novels but a quote from his own autobiography. In the same passage, which describes his seven years in the Ohio State Penitentiary (1929–36), Himes talks about convicts being stabbed, cut, slashed, brained, maimed, and killed almost daily and for the most nonsensical reasons. For example, a man was killed for not passing bread, and black convicts cut each other to death over a dispute as to whether Paris was in France or France in Paris (*QH* 63). These and other true stories from Himes's past suggest the nihilistic absurdity of much of his later detective fiction. Himes was incarcerated at the age of nineteen for robbery at gunpoint. Under the cover of darkness he had entered a suburban Cleveland home and robbed a white couple of $20,000 in cash and $28,000 in jewelry. While serving his sentence, he was involved in the famous Ohio Penitentiary Easter Monday fire of 1930 in which hundreds of men lost their lives.

I emphasize the details of Himes's life because I believe they help readers to understand his wild, absurd, chaotic detective novels and how they represent a perception of black America that has its roots in horrible reality, not heroic fantasy. The most meaningful way to understand these *black* novels—black both in the sense of the African American experience and in the black humor of their strange catalogue of adventures—is to understand that Chester Himes lived what others only dream about. His life was as full of absurd and dangerous incidents as any hardboiled detective novel written as an exercise in entertainment. He wrote his first stories in prison and began to publish them in various newspapers and magazines, including *Esquire*, which published his first short story, "Crazy in the Stir," in 1934.

Himes writes: "I grew to manhood in the Ohio State Penitentiary. I was 19 when I went in and 26 when I came out. I became a man, dependent on no one but myself" (*QH* 60).

A full analysis of his life is not necessary for this work; there are many authors who have done justice to his biography.[2] However, I do believe it necessary to give a short overview of Himes's early years to allow further insight into the world of the Harlem series. Before he turned to Harlem for the fictional landscape of his black detectives Coffin Ed Johnson and Grave Digger Jones, Himes lived and suffered racial prejudice and discrimination in many cities in the United States. The son of a teacher in a middle-class black family, Himes turned to crime not so much because of poverty but out of a psychological need for revolt. Whatever the cause, Chester Himes was a criminal before he was a writer and, in fact, might never have become a writer if he had not been imprisoned for the robbery of the white couple from Cleveland.[3] Himes was nineteen when he stood in a pawnshop trying to fence jewelry from the robbery. His pockets were full of hundred-dollar bills, and his mind was clouded after his escape through the snowy night. The pawnbroker went to the back room and called the police. Himes remembers that he could have run, but his pride would not allow him to back down even when he had the chance. "I could have run. I should have run. But, unfortunately, I never did run. Maybe that was the inspiration for my book *Run, Man Run* which I wrote thirty-two years later" (*QH* 47). Asked why he had robbed, he answered that he had done it "to get away from here," meaning in many ways the trapped *here* of the black man in America (*QH* 57).

Good detective novel writing is like tightrope walking, or living by your wits and courage—one mistake and it is all over. Chester Himes lived on the razor's edge for most of his life. Because of his short temper and his intolerance of racism, his life was a balancing act between black and white worlds, between prison and freedom, between self-expression and annihilation:

> I remember once being refused service at the counter of a restaurant. . . . I jumped to the top of the counter and kicked everything moveable onto the floor—people's half-filled plates, glasses, pie bins, coffee cups, everything —and then struck the white girl behind the counter on the shoulder with my .44-caliber revolver and beat the white proprietor repeatedly across the head. The customers fled. I walked out and walked away. I was never arrested, never charged; as far as I know there was no inquiry. (*QH* 47)

Shortly before this incident Himes had spent one unsatisfactory year at Ohio State University when he was asked to leave because of an incident in which he took a group of innocent light-skinned students to a whorehouse serving home brew. After leaving college, Himes committed other crimes, like cashing forged checks with phony identification and stealing guns, "a case of .45-caliber Colt automatics and ammunition" (*QH* 40). The weapons belonged to the Ohio National Guard and were stored in the Negro YMCA. Interestingly, in terms of future revolutionary writings in the detective novels, Himes planned to sell the guns "in Warren and Youngstown, where blacks employed in the steel mills would buy them" (*QH* 40). Himes was arrested for the crime and given a suspended sentence.

About this time he became a pimp bootlegger bellman in a Cleveland hotel. Previously, while working in another hotel, he had fallen down an elevator shaft and broken his back, an injury that plagued him for the rest of his life. He frequented bars and dives during these early Prohibition years, and many of the characters he ran across reappeared in his detective fiction. In prison he learned that men were capable of the most despicable acts and at the same time capable of the noblest feats of heroism. During the great prison fire of 1930, he witnessed many acts of bravery as inmates tried to rescue others from ticky-tacky wooden structures engulfed in flames.

Most importantly, it was while in prison that, due to a combination of motives, he began to write.

> I began writing in prison. That also protected me, against both the convicts and the screws. The black convicts had both an instinctive respect for and fear of a [writer, and] the screws could never kill a convict who was a public figure. (*QH* 64)

In prison he wrote about crime and criminals and life in prison. Many of his protagonists were white:

> My first short stories, those I wrote in prison, were not racially orientated; I did not write about the lives of blacks in a white world. That was to come. In prison I wrote about crimes and criminals, mostly about the life in prison. (*QH* 65)

The stories from this period have been recently published in *The Collected Stories of Chester Himes* (1991).

Himes was paroled to his mother in Columbus in 1936 after serving seven years of his sentence. His mother transferred his parole to his father in Cleveland after he was caught smoking marijuana. Himes's parole was for the duration of his maximum sentence, more than seventeen years. He was married to his first wife, Jean, in 1937, and soon after he wrote that he "began to feel cornered in a black world" (*QH* 71). The growing evidence of racism in all aspects of society, coupled with the negative critical response to his first two published novels and much of his other writing, eventually forced Himes to travel the country looking for a place to live with his wife. By the time he decided to leave for France in 1953, he had already published extensively in the United States. One critic said the character of Lee Gordon in *Lonely Crusade* (1947) was "psychotic, as is the author," and his books were compared to "graffiti on the walls of public toilets" (*QH* 100–101). After a decade and more of poverty and a separation from Jean, Himes became an expatriate.

Himes's detective novels were written while he was living in Europe. Himes, like many black artists, including Beauford Delany, James Baldwin, and Richard Wright, found relative social sanity in Europe.[4] It was while living in Paris that he was persuaded by Marcel Duhamel to try and write a detective novel. Duhamel was editor of *La Série Noire,* a French publication of hardboiled detective stories written by such American authors as Hammett, Chandler, Cornell Woolrich, and Horace McCoy, among others. More for the money than for any other reason, Himes took up the challenge and finished the novel in a few months while living in a dingy Paris hotel.

In the introduction to an interview with Chester Himes in 1969, published in *Flashbacks: A Twenty-Year Diary of Article Writing* (1973), John A. Williams notes: "No other writer that I know of, black or white, has ever spoken so candidly about his profession" (311). Indeed, Chester Himes has left us numerous fascinating statements about his detective fiction. We know, for example, that he claims he began writing detective fiction for money: "That's why I began writing these detective stories, as a matter of fact. . . . The *Serie Noire* was the best paid series in France. So they started off paying me a thousand dollar advance" (Williams 299). There is evidence of not only Himes's poverty but his dedication to the task of writing. In "Traveler on the Long, Rough, Lonely Road," an interview published in *Black World* in 1972, Himes says:

> When I was writing my first detective story I was desperate. I was living in
> a little crummy hotel in Paris which became a beatnik hotel. I sat there in
> my room and worked through Christmas Day, New Year's Day, and New
> Year's Night until four o'clock. (Fuller 13)

Though Himes's monetary situation was always a problem that af-
fected his decisions, the detective novel in France enjoyed much
higher status than in the United States. As early as 1947 a major
French critic, Roger Caillois, had written an influential and definitive
book on detective fiction:

> It was Roger Caillois who was farseeing and bold enough to put the
> detective novel in France on the same footing with other novels. . . . For
> Caillois the detective novel faithfully reflects the attitudes which an individ-
> ual takes while confronting society. It is a mirror of man's reactions in the
> midst of the communities in which he lives out his existence. (Smith 20)

The respect that the French had for the detective novel was reflected
in their popular *Série Noire* editions, which published American de-
tective novelists in translation. This respect was also evident in many
French *nouvelle vague* films such as *Breathless* and *Shoot the Piano
Player,* which used American detective story plots in French settings.
There is also reason to believe, from what Himes tells us, that Duha-
mel's support and enthusiasm were as influential as the money in
Himes's decision to create detective fiction.

We also know that Himes enjoyed writing the detective novels and
took pride in his work. Speaking to Hoyt Fuller about his first book,
Himes says: "Although, I would say that I have not benefitted finan-
cially to any extent from it, it's an outstanding book" (Fuller 11). In
the interview with Williams, Himes is even more explicit:

> I was very happy writing these detective stories, especially the first one,
> when I began it. I wrote those stories with more pleasure than I wrote any
> of the other stories. And then when I got to the end and started
> my detective shooting at some white people, I was the happiest.
> (Williams 315)

The connection between Himes's violent streak and hatred of white
oppression and his use of violence in detective fiction is a fascinating
psychological issue. Himes is the first black detective novelist to use
violence by blacks against whites as both an aesthetic tool and a
social statement. Furthermore, the use of violence in Himes's work

seems a logical extension of hardboiled sensibilities as seen through black militant eyes. Himes gives at least a partial explanation for the violence in his work when he talks about the American atmosphere of the detective novel:

> There's no reason why the black American, who is also an American, like all other Americans, was brought up in this sphere of violence which is the main sphere of American detective stories, there's no reason why he shouldn't write them. (Williams 314)

Certainly, the detective stories provided a rich outlet for Himes's emotional state at this time. We have confirmation from his autobiography that the writing of the detective stories fulfilled him: "The only time I was happy was while writing these strange, violent, unreal stories. I accepted them to myself as true; I believed them to be true as soon as they sprang from my thoughts" (*MLA* 126). The paradox of "unreal" and "true" contained in the above statement reveals one of the most intriguing aspects of Himes's detective works.

These are works of fiction rooted not in fantasy but in observed reality carried to its utmost logical absurdity. Unlike Raymond Chandler, who never had any experience in detective work or the criminal milieu, Himes believes his stories are "true" because they spring from his own perceptions of how life works when controlled by racism. Evidence of this is contained in his observations about his expatriate status while writing the detective novels. Like Richard Wright and James Baldwin, both of whom he knew in Paris, Himes was still dealing with his American past. The detective novels provided a means for him to incorporate past memories and experiences into meaningful fiction:

> then I began writing these series because I realized I was a black American, and there's no way of escaping forty some odd years of experience.... Well, then, I went back—as a matter of fact, it's like a sort of pure homesickness—I went back, I was happy, I was living there, and it's true. I began creating also all the black scenes of my memory and my actual knowledge. (Williams 315)

One fascinating aspect of Himes's return to the past was the way he worked real-life characters and his criminal past into his fiction. For example, Himes reports that he played dice in the Cleveland ghetto in 1928 when he was nineteen. "Some of the regulars were Abie the Jew, Red Johnny, Four-Four, Chink Charlie, Dummy and other characters I've used in my detective story series" (*QH* 36). Robert Skinner recognizes Johnny Perry and Val in *Crazy Kill* as two other characters connected to the black gangster Bunch Boy in Cleveland. In 1955, when Himes returned from Europe for a brief spell, he gathered more material for his detective novels while living in Harlem.

> Inadvertently, it was then I learned so much about the geography of Harlem, the superficiality, the way of life of the sporting classes, its underworld and vice and spoken language, its absurdities, which I was to use later in my series of Harlem domestic stories. (*MLA* 25)

The detective novels provided a place for Himes to use the illegal, dangerous, and mysterious parts of his past in ways he had not foreseen while writing his other novels. Consequently, his detective novels become a testament to black consciousness of a different sort than that experienced in earlier black detective writers. The black underworld of criminals, dealers, religious charlatans, and other con men becomes the focus of Himes's fiction—not the detectives themselves.

It was during this period in New York that Himes, author of four published novels, was forced to take a job as a porter at a Horn & Hardart luncheonette at the corner of Thirty-seventh Street and Fifth Avenue. "It was while working there I got the experience and the background for my book *Run, Man Run,* which I was to write years later" (*MLA* 28). He also writes about this period: "I didn't realize it then, but I was storing up all the imagination and observations and absurdities which were destined to make my Harlem novels so widely read. My life itself was so absurd I saw everything as absurd" (*MLA* 29). Himes relied on personal experience for characters and incidents in his detective series. He was the first black detective novelist to attempt a portrayal in detail of the desperate and deadly side of the African American community.

What is less clear is the influence that his earlier stories had on his detective novels. While in prison, he published or wrote a number of stories with motifs used in his later fiction, for example, aspects of black religion and portrayals of white prejudice. Apparently, however, there is only one story written from the viewpoint of the detective—"He Knew," published in *Abbott's Monthly Magazine* in 1933, the first year that Himes published anything. While in prison and afterward, he published many stories about criminals, crime, and drugs. Most of these stories have black protagonists, but a good percentage are written from the viewpoint of white characters, including stories published in *Esquire*. These include "To What Red Hell" (1934), "The Visiting Hour" (1936), and "Every Opportunity" (1937). Only the early "He Knew" and two of the later stories meet any of the qualifications of black detective fiction, and no story meets all of them. That is, besides fulfilling the simple criteria of detective fiction mentioned in the first chapter, the stories must have a black detective and use the black detective tropes of altered detective persona, double-conscious detection, black vernaculars, and hoodoo. Most of Himes's other stories concerning crime and criminals were written from the viewpoint of the criminal and are interested more in character development and depiction of the atmosphere of crime than in detection.

"He Knew" is considered by many critics to be Himes's first detective story. It does, indeed, contain two detectives bearing a resemblance to Grave Digger Jones and Coffin Ed Johnson of the Harlem series. These two, called John Jones and Henry Walls, are cops on a beat who kill Jones's two sons in a dark warehouse by mistake, although the two sons are indeed burglars. Milliken feels that the two policemen bear a "resemblance to the celebrated detectives of the later novels" (39). Both detectives are black, and they are put on the job because the neighborhood where crimes are being committed is black and the criminals are believed to be black. However, the story is grim, realistic, and overly melodramatic. It barely fulfills detective conventions because of the unspecified nature of the initial crime and the blundering solution. The story functions as slice-of-life realism more than detective fiction. However, H. Bruce Franklin in his book *The Victim as Criminal and Artist* is correct in pointing out that it prefigures one important aspect of Himes's coming detective fiction —black-on-black violence.

When Himes was asked years later about his inspiration for Grave Digger and Coffin Ed, he talks about two tough detectives he knew from Watts in Los Angeles and neglects to mention "He Knew," one of the first stories he ever wrote (Milliken 210, n. 6). The existence of this story seems to conflict with Himes's own memory about the origin of his detective heroes. Edward Margolies, in *Which Way Did He Go?* (1982), claims that "Himes fused these real-life cops with the forgotten paternal cops of his early short story to create his detective heroes" (60). Curiously, "He Knew" is not mentioned or published in the latest *Collected Stories of Chester Himes*.

Two later stories, written about the time of *For Love of Imabelle*, prove more interesting comparisons to Himes's detective novels. Both stories, "Naturally, the Negro" (1956) and "Spanish Gin" (1957), were unpublished until recently (*Collected Stories*, 1991). Apparently, they were early versions of detective novels that did not pan out. Skinner reports:

> It is not generally known just how much trouble Himes had getting started in the crime fiction genre. He initially drew on an unpublished short story he called "Spanish Gin" and wrote a 119-page manuscript entitled "The Lunatic Fringe." Set in Spain, "Fringe" is a tale of multiple murders and accidental killings. Apparently it was not what Duhamel wanted, and he sent Himes back to his typewriter. (20)

Himes mentions neither of these stories in his interviews or his autobiography. The manuscript "Lunatic Fringe" has not been published or mentioned in any recent Himes work, or for that matter attested to by any critic other than Skinner. "Naturally, the Negro" has been mentioned only in the *Collected Stories* by the editor, Calvin Hernton, who claims that the "extract . . . is of particular significance, as it is taken from the first sketch Chester Himes did for Marcel Duhamel" (381). "Naturally, the Negro" takes place in 1950s Paris and does not fit the description of "Lunatic Fringe."

Himes, himself, is ambiguous about many aspects of his detective story ideas. In *Quality of Hurt* he claims that soon after reaching France he went to change money in a black-market house in which an old man lived with stacks of money and rows of female dolls. "Years afterward I remembered that first sight of Pops and his room filled with dolls and money, from which I got my first idea for a detective story, but I never wrote it" (27). Himes also makes an offhand remark in his autobiography concerning the famous interview with Marcel Duhamel, the editor of *Série Noire*, who translated Himes's first novel. *If He Hollers Let Him Go* (1945), and asked him to write a detective novel. "I got news for you, I thought. I had started out to write a detective story when I wrote that novel [*If He Hollers*], but I couldn't name the white man who was guilty because all white men were guilty" (*MLA* 102).

Margolies writes that Himes read *Black Mask* and Raymond

Chandler while in prison (59). However, in his interview with Williams, Himes is less definitive. He mentions "some of Raymond Chandler's crap out there" but fails to indicate when he read it (Williams 321). He does, however, say of Chandler's famous Central Avenue scene in *Farewell, My Lovely*, "Some of that's very authentic—it was like that. A black man in Los Angeles, he was a servant" (321). Furthermore, in *My Life of Absurdity* Himes is very definitive about his true literary inspiration—William Faulkner and in particular the novel *Sanctuary:*

> The first thing I did . . . was to reread an old beat-up paperback of Faulkner's *Sanctuary* to sustain my outrageousness and give me courage. I have always considered the fiction of Faulkner the most absurd ever written and if I couldn't get any ideas from it I was stuck. (*MLA* 106)

Himes is less than clear, however, about his knowledge of detective authors. He never mentions any of the well-known European or American detective authors. Georges Simenon was, of course, famous in France at this time. Himes claims that he in fact knew nothing about writing detective novels. When asked by Marcel Duhamel to write one, he answers, "I can't write like that" (*MLA* 102). Also, in this second volume of his autobiography Himes, referring to *Imabelle*, states that "I really didn't know how to write a detective story. It was what one might call an action story" (*MLA* 111).

Reading the two stories, "Spanish Gin" and "Naturally, the Negro," one wonders whether Himes could write either detective or action stories. To begin with, neither story contains a detective. "Naturally, the Negro" reads like a synopsis: "The story begins at 5 A.M. in the St. Germain Club" (*Collected Stories* 381). Pays, a black musician, is high on marijuana throughout the story. He is having an affair with Kitty, a white, red-haired woman from Alabama. He takes her home and makes love to her, after draping a yellow scarf "between her breasts and the V of her thighs" (382). Pays lives in a beatnik hotel next door to two lesbians. When he wakes up, he looks out the window and sees Kitty leaving in a Cadillac. That night in the club he gets "treetop" high in the bathroom. When he comes back down, he finds Kitty dead, strangled with a yellow scarf. Pays's reaction to finding Kitty murdered is typical of the static prose strangling the text. "He was too high to panic. He worked it out in his mind. His scarf. His woman. Sex Murder. Naturally, the negro. He was stuck" (383). Pays hides the body and leaves to borrow a car from a friend named Brothers. When he gets back to the club, he finds a cleaning woman and no body. The cleaning woman tells him a "grand monsieur" was there to see him and "took the parcel." He goes home, pondering the mystery of the missing body and the "Big Man," and ends up getting high with his lesbian neighbors. Pays goes back to the club that night and questions everyone about Kitty. "He then asked Thelma [Kitty's best friend] who Kitty was. Thelma was surprised he didn't know. But she wouldn't tell Pays" (384). Thelma leaves the club and gets in the big gray Cadillac. Pays gets high at 4:00 P.M. and plays the piano, "lost in a marijuana dream" (385). When he looks up, a red-haired woman is leaning over the piano. "Who are you?" he whispered. "I'm a viper," she said. End of story.

This short synopsis of "Naturally, the Negro" suggests that the story has all the earmarks of bad neophyte detective fiction writing. The hackneyed prose—"She says you pack a rod" (382)—and the reliance on narrative telescoping exacerbates the weak plot development. The lack of character depth coupled with inane complications —the mysterious disappearance of the body, the strange Cadillac, and Pays not knowing who Kitty is, even though he is having an affair with her—alienates the reader. Lastly, the conceit of marijuana smoking is used excessively, and with Kitty's last reference to being a viper (jazz jargon for marijuana smoking) the story disintegrates into a cloudy mess. If Himes did present this story to Duhamel, as Hernton suggests, there is reason to believe that Himes did not have a grasp of detective novel conventions at this time (1956). Since Duhamel asked Himes to write a detective novel in December 1955, and since Himes worked through the New Year on it, the time frame of this story is about right. Another piece of evidence is that Himes was living in a "beatnik" hotel at the time (*MLA* 110). There is also reason to believe that Himes would decide not to mention the story in his autobiography, given his success with the first eighty pages of *Imabelle* (*MLA* 106). It is my feeling, however, that the story is a fragment from a later attempt at beginning a detective novel, since in repeated references to his first detective novel Himes never mentions such a totally false start.

"Spanish Gin," dated 1957 in *Collected Stories,* does little to elucidate the issue of Himes's earliest detective fiction. There is no definitive mention of this story by Himes in either interview or autobiography. However, if the date is correct, the story is most likely part of an unfinished manuscript that Himes mentions working on in late 1957 while living in Mallorca. This work apparently was called either "The Pink Dress" or "It Rained Five Days" (taken from a blues song by Mamie Smith) and was written after Himes had written three other Harlem detective novels in France: *The Five-Cornered Square* (1957), *If Trouble Was Money* (1957), and *A Jealous Man Can't Win* (1958). The English versions of these works are, *For Love of Imabelle* (1957). *The Crazy Kill* (1959), and *The Real Cool Killers* (1959). Himes mentions that he talked to Duhamel about the Spanish book:

> Duhamel liked the title and promised to advance me some money on it, but he wasn't very happy about me writing a story about Alva with a Spanish locale. In 1954 I had written a story about Vandi while living in Mallorca with Alva; now I wanted to write a book about Alva while living in Mallorca with Marlene. I was shooting my brain on absurdity, but I wanted to write tragedy. (*MLA* 168)

"Spanish Gin," however, is farce. Albert Bernel in his history of farce says that "Farce deals with the unreal, with the worst one can dream or dread. Farce is cruel, often brutal, even murderous" (21). It is impossible to tell whether "Spanish Gin" is the 1954 story about Vandi or the newer one about Alva. Whichever it is, the story is not a contribution to Himes's detective fiction.

Again we have a story in which the characters are seen behind a distorting haze, this time alcohol-induced. Frank, Susie, and Ellie are at a party in the house of Ted and Ed in the village of Puerto de Pollensa on Mallorca. They are all Americans, and they are all drunk. Susie and Frank apparently are having an affair, but neither seems to be too enthusiastic. Susie feeds caviar canapes to a Siamese cat while Frank tries to "remember where he was" (*Collected Stories* 396). Ted and Ed are out on the terrace in a drunken revel, and Frank's real girlfriend, Ellie, sits between them. Ted and Ed have a fight, in which Ted knocks Ed out. Thereupon, Ted goes to the kitchen and slashes his wrists, and Ed gets up and trips drunkenly down a set of stairs yelling, "He struck me! He struck me! the brute!" Slamming into a wall, he breaks his neck (399). Frank and Ellie then leave for their own home, where Ellie falls down in the corridor on her way to the bathroom, breaking her shoulder. Frank cannot hear her because he is in the kitchen priming the gas stove and the neighbors are arguing.

Ellie gets up and stumbles into the bathroom, where she falls again, hitting her head on the sink. "Death came instantaneously" (401). In the kitchen, Frank is attacked by the cat and hit on the shin. He sloshes gasoline on the stove which ignites, turning "the kitchen into a solid inferno of flame". Running outside, he flings "himself down into the well" and is "submerged beneath the water". The cat screamed "through the moonlit Spanish night" (402). End of story.

Again, one can easily understand why Marcel Duhamel would be disappointed in this story. There is no unified narrative viewpoint; the deaths are freakishly accidental and apparently have no relation to one another. Furthermore, the reliance on alcohol as a catalyst to these deaths again alienates the reader's sympathy. As in the earlier story, "Naturally," it is impossible to determine or even get serious about the plot development. "Spanish Gin" is even further removed from detective fiction than the previous story. Certainly, as we shall see, farcical violence will play an important role in Himes's detective fiction. However, in this story fragment the absurdity of the three deaths seems superficially linked to the background material and elicits not laughter but a sour taste of overindulgence. Skinner's claim that "Spanish Gin" was important to Himes's detective ouevre is not supported by evidence within the story. In fact, the evidence from the three stories discussed here suggests that Himes did not have a large supply of previous material to draw on, as Chandler did. Statements in his autobiography about his obsessive writing stints when composing the novels support this (*MLA* 110). Most importantly, neither of these stories adds substantially to black detective fiction. It would take the milieu of Harlem and two double-conscious black detectives with crimes to solve to root Himes firmly in the crucial African American tropes of altered personas, double-conscious detection, black vernaculars, and hoodoo.

Himes is fascinating when he discusses his interpretation of the origins and influence of the detective novel. These are opinions that he apparently developed as he continued to write detective novels and became more familiar with the genre: "But on the whole, I mean the detective story originally in the plain narrative form—straightforward violence—is an American product. So I haven't created anything whatsoever; I just made the faces black, that's all" (*MLA* 314). This famous statement about making the faces "black" seems on the surface to make a lot of sense. The ten detective novels do share characteristics with hardboiled fiction, particularly in their use of violence, uneven handling of gender, and cynical attitude concerning corruption and class. However, contrary to Himes's own statement, he did create something different. He continued to alter the detective persona as had black detective writers before him. Second, he joyfully played with double consciousness, masquerade, and trickster figures. Third, he elaborately extended the use of black vernaculars in his Harlem environment. Finally, though his use of hoodoo elements was generally satirical, he developed a consistent worldview that radically altered the face of black detective fiction.

Notably, Himes's highly developed social conscience moved his novels in a radical direction. He did not simply paste black characters into white detective formulas, as his wry statement would have it. For one thing, by Himes's own testimony, he was not familiar enough with detective stories to execute such a simple transposition. His first novel *For Love of Imabelle,* was half written before he even thought of putting a detective in it—at the urging of his editor, Duhamel. In fact, the ten novels of Himes's detective series form a unit that adds support to my thesis, stressing the important differences generated in African American detective fiction. Himes's Harlem is a distinct district of the mind as well as a physical reality. Himes delineated this Harlem through a combination of the four African American detective tropes, creating the blackground atmosphere so special to these novels. In addition, he altered the use of violence in his fiction. In hardboiled detective novels violence is used to generate suspense and to create a background ambience of danger, but Himes added humor to his violent episodes, suggesting the absurd and at the same time giving violence a deeper meaning. Violence in his novels becomes both an indicator of a world gone awry due to racism and economics and a political tool that is used against the oppressor.

I have noted that Himes found the writing of these detective stories fulfilling on a number of levels: "I liked writing, not only of the visual scenes, which I could always see plainly, and the dialogue, which I could hear clearly spoken, but of the thoughts which were always mine in any given situation" (*MLA* 150). It is interesting that Himes found these "strange, violent, unreal" stories so rewarding (*MLA* 126). It may be that, although he was reluctant to begin writing the stories ("I can't write like that"), he found himself able to tap a reservoir of feelings about black life in America once he began (*MLA*

102). Finally he had found a vehicle that allowed him to use writing skills that in his social-realist fiction had offended many people. For example, Milliken notes one of Himes's fictional editors in *The Primitive* (1955) criticizes Himes as well as other black writers for a "complexity" that makes the humor "extremely difficult to grasp" and for "excessive subjectivism, a compulsive preoccupation with self verging on narcissism," that never strays "far from straight autobiography" (9). In the detective fiction Himes's humor pinpointed crucial social behaviors clearly while escaping the charge of subjective narcissism, since none of the stories is written in the first person or concentrates its narrative on one viewpoint.

Himes broke with his literary past in a number of ways in writing detective fiction. "The Harlem of my books was never meant to be real; I never called it real; I just wanted to take it away from the white man if only in my books" (*MLA* 126). With this mythical cityscape to work with, Himes constructed a world that reflected truth in a more complex way than did his previous social-realist fiction. Detective fiction allowed him to work at the Archetypical level, utilizing the important moral scenario that myth allows. When Himes talks about the "true" in his detective fiction, he is suggesting truth on a metaphorical rather than a historical level. The Harlem series has more to do with mythic blackground than reality. Himes's unsparingly satirical yet humorous view of the greed, religious duplicity, and violence of black Americans was part of his mythical worldview. Muller writes that the "crimes committed in Harlem therefore were not exclusively temporal but mythic" (86). As Skinner notes, however, Himes's detective fiction alters the pattern of detective representation initiated by Hammett and Chandler in one important way: "In spite of many imitators and disciples that [Hammett and Chandler] spawned, there was still one characteristic that this detective had not had, and that was to be black" (24). As a successor to the American tradition of the hardboiled detective novel, Himes is the first black writer to break the color barrier in detective fiction on both sides of the Atlantic. "Everyone knew that I was writing for the famous detective-story series which, until then, had been the strict domain of whitey" (*MLA* 120). Right from the beginning, Himes altered the formulas handed down to him.

At the suggestion of Duhamel, Himes added two detectives to his first novel and with them began his alteration of the traditional detective persona. These detectives were different from previous white patterns in that they worked as a team, whereas most hardboiled novels project single, loner protagonists. Also, by writing his novels in the third person, Himes broke with the usual hardboiled first-person narration. He also gave more background information about his detectives, although even this scenario is limited. The fact that they are both married, have children, and live outside Harlem in Queens gives them a social history most hardboiled loner detectives do not possess. Even with this limited background and the fact that Coffin Ed had acid thrown in his face in *Imabelle*—which left a disfiguring scar that suggests his volatile nature—there is not much to differentiate the two men.[5] They dress in the same rumpled suits and slouch hats.

> [Grave Digger was] a big, rough, dangerous man in need of a shave, clad in a rumpled black suit and an old black hat, the bulge of a big pistol clearly visible on the heart side of his broad shouldered frame. Coffin Ed looked the same; they could have been cast from the same mould with the exception of Coffin Ed's acid burned face. (*Cotton* 165–166)

They both have temper tantrums (although Coffin Ed is more prone to losing it than Grave Digger), and they both display a worldly, cynical, almost fatalistic attitude toward life. Milliken sees them as "more adumbrated than defined" (227). However, they resist cardboard characterization because of their personal involvement with the people of Harlem. They are the essence of some primitive system of justice that mediates between an unjust white world and a desperate black one. They are the mightiest might in the lawless city of the Harlem night—but even in this role they are handicapped by an oppressive white judicial system. Their main connection to this system is through Lieutenant Anderson, who as their white supervisor tries to keep them in check. Muller implies that they are morally wounded by their insignificant status. "As black detectives upholding justice in Harlem, they apprehend that they are parodies of their white counterparts and are exceedingly self-conscious about their ambiguous roles" (87). A good portion of this ambiguity comes from their social conscience, which has them fighting crime in the black world but being unable to do anything about the direct causes of the poverty that necessitates the crime.

They usually make their appearance when the mayhem has reached a fever pitch, and they have a reputation in Harlem. "Unlike most of their detective predecessors, Coffin Ed and Grave Digger are legendary figures in their own community" (Muller 88). In fact, they have developed a mystique of power based in part on the folk tradition of the black badman, a legendary creature who fearlessly confronts white and black alike and does not hesitate to use violence.[6] The use of the generic surnames Jones and Johnson coupled with the deadly monikers Grave Digger and Coffin adds to their legendary aura. There is also a close connection in the folk tradition between the badman and the trickster in that both have the ability to outwit established authority. Himes himself was well acquainted with the badman mystique: "many times I would have been killed except for the aura of violence surrounding me" (QH 62). In Himes's novels Coffin Ed and Grave Digger put on a performance that is part of the total spectacle of Harlem. The two detectives use guns and threats to restore at least temporary order, and they are strikingly similar in their dual performance, behaving like guardians of justice as they try to keep Harlem in balance. Muller sees them as "instill[ing] respect and a certain amount of terror in the populace," as well as being "fantastical, Herculean figures" (88). Their morality is based on the reality of life in Harlem, and they are effective because they can function in a world that the white officers fear to approach. "Straighten up!" Grave Digger shouts, wading into the melee. "Count off!" Coffin Ed echoes, as both of them brandish monstrous guns described as capable of killing a stone. They are particularly brutal to witnesses and women, and they are fearless in the execution of their duties.

However, they are aware of the ultimate futility of their task because they know that crime in Harlem is a survival act forced on the citizens by the very nature of life in a racist country—hence their mutual fatalism. As Grave Digger says to Lieutenant Anderson,

> We got the highest crime rate on earth among the colored people in Harlem. And there ain't but three things to do about it: Make the criminals pay for it—and you don't want to do that; pay the people enough to live decently—you ain't going to do that; so all that's left is let 'em eat one another up. (*Cotton* 18)

Even so, Coffin Ed and Grave Digger are honest cops. Twelve years in precinct jobs have given them lumps and scars but no promotion.

"And yet they hadn't taken a dime in bribes" (*Blind Man* 101). They are also quite conscious of the inbred racism within the police force and will not tolerate manifestations of it. In *All Shot Up* a group of police officers examine a corpse and a misplaced wig in a gutter. " 'Looks like real nigger hair,' the flip cop said. . . . Coffin Ed planted a left hook in his stomach and crossed an overhand right to the jaw. The cop went down" (42). Overall, Coffin Ed and Grave Digger represent a volatile blend of black pride, anger, and frustration, an incendiary mixture that is often ignited either by their supervisors or by the people they are trying to protect.

Unlike traditional hardboiled detective fiction, the progress of the detectives' investigation is not necessarily the progress of the plot. In fact, Himes's two detectives have reached a stage of development approaching the existential. While trying to keep Harlem under control, they know their real task is to protect white people who are often the prey of black con artists in Harlem. In a number of the novels, Himes uses the narrative device of simultaneity, in which parallel actions are occurring at the same moment. Though this device does not lend itself to clarity of plot, it does indicate another way in which Himes experiments with the detective form. At the same time it initiates a tradition in black detective fiction that consciously ignores linear time frames and substitutes circular time. This refutation of Euro-Americentric ordering devices for more primitive African approaches to life and art becomes a major theme in the last two novels studied in this work.

Along with reworking the traditional linear time frame, Himes alters another important facet of mainstream detective fiction. Classical and, to a lesser degree, hardboiled detective fiction are often touted as restoring the natural order of society by solving the crime and punishing the criminal. The themes of Himes's later novels suggest that a final restoration of moral order is impossible in his detective worldview. For example, *Blind Man with a Pistol* utilizes parallel action and a nonlinear time frame to show complete moral disintegration and lack of order in a series of unsolved crimes radiating from the murder of a white male homosexual. Grave Digger and Coffin Ed, after a number of witnesses have been brutally bludgeoned, are pulled off the case by Lieutenant Anderson, who is part of a larger white judicial conspiracy that is neither explained nor pursued. Muller comments on this experimentation in form by Himes:

Adding to this dissolution into a grotesque state of being is Himes's penchant for splitting the action and scenes within a simultaneous time frame so that sequences of the conflict parallel and confound each other. (92)

Influenced by Himes, Ishmael Reed continues this experimentation with nonsequential time in his novels, as we shall see in the next chapter.

Himes's detectives may play either supporting or lead roles in the plot lines of the novels, with varying degrees of success. In the first novel they appear a third of the way through almost as an afterthought. In the books after *Imabelle*—except for *Run, Man Run* in which they do not appear at all—the detectives function as intermediaries between white law enforcement and Harlem residents. By the ninth book, *Blind Man with a Pistol*, the two detectives are completely ineffectual. The final insult to their positions as law enforcers occurs in *Plan B* when Grave Digger is suspended from the force for killing a witness and Coffin Ed is assigned a desk job after a knee injury. Worse still, the detectives find themselves on opposite sides of the black revolution question, and in the end both detectives die. However, in a majority of the novels these two characters, with their vast network of stoolies and informers, have an intuitive understanding of the machinations of life in Harlem. In a certain sense they are also spokesmen for trapped black Americans protesting the desperate injustices caused by racism. In *Cotton Comes to Harlem* the two detectives have the following exchange after treading a typically depressing Harlem cityscape:

"All I wish is that I was God for just one mother-raping second," Grave Digger said, his voice cotton-dry with rage.
"I know," Coffin Ed said. "You'd concrete the face of the mother-raping earth and turn white folks into hogs."
"But I ain't God," Grave Digger said, pushing into the bar. (47–48)

Himes's African American sensibilities are attuned to the essential realities of black people's existence in Harlem, predicated, as Muller suggests, on "the divorce . . . between any unifying principle of justice and the irrational and meaningless nature of existence" (87). The two detectives attempt to bridge this gap. They are more successful in the early novels.

All of the novels, however, show African American culture as a distinct aspect of American life. Himes accomplished this primarily by constructing the "city within the city" where Harlem becomes a microcosmic metaphor for segregated culture throughout American society. Ishmael Reed comments on this aspect of Harlem in "Chester Himes: Writer" when he says that "Himes's Harlem [is] a kind of every ghetto, as the professors might say" (93). At the beginning of the screen scenario "Baby Sister," published in *Black on Black* (1973), Himes describes Harlem this way:

> This is Harlem, U.S.A., a city of contradictions. A city of Negroes isolated in the center of New York City. A city of incredible poverty and huge sums of cash. A city of the meek and the violent. A city of brothels, bars and churches. (11)

Himes is fascinated by the paradoxes of Harlem existence, which lead to the complex behavior of its inhabitants. The Harlem of Himes's novels reflects a specialness of place and people, both imagined and remembered.

Himes describes Harlem from the viewpoint of one above it, as if he were a god looking down on the fantastic world below him. It is interesting to note how this corresponds with his expatriate status and his emotional distance from Harlem while he was writing the novels:

> Looking eastward from the towers of Riverside Church, in a valley far below, waves of gray rooftops distort the perspective like the surface of the sea. Below the surface, in the murky waters of fetid tenements, a city of black people who are convulsed in desperate living. Like the voracious churning of millions of hungry cannibal fish. Blind mouths eating their own guts. Stick in a hand and draw back a nub.
>   This is Harlem. (*Imabelle* 111)

The swollen, overpopulated, overpriced, and dangerous Harlem forms the blackground of all the detective novels. This city within a city contains both positive and negative qualities. The attractiveness of Himes's world derives partly from the way his characters cope with and overcome adversity. Harlem becomes a metaphor for a separate culture with its own laws and rules of behavior where issues of race and class are expressed in specific African American ways. Harlem is a state of mind as well as a physical place. It possesses its own mad magic, its own allure, and its own boundaries outside the strict perimeters of streets. For example, in *Imabelle,* Jackson escapes from Harlem driving a hearse with a cargo of what he believes is gold ore. Under this fake pile of gold lies the throat-sliced body of his brother Goldy dressed as a Sister of Mercy. Jackson eludes the detectives chasing him and emerges from Harlem on Sixth Avenue. However, when he attains the white reaches of Manhattan around the Plaza (Fifty-ninth Street), he turns and retreats into Harlem. Jackson is more afraid of the white city than of being captured in Harlem by the detective duo of Coffin Ed and Grave Digger.

Himes treats the physical descriptions of Harlem with lavish attention. This blackground is at times graphically presented, as the lives of incidental characters, the alleys and the streets, the neon-lit bars and whorehouses become the center of attention:

> Children ran down the street, the dirty street littered with rotting vegetables, uncollected garbage, battered garbage cans, broken glass, dog-offal —always running, ducking and dodging. God help them if they got caught. Listless mothers stood in the dark entrance of tenements and swapped talk about their men, their poverty, their hunger, their debts, their Gods, their religions, their preachers, their bad luck with the numbers and the evilness of white people. Workingmen staggered down the sidewalks filled with aimless resentment, muttering curses, hating to go to their hotbox hovels but having nowhere else to go. (*Cotton* 47–48)

Long asides like this function both as atmospheric devices and as political and social statements. Certain intersections loom larger than life in their importance to Harlem citizens, almost like ancient tribal path crossings where social rituals are performed:

> Where 125th St. crosses Seventh Avenue is the mecca of Harlem. . . . The air and the heat and the voices and the laughter, the atmosphere and the drama and the melodrama, are theirs. . . . The black people have the past and the present, and they hope to have the future. (*Blind Man* 24)

The two-page description of the intersection of 125th Street and Seventh Avenue resonates with racial tensions because it is a major point of entry for whites. In *Blind Man,* this is where a white homosexual is picked up by a black one and eventually murdered. Murder is the one crime that Coffin Ed and Grave Digger cannot allow. "If white citizens wished to come to Harlem for their kicks, they had to take the . . . risks. . . . Their only duty was to protect them from violence" (*Blind Man* 34). In fact, it is not the detectives' job to keep whites out of Harlem because they provide sustenance for the whores, pimps, club owners, and con artists "who would turn on them if they tried to keep the white man out of Harlem after dark" (34). In the end the special atmosphere of Harlem depicted by Himes directly affects his concept of the detective persona. His two detectives are a product of the environment of Harlem. As such, they bring new personas to black detective fiction, in part based on their double-conscious ability to detect.

Pauline Hopkins and J. E. Bruce introduced the rich theme of double-conscious detection to black detective fiction, and Rudolph Fisher elaborated on the trope. By demonstrating how black detective fiction incorporated aspects of masking and the trickster tradition into texts these authors opened up avenues of expression not explored in white detective fiction. Himes uses double-conscious detection by connecting his concept of absurdity in African American life to the initial concept of double consciousness as posited by Du Bois. Obviously, Himes was well aware of the absurdity of racism and the double-conscious behavior it engendered. Coffin Ed and Grave Digger are double-conscious detectives in the sense that they themselves are trickster figures who bridge the white and black worlds, using both to their advantage. Their blackness gives them a special insight into black behavior in Harlem that is relied on by their white superiors. Himes further expands the trope of double-conscious detection by giving masking and trickster qualities to a wide range of characters in the novels. Progressively complicating the trope, double consciousness represents not only African American identity problems initiated by white racism but also black-on-black trickery. Double-conscious detection in Hopkins is carried by the conceit of passing and in Fisher by the legerdemain of conjure. With Himes double-conscious detection becomes increasingly darker as the tricksters dupe fellow blacks and, in the end, themselves. Harlem manifests a carnival atmosphere in the early novels, but as the books progress the spectacle turns more and more ominous, leading in the end in *Plan B* to total chaos, instigated by the ultimate trickster of the armed black revolution, Tomsson Black.

Double-conscious detection in detective fiction implies, as I have suggested in earlier chapters, the overriding consciousness of African American detective characters of both their position as blacks in America and their connection to trickster themes in black folklore. The trickster theme works especially well in detective fiction, which has traditionally utilized masquerade and hidden identity in its plots.

In Himes's Harlem, trickster schemes abound, mostly for the purpose of bilking black residents. Harlem is a concentrated environment in which various groups vie for control of money, territory, and the support of the honest, hardworking people. Within this racial community with its own laws of behavior, a competitive atmosphere develops in which parties of trickster blacks try to outwit each other. In Himes's fiction this rivalry becomes increasingly chaotic and violent, suggesting a sort of jungle mentality of survival-of-the-fittest.

In *All Shot Up* a homicide lieutenant asks about rackets in Harlem. Grave Digger answers: "Folks up here are dreaming up new rackets every day. They got the time and the imagination, and all they need is a racket to make the money" (43). The inherent suggestion in this remark is that unemployment based on racism is at the root of the scheming. A main result of the conniving is that identity becomes fluid as characters, in the best sense of the trickster mentality, assume roles and change their names. All of the Harlem stories revolve around contretemps concerning false identities, mistaken identities, masquerades, or cons. Milliken points out Himes's affinity for the "Object X" search plot, as in the *Maltese Falcon* prototype (217). Object X can be any supposed valuable entity that someone covets. In *Imabelle* it is gold ore. It is money in *All Shot Up* and *Big Gold Dream*. In *The Heat's On* it is five eels filled with heroin. But, as Milliken suggests, it really does not matter since Himes's plots are shaky constructions at best. "The fantastic incidents create an atmosphere that is a blend of humor, fantasy, reluctant horror, and . . . exaggerated earnestness" (221). This atmosphere is perfect for exploring the trickster theme. Himes's books are full of trickster figures who use all manner of schemes to con the residents of Harlem.[7]

As we saw earlier, the African origins of the trickster figure prefigure the African American interpretation of trickster characters and themes. Himes adds new elements to the tradition by emphasizing the mercenary traits of his Harlem characters. We may recall that in *The Conjure Man Dies*—a novel that Himes obviously knew—Frimbo, the conjure man, tricks the detectives and the witnesses by use of a double—his own servant who resembles him. In Himes's work the level of trickster manipulation reaches new heights in three areas: African American religious, freedom, and Back-to-Africa movements. It must be remembered that at the root of Himes's satire there is genuine respect for African American culture and a deep abhorrence of all forms of racism. However, the fact that Himes did not hold anything sacred allowed him to criticize the most intimate elements of the African American community.

Himes begins very early ridiculing black religious movements. Early on in *Imabelle* he writes, "The people of Harlem take their religion seriously" (33), but he was well aware that this seriousness could lead to gullibility. Consequently, in all of the novels, not one legitimate religious figure is presented. His teenage gang in *The Real Cool Killers* is composed of Black Muslims who dress the part but actually profess no commitment to any religious or moral values. Sweet Prophet Brown, the leader of a popular cult in *The Big Gold Dream* is perhaps Himes's consummate religious trickster. He wears a "bright purple robe lined with yellow silk and trimmed with mink. . . . His smooth black face with its big buck teeth and popping eyes was ageless; but his long grizzly hair, on which he wore a black silk cap, was snow-white" (6–7). Sweet Prophet Brown, most likely modeled on the New York cult leader Prophet Jones, is about as amoral an individual as ever worked the crowd in Harlem. During an outdoor service one of his faithful "who had drunk of the holy water had dropped dead" (10). Sweet Prophet is desperate as thousands of his followers wait to see what this religious leader, rumored to be richer than his rivals Father Divine and Daddy Grace, would do:

> Sweet Prophet knew he had to do something quick to avert catastrophe. It was the most desperate situation he had ever faced in his long and check-ered career as a revivalist. It was worse than the time he had been accused of raping three twelve-year-old girls. (10–11)

Sweet Prophet Brown, who "had the nimble wits of a confidence man and the nerve of a bank robber" (11), shares traits with other Hime-sian con artists, like the Reverend Deke O'Malley in *Cotton Comes to Harlem,* who bilks $87,000 from eighty-seven Harlem families by promoting a phony back-to-Africa movement. O'Malley, as one Harlemite put it, is "the young Communist Christian preacher who's going to take our folks back to Africa" (9). Muller considers *Cotton* to be one of Himes's most successful novels "because of its satiric portrait of white and black tricksters preying on people's lost dreams" (98).

Himes's detective novels are narratives in which extravagant ges-ture and absurd humor predominate. A black minister in *The Crazy*

Kill falls out of a three-story window into a basket of fresh bread, staggers away, and is replaced three minutes later by a dead man with a knife sticking out of his chest. In *Imabelle* a roly-poly Sister of Mercy begging alms on the street turns out to be a fat black man named Goldy who has a heroin habit and a numbers racket. In *Cotton Comes to Harlem* an upright church lady talking to a minister in front of the Abyssinian Church has her dress cut away from behind by a thief with a razor who is after the money purse strapped to the middle of her back. The church lady walks down the main avenue of Harlem without the back of her dress, revealing broad buttocks in rose-colored panties to the passersby. Finally, she is stopped by a worker who taps her on the shoulder. "Lady, . . . I just wanted to say your ass is out" (27). Meanwhile, the thief runs into the street with the church lady's money, only to be rammed broadside by a speeding truck containing $87,000 wrapped in a bale of cotton. The continuing saga of the bale of cotton, which falls out of the truck to be picked up by a black ragpicker, forms only one of the bizarre plot lines of the novel. These are just a few samples of the many tragicomic scenes in Himes's series of Harlem detective novels.

In fact, the catalogue of trickster figures and absurd scenes is endless but not unchanging. Himes's initial comic elements become darker and more satiric as the novels progress, ultimately leading to a vision depressingly apocalyptic. The sometimes very funny scenes of the early novels—as in *Imabelle,* where Jackson is duped into "cooking" his ten-dollar bills into hundreds—become more vicious and less humorous as the stories progress. As the playfulness of the episodes sours, the main characters' motivations keep pace with the pessimistic worldview that colors the last half of Himes's autobiography. By the time we get to Deke O'Malley and Tomsson Black, the playfulness has an undercurrent of despair, and the trickster figures no longer have the grace and inherent morality of their African models. There is little moral ground to stand on for African Americans in these novels. Like Ralph Ellison's Rinehart in *Invisible Man,* they have lost themselves in a maze of contradictory personalities. Muller writes:

> The universe of *Cotton Comes to Harlem* is one of total deception. Deke, for instance, both is and is not what he seems, utilizing his multiple disguises to outwit unsuspecting Harlem residents, stay ahead of the Syndicate out to kill him, elude the police, and seduce women. (99)

Nonetheless, Himes's characters have an appeal that suggests they are only playing a game forced on them by lack of other alternatives. The very root of life in Harlem is survival, and the white power structure offers few means to survival other than cons and crime.

Himes's economic and political critique is clearly presented in these novels through his descriptions of the poverty and desperation in Harlem and by his double-conscious detective characters who must use trickery to survive. The catalogue of religious charlatans and swindlers is long, running from Sweet Prophet Brown, who works his flock for money, to the Reverend Sam in *Blind Man,* who uses a harem of black nuns for material and sexual ease, to Tomsson Black (George Washington Lincoln), who in *Plan B* creates chaos on a grand scale. Across the board Himes, as Skinner notes, depicts "the purveyors of religion as charlatans and thieves and the worshippers as upstanding but naive fools" (159). Perhaps the prime example of Himes's jaundiced worldview is Sister Heavenly in *The Heat's On.* This woman has all the trademarks of the conventional African American hoodoo priestess. "Sister Heavenly prided herself on being an old-fashioned faith healer with old-fashioned tried-and-true methods" (38). Although these methods appear on the surface to be the traditional elements of roots, portents, and prophecy, Sister Heavenly actually runs a profitable drug emporium. Her pods of "Heavenly Dust" are heroin, and her longtime companion, Uncle Saint, periodically shoots himself up with speedballs. When Pinky, the giant albino, comes to her for help, she directs him to the rabbit cage in her yard where the drugs are stuffed up the rabbit's anus. "And don't take but one, it's all you'll need. . . . The Spike is in my bureau drawer" (39). Himes's depiction of the African American folk tradition, as well as more traditional black religions, is a comic satire of types that had a large influence on Ishmael Reed's fiction.

Himes also had little use for black politics, especially the Back-to-Africa movement: "I thought the Back to Africa program in the U.S. was one of the most absurd things the black people of America had ever supported" (*MLA* 258). In his detective novels Himes voices his contempt for such contemporary movements as the Black Muslims and Black Power. The killer of a white homosexual in *Blind Man* is a black homosexual who wears a fez with "BLACK POWER" written across it. "He might have been a Black Muslim but for the fact Black Muslims avoided the vicinity of perverts" (22). However, as we shall see, Himes's satiric treatment of black politics is based on a radical viewpoint that leaned more toward revolution than assimilation.

Another distinctive aspect of Himes's detective fiction has to do with concepts of class and gender within the Harlem community. Harlem is a product of racism and is a world unto itself with its own African American laws of cultural behavior. Himes breaks down class behavior into two groups: those executing the con and those being conned. Himes's African American characters range in color from deep black to albino. Class, just as in white society, is based on color as well as money. Most of the respected and successful members of the black community are light-skinned, as are Himes's con-artist preachers. Himes's understanding of covert racism within African American society goes back to his early years when he rebelled against class distinction based on color. He writes about his first and only college year:

> But even then I despised the in-group class distinctions based on color and the degree of white blood in one's veins. In those days light-complexioned blacks were more prejudiced towards darker blacks than were many white people. (*QH* 29)

Some of Himes's awareness of this issue stems from his own family situation in which his mother made an issue of her light skin while criticizing her husband for his darker color (*QH*). Himes's view of this borrowed sense of white prejudice is heavily satirical. In *Cotton Comes to Harlem* Deke O'Malley's use of the back-to-Africa movement to dupe honest black citizens shows how far a black man with symbolically white hair will go to manipulate his own kind. Sister Heavenly in *The Heat's On,* in the course of her long and corrupt life, has used skin-lightening creams to alter her skin color. As Skinner points out, "As she became lighter in color, her means of supporting herself became more pernicious" (149). Himes shows how light skin equates with immorality, and Skinner confirms this: "Even more interestingly, the people with the lightest skins in the Harlem crime stories, women and men alike, are typically the most evil. The characters with the blackest skin are the 'squares' and therefore the victims" (7).

Lundquist sees the two detectives moving through a "milieu that contains an incredible gradation of speech and class" (109). As I have suggested, some of this gradation is based on skin color, and a lighter skin color becomes particularly dangerous when possessed by a young woman. Himes's social critique is perhaps weakest in his use of gender stereotypes. As Skinner notes, "In his Harlem crime series . . . he equated light skin color with irresistible sexuality in Black women" (7). In terms of gender difference Himes shows little progressive attitude in these novels. Milliken points out that "in each of Himes's detective novels there is also at least one stunningly attractive black woman [and] the function of these women is possibly even more limited" (249). In the introduction to *Black on Black*, Himes says, "These writings are admittedly chauvinistic. You will conclude if you read them that BLACK PROTEST and BLACK HETEROSEXUALITY are my two chief obsessions" (7). The chauvinistic writing of the hardboiled school undergoes little revision in Himes's work. The biggest difference noted is that Himes's beautiful women are usually light-skinned blacks. As Skinner notes,

> The archetypal Himes woman is a seductive, curvy, amoral sexpot with very light skin. She is a character who has many names but who shows up in virtually every story. At worst she may be a murderess but at best she will be a liar, a cheat, or a faithless lover. (22)

Following Himes's self-professed attitude toward females, Coffin Ed and Grave Digger show little respect or restraint in dealing with female witnesses. In *The Heat's On* Coffin Ed strips a recalcitrant witness named Ginny of all her clothes and ties her to a couch. "Then he leaned over and took her by the hair again. Pulling her head back until her throat was taut, he cut the skin in a thin line six inches across her throat" (160). Even while Coffin Ed executes this physical threat, he debates with himself. "He knew he had gone beyond the line; that he had gone beyond human restraint. . . . But he didn't want any more lies" (160). Imabelle, the first of Himes's seductive, amoral women, appears early in the story as a foil to Jackson's naive worship. She was "a cushioned-lipped, hot-bodied, banana-skin chick with speckled-brown eyes of a teaser and the high-arched, ball-bearing hips of a natural-born *amante*" (*Imabelle* 6). Imabelle, like others of this type, is a ruthless, greedy female who leads suckers to the slaughter. In Jackson's case she sets him up for "the blow," in which ten-dollar bills are chemically cooked into brand new C-notes. Like many another hardboiled character, Jackson was "an honest man, just led astray by a woman" (11). Milliken points out that "the function of these women in the novels is quite simply, to be desired and to be frightened" (250). A good example is Dulcy in *Crazy Kill,* who runs through the narrative with little or no clothes on. Grave Digger and Coffin Ed fall back on the stereotypical hardboiled attitude in this case. Dulcy asks, "I bad hurt?" Digger sneers, "I doubt it ... you're too pretty to be bad hurt. Only ugly women ever get hurt" (Skinner 103). However, there is even more than this going on. Iris O'Malley, wife of Deke O'Malley, is light-skinned and particularly corrupt. She uses sex to con men, and she offers herself repeatedly to the detectives. Iris is more than willing to help con eighty-seven black families out of $1,000 apiece. Even though she is black, she refuses to consider herself part of the community. "Eighty-seven colored families—like you and me," Grave Digger pleads. "Not like me!" is Iris's answer. Grave Digger and Ed give her coal-black dye to rub on her body to transform her into a churchgoing woman to help them find the money. "Make yourself into a black woman and don't ask any questions," Grave Digger said (*Cotton* 175). This is reminiscent of a scene in *The Heat's On* where Pinky, the huge albino, is painted with black ink for disguise. Himes's approach in these episodes suggests that Grave Digger and Coffin Ed have some concern for the black community as well as understanding that blackness can help solve the crimes. This notion of community and this fear of true blackness are things that lighter-skinned blacks, particularly women, subvert and avoid.

On the other hand, there are a few deftly drawn, powerful women who are in control of their immediate environment. These women generally fall into the category of the black madam and are either very old or of very large stature. Sister Heavenly of *The Heat's On* is a good example. She's a faith healer who was so old "her face had the shrunken, dried up leathery look of a monkey's" (42). She smokes marijuana in a "dainty, meerschaum pipe" and rules her kingdom with an iron hand.

> Her old faded eyes regarded him with cynical amusement over the rim of her cup. . . . "What you trying to con me out of? . . . And if you think any woman what knows that is fool enough to die and leave him something, you don't know the female race." (43–44)

Reba, the madam of a brothel run out of the Knickerbocker on 145th Street in *The Real Cool Killers,* is another example:

> She was six feet two, with snow-white hair cut short as a man's and
> brushed back from her forehead. Her lips were painted carnation red
> and her eyelids silver but her smooth unlined jet black skin was un-
> touched. (79)

Reba had changed her name from Sheba and stopped drinking after
she murdered her husband: "She caught the nigger with some chippie
or 'nother and made him jump buck naked out the third-story window. That wouldn't 'ave been so bad but she shot 'im through the
head as he was going down" (76). Himes's range of characters is
only suggested by the examples provided here; in general, his women
characters remain stereotypically seductive and duplicitous in the
hardboiled tradition.

In the end Himes reserves his most vitriolic attacks for black gay
men. They suffer even more absurdly violent punishment than "high
yellow" women and pale brown criminals. Black Beauty, the trans-
vestite in *All Shot Up,* is a perfect example. Dressed in women's
clothes, wearing a wig and a bra with falsies, Black Beauty is hit from
behind by a Cadillac and splayed against a convent wall where he
hangs with his smashed face imprisoned in a crack. Most homosexu-
als in the Harlem stories end up mutilated and dead. *Blind Man*
depicts the homosexual milieu with a particular vengeance. Grave
Digger and Coffin Ed alternately bait and insult a black homosexual
witness named Babson and then, through negligence, let him get his
throat sliced while the detectives watch a lesbian stripper. The mysterious Jesus Baby is the homosexual supposedly responsible for the
first murder of a white homosexual, but the detectives give up on the
case before they can solve the crime. All in all, the pervasive corruption and downright nastiness in *Blind Man* are explicitly tied to homosexuality and syndicate crime, though the story line provides no
real clues as to this connection. By failing to posit clear reasons other
than a typically prejudiced and slanted view of the sordidness of the
homosexual world, Himes does a disservice to his reader. In this
sense Himes falls back on the traditional hardboiled convention of a
masculine viewpoint that links hatred of homosexuality and sadistic
mistreatment of beautiful women and presents it as status quo, ac-
ceptable behavior.

Himes's African American detective fiction expands the groundwork laid by other black detective writers in the use of black vernacu-

lars. Muller calls Himes's work an "impressive cycle of detective novels set in Harlem [that] constitutes a unique antigenre in crime fiction" (x). Milliken places Himes's work in a "subgenre" that was "skillfully written for a popular commercial market" (214). He feels that Himes "steered clear of the . . . notorious cliches [and] kept the characters real and the language authentic" (216). While these characterizations make sense in relation to the way Himes signified on the hardboiled tradition, they ignore Himes as part of the black detective tradition. Furthermore, the detective novels are composed of characters that bear a special relation to Himes's conviction that the African American is a special breed of human being. Himes writes at the end of the first book of his autobiography:

> Obviously and unavoidably, the American black man is the most neurotic, complicated, schizophrenic, unanalyzed, anthropologically advanced specimen of mankind in the history of the world. The American black is a new race of man; the only new race of man to come into being in modern time. (*QH 285*)

In detective fiction Himes found a vehicle that helped make African American difference even clearer. Therefore, it is important to underline that this difference is connected in the Harlem novels to specific ends: "His is a special genre because of his black antiheroes and his Harlem settings, which permit him to reveal the 'American black's secret mind itself' " (Muller 15).

Himes was well aware of how he altered detective fiction with what he called "various new angles of my own" (Williams 314). Among these angles was the use of black vernaculars. In *My Life of Absurdity* he urges American blacks to "get all the protest out of their minds" and "look upon my story like they looked upon the blues of Bessie and Mamie Smith" (158). The references to black vernaculars in these ten novels are voluminous. As with the other areas under discussion, I can only use a few examples from many to make my point.[8] One interesting example of language use is the signifyin(g) executed by the two detectives. Coffin Ed's and Grave Digger's sense of social outrage smolders under the surface of their official face and often erupts in stinging passages. Signifying, as I have mentioned earlier, is an African American language act whose characteristics include irony, indirection, humor, and circumlocution.

Above all, it is a language act with a message. The following passage between the two detectives and Lieutenant Anderson concerns a riot in Harlem:

> "I take you've discovered who started the riot," Anderson said.
> "We knew who he was all along," Grave Digger said.
> "It's just nothing we can do to him," Coffin Ed echoed.
> "Why not, for God's sake?"
> "He's dead," Coffin Ed said.
> "Who?"
> "Lincoln," Grave Digger said.
> "He hadn't ought to have freed us if he didn't want to make provisions to feed us," Coffin Ed said. "Anybody could have told him that." (*Blind Man* 139)

This passage contains a creative use of language and an ironic delivery style—two important characteristics of black speech patterns.

Himes was extremely conscious of his reworking of the African American folk tradition. "I had taken much of my writing from slavery: the poem in *La Reine des Pommes* . . . 'run nigger run, the patroller will catch you' . . . is a slave chantey" (*MLA* 178). Other novels have numerous references to the black vernaculars of music, food, and dance. Look, for example, at the beginning of *Real Cool Killers:*

> I'm gwine down to de river,
> Set down on de ground.
> If de blues overtake me,
> I'll jump overboard and drown . . .

> Big Joe Turner was singing a rock-and-roll adaptation of *Dink's Blues*. The loud licking rhythm blasted from the jukebox with enough heat to melt bones. A woman leapt from her seat in a booth as though the music had struck her full of tacks. She pulled up her skirt and began doing a shake as though trying to throw off the tacks one by one. (5)

There are references to Louis Armstrong and Jimmy Rushing in *Cotton* (9, 18), and Himes uses descriptive scenes of Saturday night rent parties and blackjack games in *The Big Gold Dream* (73). In *The Heat's On* atmospheric passages of washboard and piano blues fill the rooms where Sister Heavenly's clients dance all night long.

> Sister Heavenly prided herself on being an old-fashioned faith healer with old-fashioned tried-and-true methods. That was why she used old-fash-

ioned gin-drinking musicians and directed her clients to dance old-fashioned belly-rubbing dances. It was the first stage of the cure. She called it
"de-incarnation." (38)

Himes blends vernacular music references into the narrative so successfully that music and dance are understood as integral parts of the
Harlem community.

The references to African American food are also too numerous to
document throughout the ten novels. In *The Heat's On* the detectives
search out a place to eat where "you can smell the girls' sweat"
because their usual spot, Mamie Louise, is closed (29). When they
enter the Great Man nightclub on 125th Street, "Faces bubbled in the
dim light like a huge pot of cannibal stew, showing mostly eyes and
teeth" (29). They choose gumbo to eat, which was "made of fresh
pork, chicken gizzards, hog testicles and giant shrimp, with a base of
okra and sweet potatoes, and twenty-seven varieties of seasonings,
spices and herbs" (30). In the first few pages of *All Shot Up* Grave
Digger and Coffin Ed are in Mammy Louise's pork store eating "hot
'chicken feetsy,' a Geechy dish of stewed chicken feet, rice, okra and
red chili peppers" (17). Mammy Louise is a common hangout for the
two detectives, and Himes comments on the Geechee origins of the
owner, "Geechies are a melange of runaway African slaves and Seminole Indians, native to the Carolinas and Florida. Their mother
tongue is a mixture of African dialects and the Seminole language"
(19). The Gullah or Geechee language patterns have been discussed
extensively by language critics, who demonstrate conclusively the
African origins of both Gullah words and Gullah grammar (see J. L.
Dillard, Geneva Smitherman, and Lorenzo D. Turner, who concentrates on the languages spoken by slaves in South Carolina and Georgia). In short, it is quite clear that Himes's conscious use of various
African American vernaculars was an attempt to differentiate his
detective fiction by grounding the narrative in the experience of black
people. Consequently, many of the characters fall back into their
folk ways when confronted with danger. One example is Jackson in
Imabelle, who when in fear of arrest drops his educated tone and
speaks a more common language. Himes writes: "Jackson had at-
tended a Negro college in the South, but whenever he was excited or
scared he began talking in his native dialect" (9).

Although the African American cultural vernaculars occur mostly
as blackground to the main action, Grave Digger and Coffin Ed make

an interesting comment about jazz in *Cotton*. As they listen to two saxophones trade jazz solos, Coffin Ed says, "Somewhere in that jungle is the solution to the world." Grave Digger answers, "The emotion that comes out of experience. If we could read that language, man, we would solve all the crimes in the world" (46). In all of the novels black vernaculars such as music, dance, and food are shown to be important cultural restoratives, creatively complex and indigenous African American creations.

Compared with other black detective writers such as Hopkins and Fisher, who find redeeming qualities in particularly black American cultural worldviews such as hoodoo, primitivism, and ancestralism, Himes proffers less optimism. His sweeping critique of black behavior in Harlem is laced with cynicism. However, as with hoodoo, Himes refers to Africa in oblique ways. For example, Goldy in *Imabelle* is described this way: "With his round black head poking from the bulging black gown, he looked like an African sculpture" (103). While such descriptions help establish the link between African American culture and African culture, Himes devotes little attention to constructing a network of Afrocentric influence. As we have noted, Himes distrusted the Back-to-Africa movement and saw hoodoo more as a scam than a powerful tool of survival. It is important, however, that we do not associate critique with negativity. Himes was proud of black people and black culture and proved himself a pioneering detective writer through his use of black detective tropes as well as his willingness to critique black behavior satirically. In my view this does not in any way diminish his artistic stature as a black writer. The important point is that Himes was aware of the shared values that help define African American culture and, through satire, possibly hoped to strengthen and improve these values. As we will see, Himes's concerns about the future of African American culture come from a different direction.

Himes's detective novels as a whole are satires of white and black behavior. Inherently critical of white power structures, Himes indicates that racism and one of its children, poverty, are directly responsible for the craziness of his Harlem world. His worldview suggests there is little hope for improvement in Harlem. Interestingly, the progress of Himes's satiric vision resulted in a different and rather drastic solution to America's racism. His new solution evolved out of his fascination with a characteristic of detective novels in general—

their use of violence. Speaking about the detective form, Himes says, "It's just plain and simple violence in narrative form, you know. 'Cause no one, *no one*, writes about violence the way the Americans do" (in Williams 314). And further on in the same interview, Himes urges fellow blacks to write detective novels because "American violence is public life, it's a public way of life, it became a form, a detective story form. So I would think that any number of black writers should go into the detective story form" (314). Himes utilized this fascination with violence in his stories, initially as a technique to help him to write detective fiction. But as he stated more than once, he recognized America's violence as being rooted in slavery: "there is no way that one can evaluate the American scene and avoid violence . . . it comes straight from the days of slavery" (329).

Himes's use of violence in the novels moves from comic vision to a serious confrontation. Often the two are mixed in a way that is hard to distinguish. Early in the detective series Coffin Ed and Grave Digger function as ordering devices in the novels, but as the series progresses, attitudes change. Coffin Ed and Grave Digger lose more and more control, and other forces outside and inside Harlem take over. The primary evidence of change is in the level and use of violence. Himes's theory on uses of violence and the literary imagination altered over the period in which he was writing the detective novels. In the early narratives violence was used in a comical and/or retributive fashion. His use of violence was stylized and in most cases elicits a contrary response of both humor and horror from the reader:

> Big Smiley countered with a right cross with the redhandled axe. . . . The severed arm in its coat sleeve, still clutching the knife, sailed through the air. . . . The little knifeman landed on his feet, still making cutting motions with his half arm. . . .
> "Wait a minute, you big mother-raper, till ah finds my arm!" he yelled. "It got my knife in his hand." (*Real Cool Killers* 8)

By the time we reach the later novels the equation has changed somewhat, and Himes's violence, although eloquently represented, begins to disturb with its underlying sinister tone. Rather than being humorous, the violence suggests vindictive bitterness underpinning all racial interactions. Himes suggests that relations between blacks and whites and blacks and blacks have progressively worsened. In *Cotton* a black attendant to the Reverend Deke O'Malley is gunned down by a white gang wearing black masks: "There was a burst from a machine gun. A mixture of teeth, barbecued pork ribs, and human brains flew through the air like macabre birds. The young man, with half a head gone, sank down out of sight" (11).

Many examples from the novels suggest that the violence in Himes's works moves from a random pattern of absurdist incidents toward a pointed political message. Himes's theory of detective narratives based on violence becomes more sophisticated in the later works. In the last novels and especially in his last stories, "Prediction" and "Tang," the level of violence reaches new highs. These stories are later incorporated into *Plan B*, Himes's ultimate statement on violence in black America. What is interesting, however, is that the violence in these stories differs from his first use of violence in that it now represents a coherent viewpoint. Forced to extremes of behavior by racist practices, American blacks now answer back in bursts of violent activity.

Run, Man Run and *Blind Man with a Pistol* are the primary texts among the detective novels which demonstrate Himes's evolving interpretation of violence. With *Run, Man Run,* Himes's worldview noticeably darkens. I include this novel in the corpus of detective novels because, even though it does not contain the black detectives, it illustrates Himes's growing sophistication in signifying on the detective form. It also initiates his growing conviction that African American survival depends on directed violence against the white oppressor. As we shall see, it is in part due to Himes's aesthetic ability in using the detective form that this radical viewpoint has a certain inner logic and moral quality.

In *Run, Man Run* (1966) a drunk, corrupt white detective named Matt Walker goes berserk and, because of racial hatred, indiscriminately kills two black cafeteria workers and tries to kill a third. The novel works on two levels and forms a logical bridge to *Blind Man* (1969). *Run, Man Run* was written after Himes had achieved some success with the detective form and came at a time in his writing career when he was bored with what was becoming for him a formulaic pattern. *Run* is a biting indictment of racism as well as a clever, twisted critique of detective novels in general. In the beginning of the novel the white detective Walker is enraged when he is taunted by a black porter: "Here you is, a detective like Sherlock Holmes, pride of the New York City police force, and you've gone and got so full of holiday cheer you've let some punk steal your car" (15). From the start, then, we are given to understand that the novel is a conscious attempt to parody expected conventions of detective fiction.

Matt Walker, a white detective working the Times Square beat, suffers from alcoholic blackouts. The novel opens with Walker staggering down the street in the early morning hours looking for his car. He is angry and frustrated because he has been robbed by a prostitute after he forced her to sleep with him as payment for not arresting her. Walker spots two black porters taking garbage out of a cafeteria and immediately rushes to the insane conclusion that they have stolen his car. He shoots one of the porters in the back of the head in a moment of racist anger. The second porter is killed after he finds the body of his fellow worker but not before Walker tries to explain himself in a terrifying scene that reveals a brutal streak of perverted prejudice. Just before shooting the second black porter between the eyes, Walker tells him: "I never had anything against colored people. I don't know what made me think like that—suspecting you porters. I guess I must have just picked it up" (22). But the first porter has already witnessed Walker's transformation into a monster:

> Fat Sam had never seen a white man go insane like this. He had never realized that the thought of Negroes could send a white man out of his head. He wouldn't have believed it. And now this sight of violence unleashed because of race terrified him. (16)

A third porter, Jimmy Johnson, manages to escape before Walker can kill him. The novel documents the perverted judicial process by which Walker is assigned to find the murderer of the black men he killed. Because Jimmy is the only witness, Walker must find and kill him.

Besides being an exciting detective novel with an uncommon self-reflexive critique, *Run* succeeds in presenting Himes's developing worldview concerning African American survival. Himes develops Jimmy's character, moving him from innocent bystander and witness to determined protagonist representing not only his own survival but that of his race. After Walker is put on the case, he has legitimate authority behind him. We follow Jimmy's escape tactics with increasing dread as he futilely tries to outwit the power and control of white authority. In this novel the primary motivation is Jimmy's growing awareness that he alone can save himself; the white detective has even seduced Jimmy's black girlfriend. Jimmy has to arm himself and prepare to kill the white detective, a difficult course of action for this educated and sensitive man. Jimmy works nights as a porter, but he is also a graduate of a college in North Carolina and is studying law at Columbia. One of the many ironies of *Run* is the fact that Jimmy, a law student, must break the law by illegally purchasing a gun in order to prevent his own murder by a detective.

Himes's last three novels all contain examples of the four tropes of black detection, but it is his accomplished critique of detective novels as a whole that separates him from previous black detective novelists. This critique of the detective form, glimpsed at times in the other detective novels, blossoms forth in these last three novels where traditional detective personas and investigations are brutally mocked. For example, Matt Walker, as the presiding homicide detective on the case, carelessly rubs his hands all over the stainless steel that one of his forensic experts is trying to dust for fingerprints. *Run* is a bitter spoof of the police procedural as well as a satire of the independent detective hero of the hardboiled tradition. The violence in *Run*, no longer stylized, is totally terrifying in its absurdity. Furthermore, the absurdity of the violence is explicitly linked to racial prejudice, making this novel one of Himes's best in terms of social commentary. The Herculean detective gambits of Coffin Ed and Grave Digger are inappropriate to this suddenly inverted situation where the victim is the hero and the detective the criminal. As Jimmy desperately maneuvers to extricate himself from a web of racial hatred intent on destroying him, Himes's position concerning African American survival in a racist society becomes clear.

> What did a man do when he knew someone was going to kill him? Kill the killer first? That was what men did in the western movies. But this wasn't a movie. Not even a gangster film. This was real life. (91)

When Jimmy sets out to stalk Walker and kill him, we understand Himes's message of self-empowerment.

In this novel, as in *Blind Man* and the posthumous *Plan B*, Himes clearly begins to use the detective novel as a vehicle for a radical political message. Embittered by racial violence in his own life, Himes gives his characters more and more autonomy, urging them toward violent retribution. Harlem represents a place of refuge for Jimmy, and he realizes that to kill Walker he must lure him back into Harlem. Symbolically, the final confrontation between Walker and Jimmy takes place at 149th Street and Broadway in the heart of Harlem. Jimmy is ambushed and shot two times, falling face forward to the pavement while getting off one useless shot. Eventually Walker is caught and killed by his brother-in-law, also a detective. Jimmy, however, wakes up in the hospital seriously wounded but alive. When asked by his girlfriend why he had attacked so foolishly, he replies, "I just wanted to kill the mother-raper and keep on living myself. . . . What's a man going to do? I couldn't keep running all my life" (*Run* 191–92).

Blind Man with a Pistol was the last novel in the detective series to be published before Himes's death. The form and political message of the novel suggest that Himes was through with his detectives and his series. To begin with, the plot is almost incomprehensible. Simultaneous time has been forced to the point that episodes apparently have no relation to each other at all. Critics such as Muller and Lundquist are quick to note that Coffin Ed and Grave Digger are reduced to impotent frustration in this novel. They are unable to solve any of the crimes in the book, and the overall chaos of the narrative elicits a sense of futility in the reader. However, if we look at Himes's novel as a vehicle for a critique of the detective form and a cautionary message about African American worldviews, it begins to make more sense.

Blind Man revolves around three messianic figures who eventually lead their followers to death and destruction in one of the most chaotic episodes of all the novels. The characters in *Blind Man* signal the end of the Harlem detective series completely extinguished in *Plan B*, and in many ways the novel can be seen as the culmination of directions that Himes suggested in the earlier novels. Marcus Mackenzie is a naive "square" who plans to lead a brotherhood march through Harlem accompanied by his white Swedish female companion. Doctor Moore is head of a Black Power movement that exhorts citizens to march—and donate funds to his cause, which is supported in part by a covey of black prostitutes he manages. Prophet Ham is another black leader who worships the Black Jesus and manipulates a group of fanatical followers to fight rather than pray. As Skinner points out, Harlem has changed:

> Himes paints Harlem in different colors than he ever has before. It is no longer a colorful place filled with suckers and criminals. Harlem has become a kind of socio-political powder keg, waiting for a stray spark to set it off. (177)

When the three groups converge at a Harlem intersection on Nat Turner Day, total pandemonium erupts as followers of all three groups fight each other.

Even Grave Digger and Coffin Ed are drawn into the melee, unable to use their guns, but fighting with their fists. The level of indiscriminate violence escalates until the detectives have to flee, and the citizens begin to riot, looting their own neighborhood. *Blind Man* ends in futility as the detectives, unable to solve the crime, resort to shooting their pistols at rats in the abandoned tenements. They have been outwitted by Lieutenant Anderson, their white superior, who, it is suggested, misdirects them for personal gain. This final comment on white supremacy is particularly revealing since Anderson originally had a rather avuncular relationship with the detectives. Both Anderson and the world of the detectives have changed since the earlier novels. By having the two black detectives handcuffed in their duty because of Anderson's connection to organized crime, Himes suggests the increasing horror of racial control verging on extermination, foreshadowing his last novel, *Plan B*. Moreover, *Blind Man* demonstrates how the corruption of values in the white world mirrors an increasing sense of disorder in the black world. This novel also illustrates the ultimate interaction between Himes's social and aesthetic theories. As the meaningless violence in the book increases, the structure of the detective novel as we know it disintegrates. Himes's message is now both thematic and structural, suggesting a move into the postmodern world of detective fiction to be discussed in the next chapter.

Finally, Himes's bitter and cautionary worldview can be seen as a logical progression through his detective fiction. Initially, he attempted through poignant blackground passages to illustrate how blacks live and create within their own communities. His fond eye for the absurdities of behavior suggested a love of spontaneity and change and an appreciation for the powers of black vernaculars and double-conscious trickster qualities. In the final novel blackground has become foreground, and the moral center represented by the two detectives has dissolved. Black vernaculars and political movements now seem outrageously intense. Worst of all, nothing works in this universe. All the traditional African American survival systems are symbolically laid to waste. The overall pessimistic view in this book reflects Himes's despair over racial politics in America. *Blind Man* and *Plan B* carry the mythical and metaphorical aspects of Himes's Harlem to their ultimate and, for Himes, logical end.

In previous chapters I have discussed how black authors used detective fiction to provide social, political, and moral alternatives to the dominant white culture. Himes recognizes these alternatives as being part of African American society, but he also reserves the right to criticize black people. Consequently, he sees vernaculars, double-conscious detection, and religion as African American survival systems having their own problems. Furthermore, these tropes provide only temporary relief from the complex, unsolvable problem of racism. Himes is best at describing black characters and the cityscape of Harlem in ways that indict racism by negative example. None of the absurdity of his world would exist if it were not for the first absurdity of racism. In the end, Himes suggests that a vicious world controlled by racism demands a vicious answer. In the last works of his career Himes offered the final solution—on his terms.

"Prediction" and "Tang" are taken from what was to be Himes's final Harlem series novel, *Plan B,* a work that was never finished or published in his lifetime.[9] In the last part of his autobiography he writes about starting the book: "I began writing a book called *Plan B,* about a real black revolution in which my two black detectives split up and eventually Grave Digger kills Coffin Ed to save the cause" (*MLA* 361). But one page later the evident outcome of the project becomes clear. "I would work on my book ... which was gradually heading for disaster" (362). Himes died before he could finish the book. After his death Michel Fabre edited his papers and, with the help of Robert E. Skinner, produced a manuscript that was published in both France and the United States. Fabre and Skinner contributed a long introduction to the American version in which they describe the book as "an incandescent parable of racial madness as well as a retrospective of American racial history" (xxvi). "Prediction" and "Tang," the short stories that form a part of *Plan B,* have been published separately in *Black on Black* (Muller 113). As Muller suggests, these two stories are a culmination of Himes's violently radical political philosophy as it developed in the 1960s. Himes writes in the introduction to *Black on Black* that he wrote "Tang" in 1967, "when my thoughts had concentrated on BLACK REVOLUTION" (7). "Prediction," his last short story, was written in 1969 when he had "become firmly convinced that the only chance Black Americans had of attaining justice and equality in the United States of America was by violence" (*Black* 7–8).

Although the stories were published separately, I attempt to analyze them as part of the larger novel, *Plan B,* and to show how they help define the ultimate message of Himes's last work. *Plan B* continues the parallel time structure increasingly used in his last detective novels. One of the parallel stories provides a revisionist history of white and black relations from early slavery to the twentieth century. Written in broad satirical strokes, it indicts southern whites for their racial prejudice and sexual immorality. Fabre and Skinner suggest that these sections "parody the Southern Gothic tradition of Erskine Caldwell and William Faulkner" (*Plan B* xxvii). By tracing white and black genealogies, Himes sets the stage for the main focus of the novel, which takes place primarily in Harlem, and outlines the progression of an armed black revolution called Plan B (for black), organized by one Tomsson Black, a self-made black revolutionary who hides behind the mask of an integrationist and black capitalist. Under the guise of his businesses, Chitterlings Inc. and Black for Blacks, largely funded by white philanthropy, Black is providing free weapons to black males. A large portion of the novel depicts in brutal detail armed attacks of blacks on whites and white retaliation.

Himes's aesthetic use of violence in this last novel is in part reflected by his own hardening stance concerning black revolution and black violence. As expressed in his interviews. Himes saw armed revolution as the only political solution to racism in America. This radical viewpoint may have been a consequence of his own difficult and violent life. However, Himes's expatriate status in his last years did not allow him firsthand experience of the American scene, and many of his opinions seem based on interpretations of political activity received at second hand. Certainly, his radical ideas, like much of Himes's life, seem extreme and romanticized when viewed through his own words. Aesthetically, Himes allowed expression of these ideas to develop along hardboiled detective lines. In the last two stories and in the rest of *Plan B,* violence begins to take the place of religion, sex, and even money in its power to control the narrative. Himes gave a legitimacy to violence that goes beyond the initial legitimacy that it was given in detective works by Hammett and Chandler. Hammett's *Red Harvest,* considered by most critics to be the first hardboiled crime novel, contains an amazing amount of violence, most of it perpetrated by gangsters on themselves. Hammett's violence is cartoonist and chaotically misdirected, and Chandler's violence is more a narrative technique for plot progression than anything else. Himes redefined the use of violence in the detective novel tradition, using it not only for drama but as a weapon for political change. Himes's use of violence in his detective series starts off as a reflection of white and black culture out of control. As he states in his interview with Williams, he had violence in mind when he started writing the series. "American violence is public life, it's a public way of life, it became a form, a detective story form" (Williams 314). From these initial reflections on the quantity of violence in black and white cultures, Himes's last works begin to consider its quality. His sense of the purpose of violence in his books and in life had changed, and by the late sixties he began to consider violence—that is, black violence as retribution for white racism—as the only legitimate response for black America. He was willing to proclaim this while at the same time preaching against personal violence of any kind in his own life (*QH*). Himes was often a man of contradictions. However, violence in his stories moved at this time from random comic horror to an overt radical means to political ends. The last detective novels, such as *Blind Man,* point in this direction although the violence there does not have the direct function of retribution it will achieve in "Tang" and "Prediction," two important representative sections of *Plan B.* Himes's moral and political thinking has reached the point where, as he tells Williams,

> It's just an absolute fact that if the blacks in America were to mount a revolution in force, with organized violence to the saturation point, that the entire black problem would be solved. But that is the only way the black man can solve it. (Williams 325)

There are many similar statements in the last volume of Himes's biography. The violent revolution that boiled under the surface of *Blind Man with a Gun* finally explodes in Himes's last pieces of fiction, including his short stories and his posthumous novel.

The short story "Tang" becomes chapter 1 in the novel and sets the tone for the rest of the book. The chapter opens with a down-

and-out black couple in Harlem named T-Bone and Tang receiving a mysterious package which contains an M14 army rifle and an unsigned note reading, "WARNING DO NOT INFORM POLICE!!! LEARN YOUR WEAPON AND WAIT FOR INSTRUCTIONS!!! FREEDOM IS NEAR!!!" (*Plan B* 8). T-Bone, fearful and cowed, wants to turn the rifle over to the police. Tang, strong, independent, and fed up, wants to keep it and follow instructions. " 'You call this living?' She drew the gun tight to her breast as though it were a lover. 'This the only thing what made me feel alive since I met you' " (10). They fight after T-bone tells her, "You been lissenin to that black power shit, them Black Panthers 'n that shit" (10). Tang points the gun at him and shoots, but it is not loaded. T-Bone, in a blind rage, cuts the rifle out of her hands and stabs her to death. Although, once again, the ultimate outcome is black-on-black violence, in this case a female's willingness to join a black, violent revolution gives a chilling note of desperation to the opening of the novel. The abject poverty and ruined lives of Tang, the prostitute, and T-Bone, the shiftless pimp, permeate the atmosphere of Harlem. Unlike the other detective novels, in this case there is no sense of the absurd. Even though Tang is killed, her honest attraction to the power of revolt is the message that is carried into the rest of the novel. Coffin Ed Johnson and Grave Digger Jones investigate the crime. While interviewing T-Bone about the murder of his girlfriend, Grave Digger becomes so enraged that he hits T-Bone over the head with his pistol and kills him. Grave Digger is then suspended from the force, and soon after Coffin Ed falls into an open manhole and is put on the disabled list. Both detectives are quickly put out of action and do not appear again until the end of the novel.

Plan B is a frightening portrayal of desperate people pushed to the edge of their sanity by conditions of racism. The travails of this one black couple suggest the extreme condition of the entire black community of Harlem. Himes has elevated his use of violence to incorporate an indictment of a whole social system. As the novel progresses, the acts of violence increase in intensity, bewildering both white and black segments of the population in Harlem and the United States. These acts include a massacre on Eighth Avenue in Harlem of black men, women, and children by the police in retaliation for the gunning down of two white police officers by an unnamed black revolutionary. A black man is lynched in Central Park during a concert. A black doctor in Chicago, a black HEW adminstrator in Cleveland, and a black Baptist minister in Washington attack and shoot any number of white citizens. The proponents of law-and-order perpetuate the violence by indiscriminately killing black people everywhere. The senseless, unorganized mayhem affects the whole country and leads to forced containment of the black population. The blacks in Harlem are divided in their reaction to the offer of organized revolution presented to them by some unknown hand. The tension increases until it finally explodes in chapter 21 (the short story "Prediction"). In this chapter the progression toward armed revolt is taken one step farther, as a single armed gunman hiding in a cathedral lays waste to a large number of whites during a "unity" parade by police. The writing has the eerie tone of a futuristic fantasy set in an unnamed big city positing a universe where whites and blacks are completely segregated. "At no time had the races been so utterly divided despite the billing of unity given to the parade" (*Plan B* 172). The marchers are all white policemen, and the spectators are also white. The parade has been "billed as a parade of unity to demonstrate the capacity of law enforcement and reassure the 'communities' during this time of suspicion and animosity between the races" (172). Whereas the violence in the opening chapter was misdirected as T-Bone kills Tang, the violence in this chapter is explicitly directed at whites.

A black janitor hides in a church vestibule with a rifle pointing at the street through the "poor box" in the door. It is Sunday afternoon in Harlem, and the huge police parade of 6,000 officers, led by commissioners and subalterns, commands the center of the boulevard. When the white police in full uniform, cheered on by a white crowd, march by the church, the lone gunman pokes his rifle through the opening. This chapter brings Himes to the end of his metaphorical journey through racist America. Himes uses this mythical urban landscape to make his final point concerning the races. Rather than amalgamation or unity, Himes sees even more racial alienation in America's future. The white police and the white spectators are representative of all of white America, and the "crowd of all-white faces seemed to deny that a black race existed" (172). Himes has carried the premise of enforced segregation that he so often toyed with in the detective series to its logical conclusion. The lone gunman, too, is obviously a stand-in for his race:

> He had waited four hundred years for this moment. . . . He would have to
> assume the authority which controlled his life. . . . He would have to be-
> lieve that although blacks would suffer now, there would be those who
> would benefit later. . . . If his death were in vain, and whites would never
> accept the blacks as equal human beings, there would be nothing to live
> for anyway. (*Plan B* 174–75)

The parade passes in front of the Catholic cathedral, and the lone
black gunman opens fire. What follows is the longest exposition of
violence in all of Himes's work and perhaps in any detective work by
a black or white writer. The writing is superbly disturbing as the
mayhem continues for a total of five pages of gore and destruction:

> Snot mixed with blood exploded from their nostrils and their caps flew off
> behind, suddenly filled with fragments of their skulls and pasty brain
> matter streaked with capillaries, like gobs of putty, finely-sculpted with
> red ink.
>   . . . Men, women and children dashed about, panic-stricken, screaming,
> their blue eyes popping or squinting, their mouths open or teeth gritting,
> their faces paper white or lobster red.
>   . . . In a matter of seconds the streets were strewn with the carnage,
> nasty gray blobs of brains, hairy fragments of skull looking like sections of
> broken coconuts, bone splinters from jaws and facial bones, bloody, gristly
> bits of ears and noses . . . squashy bits of exploded viscera. (176–78).

It is as if Himes was venting a lifetime of anger and aggression. The
pent-up rage of 400 years of oppression erupts on the page, and the
excessiveness of the prose seems to me to reflect an anger so pure
that it transcends polemic. The pure joy of apocalyptic destruction
reverberates on the pages. Himes's glee can hardly be contained as
the poetic prose describes total mayhem and bodily destruction. The
ever-cascading tumble of destructive imagery amazes and outrages
the reader. Finally, the police send in a tank as the people on the
street desperately search for the sniper they knew must be a black
man. "But all were decided, police and spectators alike, that the
sniper was a black man for no one else would slaughter whites so
wantonly" (179). The black man, a poor janitor who works in the
church, is beyond caring about his own death. He has sacrificed
himself for a higher cause:

> But it was the most gratifying episode of the black man's life. . . . Hate
> served his pleasure. He thought fleetingly and pleasurably of all the humili-

ations and hurts imposed on him and all blacks by whites. The outrage of
slavery flashed across his mind. (180)

The whites finally blow up the cathedral and reduce the black janitor
to a "few scraps of bloody black flesh" (182).

The one flaw in the story seems to be the gunman's own alienation
from other African Americans. His lone stand could be construed as
random insanity, no matter how rational his reasoning. "[H]e would
have to do it alone, without comfort or encouragement, consoled
only by the hope that it would make life safer for the blacks in
the future" (174–75). Himes adds a final paragraph, however, that
metaphorically extends this nameless man's sacrifice: "In the wake of
this bloody massacre the stock market crashed. The dollar fell on the
world market. The very structure of capitalism began to crumble"
(*Plan B* 182). By connecting the wholesale slaying of white people to
a total collapse of what Himes sees as an oppressive capitalist system
supporting racism, the story suggests a positive and immediate result
to armed black revolution. What the man with the pen couldn't do,
the man with the rifle does. Regardless of the credibility of such a
connection, Himes obviously had reached a breaking point in his
writing. The last messages of his writing life confirm in extreme what
he had been saying all along—that racism lies at the root of America's
problems. Himes saw Harlem and African American life rooted in a
racism that killed, maimed, and destroyed as effectively as a rifle
blast. In this last frightening and painful flurry of rage we can sense
Himes's ultimate retribution for the absurdity of an existence colored
by racism.

White authority reacts by indiscriminately killing blacks, and
blacks attack in return or retreat to the sewers and tunnels under
the city. From there they sabotage the water, telephone, and electric
systems. This leads to the final solution or "The Black Hunt," in
which black males are hunted down and killed by bands of white
"sportsmen." Unable to control the widespread civil disobedience,
the government asks Tomsson Black, the black president of Chitterlings Inc., to appeal to the black masses. Throughout the novel, in
alternating chapters, Himes has outlined the growth of violent insurrection among black citizens, armed and encouraged by some unknown hand, and the growth and development of Tomsson Black.
Black has been falsely imprisoned for "raping" a rich white woman

who later becomes his benefactor. While in prison he educates himself and becomes a black revolutionary, forming a group called the Big Blacks. After his release he travels to other countries, where he studies Marxist theories of revolution. He goes underground but later resurfaces as a black capitalist who applies for grants-in-aid to start up his own company. Tomsson Black is Himes's ultimate trickster figure. In the final part of the novel he plays the Uncle Tom to white benefactors and capitalists, and in his appeal to black citizens he encourages them "to be orderly and law-abiding, to trust their government and do the right thing" (*Plan B* 191). Meanwhile, he has been gathering enough funds to provide weapons to blacks in Harlem and throughout the United States. The editors make a note in the text at this point that no formal conclusion exists for *Plan B* and that the conclusion has been reconstructed from an outline.

In the final scene of the novel, Coffin Ed and Grave Digger are called back to duty and put into an undercover operation to try and determine who is masterminding the armed black revolution. They conclude that it must be Tomsson Black, and in a meeting with the New York police, the FBI, and the CIA, the two black detectives present their evidence. They are not believed and are dismissed from the force without benefits. Soon after, they are arrested for being armed and sent to jail. A representative of Tomsson Black provides their bail, and they are brought to White Plains to meet the man. In the final recognition scene Tomsson Black reveals that he has indeed masterminded the insurrection but adds that he failed to organize blacks into guerrilla units before arming them. Coffin Ed protests against Plan B and draws his pistol to kill Tomsson. Grave Digger shoots the gun out of his partner's hand and says: "You can't kill, Black, man. . . . He might be our last chance, despite the risk. I'd rather be dead than a subhuman in this world" (202). They argue, and Grave Digger kills Coffin Ed. Tomsson Black then draws a gun and shoots Grave Digger because he knows too much. The novel ends on an ambiguous note as Tomsson's black secretary says to him, "I hope you know what you're doing" (203).

Although *Plan B* is an uneven novel whose juxtaposed stories sometimes strain credibility, it shows Himes's developed sense of black outrage and reflects the political climate in the United States during the sixties and seventies when it was begun. The novel also brings an end to the detective series by having both detectives die, one at the hand of his partner. This shocking denouement makes sense in the fractured worldview presented in the novel and in the progression of the detectives' disintegration traced in the last few novels. *Plan B* satirizes racial relations in the United States, using the detective format as a weak structural device that signals the end of the genre for Himes. Coffin Ed and Grave Digger are completely ineffectual in this novel. There is no longer even the pretense of maintaining social stability in Harlem. I have tried to show how the progression of the series of detective novels leads almost inevitably to this grim conclusion. As the detectives prove less and less important to the structure of the novel, the content of the last works changes also. In *Blind Man* and *Plan B* Himes has come almost full circle from his earlier social-protest fiction. In his last works he fuses the crime novel with social critique, using the detective format as a device to describe black life and to construct a powerful indictment of racism in America. Violence in the detective novel has now become not so much a social statement as a concentrated effort to depict a world gone awry. The inevitable armed confrontation between blacks and whites is something that Himes has hinted at throughout his detective series. The difference is that in *Plan B* this confrontation has moved beyond individual conflict into collective mayhem—which Himes has seen lying on the outskirts of black/white relations and which in this novel takes center stage. Although removed from actual reality, the armed revolution described in *Plan B* has a certain validity in Himes's worldview, which sees racism as lying at the root of all that is evil in human relations.

Himes is often considered to be a hardboiled detective writer who wrote entertaining detective thrillers. This is hardly the case. Himes transforms the tradition handed down to him from American masters Hammett and Chandler. Following a precedent established by the black detective writers before him, Himes continues a tradition of black detective tropes and redefines the use of violence in detective novels. Himes applies the African American tropes of detective fiction with a unique voice. His novels boil with ludicrous incidents that teeter on the edge of chaos. The comic and the violent merge and grow out of each other like wild vines struggling over the stones of disintegrating Harlem buildings. Himes was conscious of what he was doing, defining the African American culture in his own way and presenting through the detective genre a new appreciation for the complexity of black America. Furthermore, the political and moral message behind the violence in Himes's narratives suggests a radical sensibility not yet seen in the black detective tradition. Himes successfully changed the way blacks would deal with the detective form, opening up the field for further creative experimentation that will be reflected in the works of Ishmael Reed and Clarence Major.

6

The Black Anti-Detective Novel

Ishmael Reed and Clarence Major extend the tradition of black detective fiction into the postmodern era. Working in the 1970s, both writers wrote experimental narratives in what has been called the anti-detective tradition.[1] In the 1980s and 1990s new black writers have emerged, and although I will not discuss these new novelists until my Afterword, it is important to mention such writers as Dolores Komo, Barbara Neely, Eleanor Taylor Bland, and Walter Mosley, who have brought interesting new perspectives to the black detective novel. In particular, these writers have shown how black detective fiction can reach a new and wider audience as the novels comment on a tradition of mainstream detective writing in America while continuing aspects of the black detective tradition. In this chapter I am more concerned with analyzing the intriguing narrative experimentations of the black detective writers Ishmael Reed and Clarence Major.

In the novel *Mumbo Jumbo,* Ishmael Reed creates PaPa LaBas, an idiosyncratic black detective who challenges both classical and hardboiled detective personas. As the head of a private detective agency called Mumbo Jumbo Kathedral, LaBas represents African American sensibilities in an experimental novel of postmodern complexity. Reed writes that his work "includes features one finds in postmodernist writing" (*Writin' Is Fightin'* 137). Bernard Bell sees black postmodernist writers as "concerned with . . . the truths of the perversity of American racism and the paradoxes of Afro-American double-consciousness," as well as "reaffirming the power and wisdom of their own folk tradition . . . especially black speech, music and religion" (284). *Mumbo Jumbo* fully supports Reed's reputation as a daring writer who combines aspects of postmodernist experimentation with African American themes in a series of satirical novels.

179

Reed satirizes both white and black characters in fictions that also parody popular culture forms and question accepted literary discourse. With *Mumbo Jumbo* Reed continues his postmodernist experimentation by writing an anti-detective novel that expresses a new level of social and political awareness of African American culture. Clarence Major moves away from the social and political criticism of Reed toward a more abstract exploration of African American artistic methods. In *Reflex and Bone Structure* (1975), Major pushes the detective novel to the farthest limits of the postmodern literary frontier in a work that uses detective fiction as a catalyst to challenge traditional fictional perspectives. Major continues the anti-detective tradition in black fiction by combining anti-detective themes and metafictional techniques. Reed and Major are post-World War II writers who recognize the past accomplishments of other African American detective novelists but who transform detective conventions in specifically postmodern ways.

Reed and Major share a number of similarities in the way they approach the detective novel. Like the earlier writers we have discussed, both authors revise the traditional classical and hardboiled formulas in the areas of detective persona, double-conscious detection, and hoodoo. It is with the trope of double-conscious detection, however, that these writers effect a major change in black detective fiction's approach to its themes. The depth of Reed's and Major's experimentation with the double-conscious detective trope is unparalleled in other African American detective fiction. Not only is double-conscious detection used by these two writers in relation to detective tropes such as disguise and masking, but it is extended to include experimentation with narrative methods. Detective conventions are used by these writers as the armature on which they build novels that ask questions about modes of literary discourse as well as presenting the political, social, and artistic issues important to African Americans. Double-conscious experimentation in the black anti-detective novel revises history from a different perspective, questions accepted notions of time, and elevates the trickster motif to include narrative as well as character masking. This amplified use of the double-conscious detective theme shares many of the concepts of postmodernism, forged into new patterns by African American sensibility. The black anti-detective novel extends the black detective tradition by redefining the African American themes of detective fiction we have discussed in earlier chapters.

Although there is no distinct definition of postmodernism that all critics agree on, there is a consensus of opinion on a number of its defining traits. Robert Elliot Fox in *Conscientious Sorcerers* (1987) cautions that "whatever post-modernism is—and despite certain contiguities, there is no complete agreement on a definition—it is, in any event, useful in forcing us to rethink what modernism was" (121). Fox goes on to list a series of features that help delineate postmodernism for him. These include indeterminacy, fragmentation, decanonization, irony, hybridization, and carnivalization (120). The fictions of both Reed and Major share enough of these features to place them definitively within the postmodernist literary tradition. Linda Hutcheon, in *A Poetics of Postmodernism* (1988), illustrates most effectively the postmodern imagination. She points out that postmodernism is not simply "a synonym for the contemporary" but a movement that she calls "fundamentally contradictory, resolutely historical, and inescapably political" (4). Furthermore, Hutcheon recognizes that postmodern art is "both intensively self-reflexive and parodic" (x). In attempting to define the postmodern literary world, Hutcheon must redefine her own expectations of twentieth-century fiction:

> [A]pproaches . . . would need expanding to include historical and ideological considerations demanded by these unresolved postmodern contradictions that worked to challenge our entire concept of both historical and literary knowledge, as well as our awareness of our ideological implication in our dominant culture. (x)

It is within the concept of parody that Hutcheon finds postmodernism most accessible. "Parody is a perfect postmodern form, in some senses, for it paradoxically both incorporates and challenges that which it parodies" (11). Reed and Major both consciously parody the detective form in novels that question the accepted literary and social values of Western culture. Like the other authors in this study, Reed and Major utilize detective fiction conventions to express African American themes. Furthermore, detective fiction to these authors is a Euro-Americentric convention that in itself deserves satirical or parodic treatment.

Stefano Tani in *The Doomed Detective* sees the anti-detective novel as one that

> frustrates the expectations of the reader, transforms a mass-media genre into a sophisticated expression of avant-garde sensibility, and substitutes for the detective as central and ordering character the decentering and chaotic admission of mystery, of nonsolution. (40)

Other critics also concentrate on the idea of nonsolution of the mystery while calling anti-detective novels metaphysical detective stories. Reed and Major write metaphysical detective stories as defined by Michael Holquist in "Metaphysical Detective Stories in Postwar Fiction."[2] As Holquist sees it, "Postmodernists use as a foil the assumption of detective fiction that the mind can solve all; by twisting the details just the opposite becomes the case" (173). Major's work carries this idea to the ultimate conclusion since nothing at all can be solved in *Reflex,* not even the most elementary issues of character, plot, and action. Holquist sees the defining attribute of metaphysical detective stories as "adopting the 'method' of the detective novel but not its 'telos,' forcing the reader to put together clues, not to reach a solution, but to understand the process of understanding" (149). Reed and Major use the metaphysical detective novel, or what I prefer to call the anti-detective novel, to question accepted Euro-American sociopolitical worldviews as well as traditional narrative methods.

Through the use of self-reflexive narrative ploys, both authors debate the process of perception and the nature of learning. Gates comments that Reed "write[s] self-reflexive texts which comment upon the nature of writing itself" (*Figures in Black* 249). Similarly, both Reed and Major are fascinated with sabotaging the usual compliance among author, reader, and text, thereby questioning accepted modes of understanding and methods of communication. The nature of Reed's and Major's work forces a new alliance between reader and text not yet seen in black detective fiction. Reed and Major parody typical detective conventions and content in texts that experiment with narrative form, alter character and language representation, and challenge conventional notions of time and history. Black postmodern detective fiction examines issues of race and class through political and social satire while questioning literary and artistic conventions.

Mumbo Jumbo is Reed's initial attempt at using detective tropes, and it serves as a fitting model for this last chapter in *The Blues*

Detective since it synthesizes and comments on the tradition of b
detective fiction up to this time. Reed's *Louisiana Red* (1974) ¿
has PaPa LaBas as a character, but it does not extend the use of ι
detective beyond the parameters set up in *Mumbo Jumbo*.

Ishmael Reed is very conscious of the black detective tradition. He
was one of the first black authors to recognize the importance of
Chester Himes's Harlem detective series: "It won't be long before
Himes's 'Harlem Detective series,' now dismissed by jerks as 'potboil-
ers,' will receive the praise they deserve" (*Shrovetide* 96). Furthermore, Reed realized that Himes was also helping to define a tradition
of black detective writing that insisted on a difference between white
and black approaches to the detective persona. "He [Himes] taught
me the essential difference between a Black detective and Sherlock
Holmes" (97). Reed also knew the earlier black detective novel,
Fisher's Conjure Man Dies, and consciously makes allusion to it when
he has Woodrow Wilson Jefferson rent a room above "Frimbo's Fu-
neral Home" (*Mumbo Jumbo* 75). Reed combined his understanding
of African American reinterpretation of detective tropes with a satiric
sensibility that cleverly parodies the detective form. His obvious interest in popular culture forms, evidenced by books such as *Yellow-Back
Radio Broke-Down* (1977), which parodies the Western, made him a
likely candidate to rework the detective novel. He has stated in
Shrovetide in Old New Orleans that "being a Negro in this society
means reading motives in a complicated way. We write good detective
novels" (13). Reed further elaborates on his conscious experimentation with the detective form in "Serious Comedy in Afro-American
Literature":

> If there exists a body of mysteries in Afro-American oral literature, then
> included among my works would be mysteries like *Mumbo Jumbo*, which
> is not only a detective novel, but a novel concerning the mysteries, the
> secrets, of competing civilizations. (*Writin' Is Fightin'* 138)

Mumbo Jumbo is very much an anti-detective novel in that it ambitiously posits a mystery that can be solved only in abstract terms
and so fails to satisfy the primary detective convention of positive
resolution. As we saw in relation to Himes's last detective novels, this
elementary concept of detective fiction was dramatically questioned.
Himes replaced resolution with a fragmented ending that offered no
positive solution to questions posited in the beginning. In *Plan B*

Himes's detectives are killed off, signaling the end of a phase in the black detective tradition. After Himes, both Reed and Major take the black detective novel in a new direction.

As a novel of ideas and satirical criticism, *Mumbo Jumbo* works on a number of levels. Primarily, it is a postmodernist anti-detective novel that continues the use of the black detective tropes of altered detective personas, double-conscious detection, black vernaculars, and hoodoo while parodying the detective form. The metaphysical central mystery and revisionist approach to history of *Mumbo Jumbo* are additional indications of postmodern detective viewpoints. On another level the novel is a witty indictment of extreme behavior of all types. The characters in *Mumbo Jumbo* suggest allegory rather than social realism. Each character represents a philosophical viewpoint from either side of the basic conflict. Few of the characters actually change or develop from their initial depictions in the text, and they read like a composite of ideas more than flesh-and-blood people. For example, Woodrow Wilson Jefferson, a rural African American from Re Mote, Mississippi, is used by the Knights Templar to falsely represent the black viewpoint. He never matures or questions his role, even after being exposed to urban living and more sophisticated ideas. Black Herman and Von Vampton are both occultists, but Black Herman strictly pursues positive African American values with his powers whereas Von Vampton is corrupted to the core. Thus many of the characters are easy marks for ridicule and satire since they represent types rather than individuals. Hinckle Von Vampton and Biff Musclewhite, for example, are obviously meant to be seriocomic or allegorical characters; Von Vampton is thousands of years old, and Musclewhite acts and thinks just as his name implies. Characters such as these suggest caricatures or cartoons representing radical racial, political, and cultural attributes. The satire also works on an abstract level because the characters stand in for ideological viewpoints of a broader nature. Reed shows the hypocrisy of many aspects of Western civilization through this type of character presentation. The white characters such as Hinckle Von Vampton and Biff Musclewhite are extreme examples of racist mentality. In turn, some black characters are criticized for their positions. For example, Abdul, sounding his clarion call of Black Power, is ridiculed in the end as a black puritan who burns the sacred text because it is in his estimation too lewd and scandalous. Characters move magically through the text regardless of obstacles like time or borders between countries. Thus a character like the Haitian rebel Benoit Battraville can appear in his large ship *The Black Plume* on the shores of Manhattan simply because Reed needs someone to represent the revolutionary politics of Haitian life. Reed's satirical approach is at times extremely funny and revealing. At other times the didacticism of the text intrudes on the narrative flow and seems perhaps too obvious. Overall, the characters in this novel have to be appreciated on the level of satirical fantasy.

On yet another level, the book suggests a larger landscape against which the ancient conflict between eros and thanatos is played out. Put in its simplest terms, *Mumbo Jumbo* reflects humankind's constant war with itself. On one side lies love and life-affirming revitalization, and on the other an urge toward hatred and self-destruction. The crisis of the epidemic "Jes Grew" heightens the intensity of the conflict as the United States moves into the second decade of the twentieth century. The social and political structure of Western civilization, based on a death-seeking ethos called Atonism, is portrayed as contemptible. For example, Hierophant I, the chief Atonist, is overjoyed to learn that the watercress darter has become extinct, further proof that the Atonist cause is winning the fight for control of the planet. The Atonists, who represent the deadliest aspects of Western civilization, are predominantly white and are in direct competition with Jes Grew and JGC (Jes Grew Carriers), who represent the life force and are mostly black.

The continuous struggle between different ideologies and groups in the novel suggests a modern society in conflict. Buddy Jackson is a black gangster fighting the white gangsters led by Schlitz. Berbelang is a black revolutionary fighting the racist practices of institutions such as the Museums. There is even division among ranks as the Knights Templar quarrel with the death-dealing Wallflower Order. Amid this chaos there is little manifestation of sanity and continuity. The broad condemnation of Western civilization is construed through the eyes of an educated, sensitive African American represented in the text by PaPa LaBas, and Reed's basic critique takes a new turn as the novel posits a positive approach to African American consciousness, based in part on African American and Afrocentric, not Euro-Ameri-centric, worldviews. One way Reed accomplishes this is by reinterpreting the whole history of Western civilization, redefining its myths and reconstructing its gods.

The novel revolves around the central mystery of the missing Jes Grew Text, the written record of the origins of the life force. Von Vampton, one of the main characters in the novel, represents the Atonist, anti-Jes Grew viewpoint. He is editor of the *Benign Monster,* a magazine that attempts to destroy the emerging black arts movement of the 1920s in Harlem. Von Vampton is a Knight Templar from 1118 who reincarnates himself each time the Atonist civilization is under attack. He is also the illegal owner of the Jes Grew Text, which he has dispersed in installments to fourteen African Americans in Harlem. He makes a deal with the Atonists, promising to turn over the Text if they will make the Knights Templar the leading eradicators of Jes Grew. When the Text ends up in Abdul Hamid's hands, Von Vampton tries to get repossession; Abdul resists and is killed. PaPa LaBas discovers Abdul's body, his hand still clutching a clue to the whereabouts of the Text. As an "astrodetective," LaBas is intrigued by the philosophical implications of the Text for liberating African Americans and all of Western civilization. Intent on protecting the ancient mysteries of Haitian hoodoo, LaBas is disturbed by the defection of his assistants, Berbelang and Charlotte. He had also argued with Abdul Hamid, who urged a more pragmatic approach to African American organization and behavior.

Berbelang and his gang of art snatchers, the Mu'tafikah, kidnap Biff Musclewhite, the former police commissioner. Musclewhite escapes and kills Berbelang, but the Mu'tafikah reconfiscate important pieces of ethnic art and deliver them to Benoit Battraville's ship, which is docked on the outskirts of Manhattan. LaBas and Black Herman arrest Von Vampton for the killing of Abdul. They also arrest the "safecracker" Gould, another Knight Templar, who is in blackface, acting as a "talking black android" and urging blacks to resist Jes Grew, and they deliver the two to Battraville for punishment. Suddenly Jes Grew starts to disappear. LaBas and Herman dig up the ornate box from under the Cotton Club where Abdul had hidden the Text, but the Text is gone, and in a letter Abdul explains that he burned the Text because it would have a bad influence on African Americans. In an epilogue LaBas lectures students at a university in the 1970s and predicts that the conflict between the Atonists and Jes Grew will continue and that Jes Grew will eventually triumph.

Reed cleverly utilizes detective conventions such as the detective persona, the murdered witness, the strange clue, and the final recognition scene to structure the novel. The story of Jes Grew and the Text, for which PaPa LaBas so desperately searches, is on one level a mystery capable of being solved in the normal detective fashion. That is, there is a murder and a clue to the identity of the murderer. But on another level the story is a metaphysical conundrum that parodies the detective novel, since the central mystery of the novel, the true identity of the Jes Grew Text, is impossible to ascertain. The term "Jes Grew" itself seems to have been taken from James Weldon Johnson's phrase "jes' grew," referring to the anonymous and undefinable creation of secular music and songs from the black folk tradition. Reed connects the current outbreak of Jes Grew to an ancient sect formed around the Egyptian god Osiris. The Text of that sect was written into the Book of Thoth, which is now known as the Jes Grew Text. However, what this Text consists of remains a mystery beyond the end of the novel. This lack of definition posits a metaphysical question that parodies the traditional detective novel, which demands resolution of conflict and restoration of natural order. It is only by looking at the metaphysical question in light of Reed's Neo-HooDoo philosophy that we get a solution to the case of the missing Jes Grew Text.

Unlike the traditional detective novel, *Mumbo Jumbo* does not move forward and backward at the same time, as outlined by Porter in *The Pursuit of Crime*. The murder of Abdul occurs halfway through the book rather than at the beginning, complicating the common detective novel design. Furthermore, *Mumbo Jumbo*'s experimental construction with its prologue, epilogue, and jumbled time frame confounds structural analysis along the lines of Tzvetan Todorov's concept of the three forms of detective fiction: the whodunit, the *série noire*, and the suspense novel.[3] One way *Mumbo Jumbo* does conform to both classical and hardboiled detective novels is in its use of the material search for Object X ("X" indicating a physical concrete such as the criminal, murder weapon, secret map or will, etc.). In this case the mysterious Text of Jes Grew functions as the Object X that pushes the story. As an anti-detective novel *Mumbo Jumbo* refuses to follow the normal chronological sequence of the detecting process leading to a final solution. Unlike most traditional detective novels, the answer in *Mumbo Jumbo* is not found on the last page but lies in the process of self-discovery that occurs during the act of reading the novel. This process is initiated as we begin to question accepted Euro-American philosophical and literary viewpoints and follow the text of the book, which instructs us in the Neo-HooDoo worldview.

The main character in the novel is PaPa LaBas, a fifty-year-old Neo-HooDoo detective who lives in Harlem at the Mumbo Jumbo Kathedral with his family of assistants, Earline, Berbelang, and Charlotte. Earline is PaPa LaBas's closest confidant: she calls him Pop and he calls her Daughter. Earline is torn between supporting LaBas in his hoodoo detective business and joining Berbelang, a radical black revolutionary, who leaves the Mumbo Jumbo Kathedral after accusing LaBas of being obsessed with political conspiracy theories. Berbelang is the head of a radical group, Mu'tafikah, which steals back art objects from Museums or Art Detention Centers. Charlotte is a white Frenchwoman who also leaves the detective agency during the course of the novel.

As we have seen, the detective family or agency is a consistent trope used in black detective fiction, and *Mumbo Jumbo* continues this alteration of the detective persona. Reed's LaBas is unabashedly religious yet perceptively political in viewpoint. As such, Reed's detective is the most spiritual and ethereal character in black detective fiction as well as the most socially perceptive. As head of the hoodoo detective agency called Mumbo Jumbo Kathedral, a temple with twenty-one shrines to loas or voodoo gods, LaBas begins the double-conscious detective alteration of the text. As a black hoodoo detective he is a decided departure from both the classical and the hardboiled detective schools. He is neither the brilliant investigator modeled on Holmes nor the gun-toting individualist of the Hammett school. LaBas is more a detective by name than by occupation. As a hoodoo priest and folk healer he is introduced as someone who "sized up his clients to fit their souls" (*Mumbo Jumbo* 23). "Many are healed and helped in [his Mumbo Jumbo Kathedral], which deals in jewelry, Black astrology charts, herbs, potions, candles and talismans" (24). He is never described as a detective who accepts payment to solve cases of criminal behavior, nor is he in the employ of any law enforcement agency. Similarly, unlike Himes's detective duo, LaBas is no hardboiled arbitrator of justice. However, he does possess powers of intimidation related to his hoodoo talents. We learn, for example, that "a little boy kicked his Newfoundland HooDoo 3 cents and spent a night squirming and gnashing his teeth," and "a warehouse burned after it refused to deliver a special variety of herbs" (23).

LaBas comes to us out of the African trickster tradition and resists definitive analysis. Akin in some ways to Frimbo in *The Conjure Man Dies,* PaPa LaBas, by his actions and by the etymology of his name, suggests connections with Haitian hoodoo and, by extension, an African past. Bell perceptively recognizes PaPa LaBas as "clearly nonrepresentational" (335). Reed calls him a "noonday HooDoo, fugitive-hermit, obeah-man, botanist, animal impersonator, 2-headed man, You-Name-It" (*Mumbo Jumbo* 45). This elusive and chameleonlike characterization functions nicely when we recognize LaBas's heredity in African myth and storytelling. Gates, Bell, and other critics clearly establish LaBas's genealogy through the Haitian *vodoun* mythological priest Legba back to the original African deities of the Fon people. Legba's role is that of messenger or divine interpreter of mysteries. Gates makes the connection between Legba and Esu-Elegbara, the divine trickster of the Yoruba myths. As Gates points out in *Figures in Black,* LaBas is a "conflation of two of the several names of Esu, the Pan-African trickster" (254–55). Through a playful corruption of the Haitian Papa Legba, PaPa LaBas becomes "the Afro-American trickster figure from black sacred tradition" (255).

Given this illustrious ancestry, PaPa LaBas can be relied on to be an agent of change in the text as well as a clever spokesman in the formulation of what Reed refers to as his Neo-HooDoo aesthetic. Also, the very nature of LaBas's indeterminacy benefits the double-consciousness narrative ploys Reed uses in the novel, which we will look at later. LaBas defines himself as "a jacklegged detective of the metaphysical who was on the case" (*Mumbo Jumbo* 212). LaBas confirms this altered black detective persona when we understand that his blackness and his double-conscious intuition allow him to solve the crime of Abdul's murder and determine the hiding place of the Text. His ability is exemplified in the way he understands the significance of the clue Abdul holds in his hand, a piece of paper containing an "Epigram on American-Egyptian Cotton," which reads:

> Stringy lumpy; Bales dancing
> Beneath this center
> Lies the Bird

By making the connection between this cryptic note and "The Dancing Bales," tap dancers at the Cotton Club, LaBas concludes that the box containing the Text is under the stage at the club. The confluence of references to African American entertainment and slave labor emphasizes the vernacular insight of LaBas's double consciousness. A further connection can be made between "the Bird" and the Maltese Falcon, the fabulous bird that forms the center of perhaps the most famous American detective novel ever written.

As the text indicates, LaBas comes from a long line of African instigators. "Some say his ancestor is the long Ju of Arno in Eastern Nigeria, the man who would oracle, sitting in the mouth of a cave" (*Mumbo Jumbo* 23). He is the grandson of a slave who possessed a mysterious power to inflict punishment on his owners and the son of a man who ran a mail-order root business in New Orleans. Thus, in terms of African American hoodoo heritage, PaPa LaBas holds impeccable credentials. He personifies the Jes Grew mentality: "LaBas carries Jes Grew in him like most other folk carry genes" (23).

In another shift away from traditional detective personas, we are given almost no physical description of LaBas, so that his presence in the novel is more metaphysical than physical. We do know that he is fifty years old during most of the novel and close to a hundred by the time of the epilogue, a passage of time, by the way, that has inflicted no apparent physical change. After the defection of his trusted disciple Berbelang and his assistant Charlotte L, LaBas undergoes a midlife crisis of sorts. Unlike the cocky Sherlock Holmes, LaBas is unsure of himself:

> PaPa LaBas reflects. Do you think we're out of date as he said?
>   I know that the politicians of this era will be remembered more than me but I would like to believe that we work for principles and not for self. "We serve the loas," as they say. (40)

Furthermore, LaBas isn't the only show in town. The reader is introduced quickly to two rivals: Abdul (a.k.a. Johnny James from Chicago's South Side), the Black Muslim, a religious militant who sees LaBas's approach as "Hoo Doo psychiatry" (37); and Herman, the black hoodoo priest, who is a numerologist and mystic. Although LaBas's and Herman's approaches to black folk religions are different, Abdul sees them both as taking advantage of the ignorance of the black population, and he attacks their reclusiveness and elitism. "You see while you are cloistered protected by your followers and patrons and clients I'm out here on the street watching what was once a beautiful community become a slave hole" (37). However, Reed sees LaBas in a more positive light. LaBas gives structure and meaning to the novel. He is a detective with problems, but he is also very perceptive, and, as a hoodoo detective, he represents African American creativity and renewal through spiritual connection to the Afrocentric past.

Mumbo Jumbo is full of references to black vernaculars. Jes Grew, an epidemic of ecstasy originating in New Orleans, is rapidly taking over the United States, causing people to dance, laugh, and love life. Jes Grew is variously interpreted as the blues, jazz, ragtime, and slang, directly connecting it to African American music. Jes Grew needs its Text to survive, and apparently the Text exists somewhere in Manhattan. The mystery of this Text's content, or what Gates calls its litany, is the puzzle that lies at the core of the novel. Although the Text is an ancient manuscript, no one knows its words. Reed seems to be suggesting that Jes Grew, or the essence of black life, has moved beyond prehistory or oral history and that its entry into the twentieth century demands a written component to make it legitimate. This passage from oral to written reality mirrors the progression of the African American culture from the oral stage of African prehistory to the modern world of written texts. As we shall see, *Mumbo Jumbo* attempts to offer an answer concerning the nature of the Jes Grew Text.

The title *Mumbo Jumbo* suggests the complexity of Reed's approach to black vernaculars. As Gates points out, "Mumbo Jumbo" is a phrase that carries many connotations (*Signifying Monkey* 221). According to Gates, the word is an Americanized version of the Swahili *mambo, jambo* (a greeting similar to "What's happening?"). It has come to represent, in the derogatory and common American idiom, all black language and black religions and carries a specific connotation of something unintelligible or mysterious. *Webster's International Dictionary* gives "gibberish" as one definition, after first defining Mumbo Jumbo as "a deity held to have been worshiped by various African peoples." Reed concentrates on the positive aspects of the African mother tongue from which "Mumbo Jumbo" is derived. Within the text itself, Mumbo Jumbo is said to come from the Mandingo language and to mean a "magician who makes the troubled spirits of ancestors go away" (7). Reed indicates by this example his intent to reconnect African Americans to their African ancestors and restore the African American identity by redefining the historical past.

The phrase "Mumbo Jumbo" means different things to different people. On one level the title of the book alone suggests that Reed, while rooted in the African American present, is equally enamored of the African past. Obviously the phrase was freely adapted by white Americans while meaning something quite different to African Americans. Reed takes advantage of these double meanings and sometimes derogatory implications by elevating "Mumbo Jumbo" to a phrase representing African American Neo-HooDoo. He takes advantage of its many connotations to suggest the multiplicity of creativity in Neo-HooDoo thought. What is seen as bad and confusing in traditional American vernacular becomes good and enlightening in Reed's revised use of black vernacular language.

The title also immerses the reader in the African American vernacular world. Vernacular references to music and dance as well as language abound in the novel as do allusions to black historical figures of the musical world. We have mention of Charlie Parker (16), James Weldon Johnson (60), and Fats Waller (72), among many others in Reed's clever inclusion of musical metaphors in the text. Throughout the novel this mixture of real people of the black musical vernacular with fictional characters is one method utilized by Reed to project his own literary Neo-HooDoo on the novel form. In fact, the novel is so rich in the use of black vernaculars that it is impossible in this short space to indicate all of his wide-ranging appreciations of black culture. On one page alone he makes connections between Haitian voodoo gods in the wood carving of ghede, nods to black vernacular speech in his use of "fagingy-fagades" as a name like "ofay" for white people, drops a mention of Jelly Roll Morton, and weaves obeah sticks, loas, and veves into his discursive analysis of Black Renaissance life (49).

Reed carries vernacular creation one step farther than previous authors by actually writing *Mumbo Jumbo* in a distinctive language of African American creativity. Jerome Klinkowitz recognizes this recreation of language as the primary issue in postmodern writing: "In self-apparent fiction, the reader's attention is directed to language" (65). Reed signifies on the typical detective prose by suggesting the mystery and suspense passages of hardboiled intrigue that are more style than substance:

> Packing their heat, the hoods begin to open the car doors to assist their Boss. But they are pinned in. Up on the roofs, firing, are Buddy Jackson's Garders. Exaggerated lapels. Bell-bottoms. Hats at rakish angles. The Sarge's men sit tight. The bullet pellets zing across the front of the automobiles and graze the top and trunk. Buddy Jackson exhorts the Sarge to leave Harlem and "Never darken the portals of our abode again." (*Mumbo Jumbo* 19)

The language and images may be straight out of hardboiled detective fiction, but the idea of a black gangster ordering white gangsters out of Harlem is not.

Furthermore, Reed continually draws attention to his parodic use of language by mixing his descriptions with allusions to popular culture: "Men who resemble the shadows sleuths threw against the walls of 1930s detective films have somehow managed to slip into the Mayor's private hospital room" (18). However, the primary method of Reed's vernacular creation is found in the interwoven complexity of the words themselves, a combination of hip, bebop, cascading improvisation on theme that ignores conventional syntax and grammar rules and goes on to create a distinctive African American voice. This attention to the artifice of language is a theme continued by Clarence Major. In one passage Black Herman verbalizes his version of Neo-HooDoo while signifying about African American creativity in the United States:

> That's our genius here in America. . . . The Blues, Ragtime, The Work that we do is just as good. I'll bet later on in the 50s and 60s and 70s we will have some artists and creators who teach Africa and South America some new twists. . . . If your heart's there, man that's ½ the thing about The Work. . . . Doing The Work is not like taking inventory. Improvise some. Open up, Papa. Stretch on out with It. (*Mumbo Jumbo* 30)

The references to African American music encoded under the totality known as The Work are samples of the way Reed laces the text with clues pointing to the real mystery of the novel. These clues, which suggest that a more comprehensive cultural system of African American attributes structures the novel, might be compared to what Michael Awkward in *Inspiriting Influences* calls the "denigration" of the text, that is, "those appropriative acts by Afro-Americans which successfully transformed, by the addition of black expressive cultural features, Western cultural and expressive systems" (9). Reed subverts the detective text with his African American consciousness and transforms both language and content with what Awkward sees as the domination of "Black cultural 'spirit' or essence" (10). In this sense the detective novel becomes an African American mystery whose clues and signs lead not inward toward some solution of a crime but outward toward a definition of black identity.

As part of this definition, the novel revisits Harlem during the Jazz Age (1920s), which is the period of the Harlem Renaissance, a great flowering of African American arts and culture. Positive attributes of African American culture are stressed through the repeated insertion of real figures from black history, black music, and black politics, and there are references to the great writers of the Harlem Renaissance such as James Weldon Johnson, Wallace Thurman, Langston Hughes, and Zora Neale Hurston. This affirmation of black personalities further extends Reed's notion of the Neo-HooDoo aesthetic by blending fiction and history. The action of the novel is also played out against historic events such as the U.S. Marine invasion and occupation of Haiti (1915–34) and the politics of Warren Harding.

As we have discussed in previous chapters, African American authors have consistently taken advantage of double consciousness in their detective texts, extending the original Du Boisan trope by combining it with detective conventions such as masking and masquerade. *Mumbo Jumbo* continues this tradition with one important difference. Reed raises double consciousness to a new artistic level through his system of Neo-HooDoo aesthetics and his stylistic recharging of the novel form. Reed has written that Neo-HooDoo is composed of many things and can manifest itself in many ways—for example, in "Fantasy, Nationalism, the supernatural, Hoodism, realism, Science Fiction, autobiography, satire, scat, Eroticism, Rock, K.C. Blues, Intrigue and Jazz" (*Conjure* 26). It might be argued that Reed touches on all of these manifestations in *Mumbo Jumbo*. Neo-HooDoo is also connected to positive African American worldviews through redefinitions of New World and Afrocentric religions. Bell sees Reed's Neo-HooDoo aesthetic as one "which is largely constructed from residual elements of syncretistic African religions [and] is a belief in the power of the unknown, particularly expressed in artistic freedom and originality" (331). This celebration of African American originality permeates the novel.

We recognize elements of Reed's Neo-HooDoo aesthetic in typically important African American vernacular creations such as language play and music as well as in the use of hoodoo sensibility. But nowhere previous to Reed has this worldview comprised such a complete and well-thought-out approach to revision of detective conventions through the transformation of the double-conscious and hoodoo tropes. In effect, Reed develops all of the four tropes into manifestations of his Neo-HooDoo philosophy in a process that consciously revises the black detective tradition. Gates has said that *Mumbo Jumbo* is "the great black intertext" written in the conscious mode "in the realm of doubled doubles" (*Figures in Black* 254). *Mumbo Jumbo,* as an anti-detective novel, presents Neo-HooDoo ideas in a self-reflexive text of double-conscious narrative strategies. We must understand Reed's Neo-HooDoo tenets in relation to both the content and the form of the novel.

Reed's concept of Neo-HooDoo was first explored in his poetry, such as "Neo-HooDoo Manifesto" in *Conjure* (1972) and *Catechism of D Neoamerican Hoodoo Church* (1970). Neo-HooDoo is an amalgam of hoodoo ritual, Afrocentric philosophy, and African American culture that affirms black consciousness. In part, it urges black Americans to accept and be proud of their difference, creativity, and survival. Although not all African American individuals are seen as praiseworthy (Reed satirizes black characters as well as white), the overall emphasis in Neo-HooDoo is on re-creation and regeneration through a celebration of black consciousness and black cultural expressions. Reginald Martin sees Reed as "proposing HooDoo as the springboard for black aspirations" and "offer[ing] a different, and black, way of transacting in the world" (84). Reed writes that "Neo-HooDoo believes that every man is an artist and every artist is a priest. You can bring your own creative ideas to Neo-HooDoo" (*Conjure* 25). Reed's reference to hoodoo terminology, concepts, and figures is perhaps the most telling motif in the novel. In fact, the very basis of the Neo-HooDoo worldview is heavily reliant on hoodoo religion. As one of the four major tropes we have discussed, hoodoo has been instrumental in helping to define the different ways in which blacks use detective texts. Reed continues the use of this trope but adds to it by consistently fusing it with double-consciousness narrative techniques, making this experiment in style the backbone of his Neo-HooDoo aesthetic.

With the creation of *Mumbo Jumbo,* Neo-HooDoo also incorporates the tropes of black detection under its banner. Reed's Neo-HooDoo philosophy welds the changed detective persona, black vernaculars, double-conscious detection, and hoodoo into a collective combination under the guise of the detective novel. The nature of Reed's Neo-HooDoo aesthetic is one, if not the primary, mystery to be solved in this postmodern anti-detective novel. Putting together the Neo-HooDoo clues offered in the novel also helps to solve the mystery of Jes Grew and its Text. Neo-HooDooism as applied to the novel is not a religion; it is a new definition of African American consciousness, that stresses the positive attributes of the African American community. Reed's Neo-HooDoo aesthetic is based on a heightened African American perception of the black presence in America and is directly related to the 1960s Black Power and Black Aesthetic movements. Furthermore, Neo-HooDoo insists on a reinterpretation of history that links contemporary black existence with ancient Africa (for example, PaPa LaBas's connection through the Haitian voodoo mysteries to the ancient mysteries of African religion). Reed's revisionist interpretation establishes the Osiris/Set conflict at the very origins of human consciousness. Africa's Egypt is seen in this sense as the progenitor of human consciousness, containing the seeds of both destruction and renewal. Jes Grew is Reed's Neo-HooDoo terminology for the positive revitalization of the African American spirit, which possesses the power to save all of humankind from total destruction.

Mumbo Jumbo extends the use of black detective fiction into a hybrid form, blending actual events with fantasy and fiction. This narrative sleight-of-hand is accomplished by including photographs, real quotes, and footnotes from actual texts. Although these are typical postmodern conceits, *Mumbo Jumbo* alters the equation somewhat by beginning with a unique viewpoint and premise. That is, history must be rewritten from an African American perspective with an Afrocentric focus if we are to gain any understanding of the present. Even though the novel takes place in 1920s Harlem, PaPa LaBas's search for the Text and the murderer of Abdul Hamid is directly linked to the ancient past of Egypt. This is connected to detective conventions through a revised use of the familiar recognition scene, which usually occurs at the end of a novel with the detective summing up the process by which the mystery was solved. In Reed's innovative recognition scene he improvises on this convention by making the last third of the novel the recognition scene and connecting it to the interpolated story of the history of Jes Grew and its Text.

In this interpolated story Reed offers a revisionary interpretation of the rise of Western civilization based on an Afrocentric worldview. The conflicts in the novel revolve around a basic split in human consciousness. Osiris, the Egyptian god, created a sect of life-affirming, Dionysian principles which resulted in Jes Grew. Set, his brother, instigated an antilife, Apollonian sect determined to destroy the world: the Atonists. Osiris's dances of fertility are recorded in the Book of Thoth, the original Text of Jes Grew. The lost Text was discovered in 1118 by the Knights Templar, a secret Christian society formed during the Crusades. Hinckle Von Vampton, an original member of the Knights Templar, steals the Text. In 1307 Pope Clement outlaws the Knights Templar, and Von Vampton escapes with the Text. Wherever Von Vampton goes with the Text there are spontaneous outbreaks of Jes Grew as people sense the nearness of the sacred book.

Reed rewrites history, restoring an Afrocentric perspective to the process of time.

If Euro-American postmodernism works against historicism, its Afro-American counterpart necessarily works in the direction of a different historical sense, one that not only puts black back into the total historical view, but which also (again necessarily) reexplores blackness in terms of itself. (Fox 8)

On its most serious level, *Mumbo Jumbo* is about the Atonist attempt to eradicate Jes Grew from the human race. Jes Grew is the essential ingredient of African American consciousness; it is linked to dance and music, vital expressions of what might be described as the ecstatic life force of the African American. Jes Grew enters New Orleans by way of Haiti, and its origins are obviously African. Its effects are described as follows: "He said he felt like the gut heart and lungs of Africa's interior. He said he felt like the Kongo: 'Land of the Panther' " (5). The crime of exterminating Jes Grew is by obvious extension an attempt to destroy the Afrocentric spiritual power of creativity and renewal, and the criminal is all of Western civilization.

Given the abstract qualities of Jes Grew, there can be no possibility of a solution in conventional detective terms. Reed takes the notion of irresolution one step farther by suggesting that in fact there should be no resolution. It is in the joyful acceptance of life's indeterminacy that true happiness lies. As Gates points out, *Mumbo Jumbo* "is a novel that figures and glorifies indeterminacy" (*Figures in Black* 260).

It is no coincidence that Charlie Parker, the *houngan* priest of improvisation, enters the text early on as an indicator of the novel's primary theme of re-creation (*Mumbo Jumbo* 16). Down through the centuries the spontaneous joy of Jes Grew has triumphed over suppression by the Atonists and the Wallflower Order, representatives of the Euro-Americentric death wish. "Jes Grew is electric as life and is characterized by ebullience and ecstasy" (6). Lance Olsen, in his book on postmodernism and the comic vision, recognizes that the Euro-Americentric "tragic" vision of life is the minority one in world cultures. Most cultures affirm a more comic vision in which "a subversive impulse is directed toward the dominant culture. The comic vision sees life not as work but festival, not as Puritan hardship but as playful pastime" (23). Martin also sees Neo-HooDoo as in part a "literary method . . . aligning . . . closely with a love of life, and the good things to be found in life" (82). Therefore, *Mumbo Jumbo* works on two planes of discourse. Within the content of the novel Jes Grew subverts intimidation through improvisation. This is mirrored in the style of the novel, which subverts traditional detective form through hybridization. This emphasis on the positive, the Jes Grew of pure life force and joy of existence, distinguishes *Mumbo Jumbo* and points the way to a Neo-HooDoo worldview. By reconstructing black history and reconnecting it to the ancient past, Reed emphasizes the great strengths of African Americans. Their survival as a culture indicates the powers of an inherent Jes Grew ability to re-create spontaneously, readapting old forms to new methods of accomplishment. The book *Mumbo Jumbo* is a case in point.

I have suggested that the thematic content of *Mumbo Jumbo*, as represented by Jes Grew through improvisation and creativity, is reflected in the narrative construction of the novel, which is a further extension of the double-conscious theme. Reed constructs a trickster text that forces the reader to revise accepted notions of the novel form. *Mumbo Jumbo* is composed as a popular culture compendium, a collage of effects lifted from the visual arts as well as literary

sources. The complicated interactions of pictures, newspaper head-
lines, quotes from history texts, and cinematic allusions organized by
an indefinite yet omnipotent narrator are richly postmodern in self-
reflexive technique. The terms "hybridization" and "carnivalization,"
which hark back to Bakhtin's notion of heteroglossia in the origins
of the novel, are appropriate for this novel. Bakhtin describes heteroglossia as

> A comic playing with languages. . . . character speech, character zones,
> and lastly various introductory or framing genres are the basic forms for
> incorporating and organizing heteroglossia in a novel. All these forms
> permit languages to be used in ways that are indirect, conditional, dis-
> tanced. (323)

Thus Reed uses the detective form, some of its language, and some of
its conventions in a mix of hybrid narrative techniques.

Gates recognizes that Reed's "form of satire is a version of gumbo,
a parody of form itself" (*Figures in Black* 256). *Mumbo Jumbo* experiments with form and style as well as introducing innovative ideas.
By pulling the reader out of the flow of narrative, it constantly refers
to itself as a conscious act of writing.

> The narrative self-referentiality is not always so simple to decipher, as all
> of Reed's novels are writerly texts; he expects the reader to be familiar
> with past fiction and non-fictional events external to the particular novel
> at issue. Reed also expects the reader to "make" the text and its im-
> plications by way of understanding the narrative games being played.
> (Martin 75)

The book breaks with common assumptions about how a novel
should be read by creating a colorful pastiche of narrative methods.
Gates in *Figures in Black* calls *Mumbo Jumbo* a book "about texts
and a book of texts, a composite narrative composed of subtexts,
pretexts, post-texts, and narrative within narratives" (252). Terry
Castle says that "the carnivalized work . . . resists generic classifica-
tion and instead combines . . . a multiplicity of literary modes in a
single increasingly 'promiscuous' form" (912). Furthermore, carnivalization suggests the elements of masquerade, celebration, and ecstatic behavior associated with Jes Grew and its entry into the United
States through New Orleans. Reed's postmodern imagination applied
to African American themes is one way of defining Neo-HooDoo.
Yet another is Jes Grew in action. All of it implies an ideological

readjustment of worldview that I suggest lies at the heart of *Mumbo Jumbo*.

Reed inserts photos of blacks, footnotes written by himself, passages from other books, and pictures to create a new type of text. Much like Jes Grew, it seems to spring spontaneously into being. The structure of the novel follows no recognizable pattern, consisting of episodes of narrative interwoven into a quiltlike pattern of interjections and illustrations. The main body of the novel is preceded by a cinematic-like prologue, and there is also an epilogue and a partial bibliography of historical and philosophical texts, which give the book a scholarly air. The novel is a blend of research, historical fact, and imagination. The linearity of the narrative is constantly under attack, suggesting the importance of circularity in time, another aspect of Afrocentric religions incorporated into the Neo-HooDoo aesthetic. For example, Reed's concern with the history and tradition of black Americans is effectively presented through the novel's fragmented time sphere, which extends backward from the 1920s in Harlem to the Egyptian era. In effect, this creates not a linear time frame but a circular one that rewrites received historical assumptions. As Reginald Martin points out in *Ishmael Reed and the New Black Aesthetic Critics*,

> Reed's version of this synchronicity incorporates a future by believing in time as a circle of revolving and re-evolving events, but the past/present concept is certainly maintained in the way characters correspond about past and present matters as though they were simultaneous. (74)

Keith Byerman in *Fingering the Jagged Grain* concurs and sees this creative play on conventional time structures as a conscious attempt to critique Euro-Americentric control of both history and literature. "His [Reed's] play with time and genre is a way of denaturalizing assumptions about these aspects of culture and revealing the underlying manipulative functions of both" (219). Finally, what is questioned here is the ultimate authority of the author to present a total fictional reality. By interrupting the flow of narrative, stressing historical asides, and positing positive African American worldviews, Reed seems to be suggesting that all texts must be examined closely for false fabrication.

Furthermore, history itself may be a fabrication that can be manipulated according to whoever is doing the interpreting of facts. This is perhaps Reed's most important point about Neo-HooDoo creativity. Neo-HooDooism demands an individualistic interpretation of the dominant culture's control of time and representations of time. Neo-HooDooism is rooted in its own African American perspective and value systems, thereby creating an alternative philosophy by which one can judge the world and act in it.

> As a literary method, Hoodoo reinterprets and reinvents; it uses time disjunctionally and synchronically to illustrate social truths by juxtaposition with their opposites and their supposed origins. (Martin 83)

Reed, then, is concerned with extending the African American consciousness backward as well as concentrating on the newly emergent creative interpretations of mainstream culture.

Although Himes also concentrated on Harlem in his detective series, depicting the struggles of the community to survive in a segregated environment, Reed, from a more contemporary vantage point, returns to the Harlem Renaissance to reemphasize the important attributes of that period. Among these are the growth of self-esteem and self-definition as well as a revitalization of the African past to the African American present. Reed sees the Harlem Renaissance as important to the consciousness of modern black Americans. But the period also contains the seeds of future black revolutionary movements as represented by Berbelang and Abdul Hamid. As the author of a revisionary text on Harlem and the Harlem Renaissance, Reed is strongly supportive of Afrocentrism yet cautionary about black cliques and power movements. Fox writes:

> Reed uses his aesthetic to retrieve the most esoteric aspects of African and world history and to fuse them with contemporary events. The combination of objective and imaginative events and analyses indicates that no one way of knowing has *a priori* precedence over another. (169)

Reed can indeed fuse a Black Muslim into a Harlem Renaissance cityscape purely for the effect of social satire and as a warning. However, the overall emphasis of *Mumbo Jumbo* is on a concentrated African American worldview that has much in common with the aspirations of the Black Power movement (1965–75) in the United States. As William L. Van Deburg points out in his *New Day in Babylon* (1992), Harlem Renaissance artists, through "promotion of black cultural distinctives, and their commitment to improving black

self-esteem, . . . provided a rich, activist legacy for what would become the Black Arts Movement of the sixties" (39).

Furthermore, in both a cultural and a political sense, *Mumbo
Jumbo* reflects Black Power principles. On the cultural front we have
already discussed the novel's activist approach to rewriting history
and affirming African American vernacular strengths. Van Deburg
considers "racial pride, strength, and self-definition" as the key elements of what "came to be called the Black Power movement" (2).
But the novel also contains characters such as Berbelang and Buddy
Jackson, who move beyond cultural warfare to actual aggressive action against the white power structure. This type of organized politics
of self-defense and reclamation of black cultural artifacts is symptom-
atic of the Black Power movement's call for blacks to "control their
own destinies" (23), "to write their own histories and to create their
own myths and legends" (27). Or as Stokely Carmichael, one of the
founders of the Black Power movement, put it, blacks had to redefine
their collective identity from "the dictatorship of definition, interpretation and consciousness" (in Van Deburg 27). *Mumbo Jumbo*'s
worldview of social and political emancipation from the Atonists by
way of Jes Grew is intricately connected to Black Power sentiments.
Witness the way in which *Mumbo Jumbo* defines African American
power through its Afrocentric interpretation of history, its reliance
on hoodoo religion, and its expression of pride in African American
vernacular creations.

As a black detective novel, *Mumbo Jumbo* extends the tradition of
previous black detective novels when dealing with conflicts of Euro-
American and African American worldviews. The book's moral position and attack on Euro-American social values are clearly manifested
through its derision of the Atonist world order. On another level, the
very structure of its language play parodies the detective novel by
enticing the reader with a mystery that cannot be solved, just as the
blend of real and imagined history creates a unique historical narrative. The tension between fantasy and reality in the novel focuses
attention on the metaphysical questions imbedded in the tale. Conflicts of philosophy and reinterpretations of history suggest that abstract questions concerning race, social relations, and politics lie at
the core of this detective novel.

In many ways the Text for which Jes Grew searches is the text
which *is Mumbo Jumbo,* that is, a text that validates and valorizes

an African American worldview. Fox points out that in *Mumbo Jumbo* there is a "mystery war ... a war *between* mysteries or between mystery and its absence" (56). In other words Reed is more interested in positing questions and questioning assumptions than he is in solving the mystery of Jes Grew, which in fact to an African American secure in understanding of self is no mystery. Reed's ultimate aim in *Mumbo Jumbo* is to produce a unique African American worldview and to question how one is taught or learns to attain a cultural identity. Reed's Neo-HooDoo is his own personalized worldview presented as a life-affirming alternative to Euro-Americentric worldviews.

The question of Reed's relation to other black aestheticans of the period such as Addison Gayle, Amiri Baraka, and Houston Baker is complicated. Reginald Martin insists that "Reed's work fails to meet the demanded criteria from the major aestheticians" because of his use of humor and surrealism and his refusal to "accommodate the demands of the adherents and the leading aestheticians" (42). Yet Reed's Neo-HooDoo has much in common with statements made by major black aesthetician editors Addison Gayle and Larry Neal in *The Black Aesthetic* (1972). "A main tenet of Black Power," they write, "is the necessity for Black people to define the world in their own terms. The Black artist has made the same point in the context of aesthetics" (257). Gayle writes in the foreword: "The Black Aesthetic, then, as conceived by this writer is a corrective—a means of helping black people out of the polluted mainstream of Americanism" (xxii). It is difficult to ascertain how Reed's Neo-HooDoo aesthetics as discussed in *Mumbo Jumbo* differs remarkably from these general voicings of black aesthetics. However, critics such as Gayle claim Reed's work changes with the publication of *Louisiana Red* (1974) and *Flight to Canada* (1976), both of which postdate *Mumbo Jumbo* and are not discussed here.

Like *The Conjure Man Dies,* the mystery at the core of *Mumbo Jumbo* involves African American consciousness. Just as Frimbo questions the nature of blackness in a white society, PaPa LaBas represents an African American viewpoint in a Euro-Americentric environment. "The rest of the world would do better to concern itself with why Frimbo was black" (230), Frimbo states when questioned about the mystery at the center of *Conjure Man.* So too *Mumbo Jumbo* explores the mystery of black consciousness caught in a white world. Martin understands that "*Mumbo Jumbo*'s mystery is the origin and composition of the 'true Afro-American aesthetic' " (85). Reed's Neo-HooDoo is that aesthetic, establishing as it does for the first time in black detective fiction a consistent black viewpoint on such important issues as the historical process, the nature of time and black identity, and the re-creation of narrative forms. As part of the creative reinterpretation of the detective novel Reed also attacks restrictive, proscriptive, and rigid definitions of African American art, character, and culture. In this way he expands narrow definitions of authentic racial or ethnic identity.

Mumbo Jumbo successfully combines detective convention alterations with stylistic innovations and satire. The bizarre plot and the confrontation of allegorical characters are interwoven into a detective format that puts PaPa LaBas at the center of the novel. Black Herman and PaPa LaBas work together as a team to solve the mystery of the missing Text and Abdul Hamid's murder. Earline consequently plays a minor role. This is unfortunate since she is one of only two female characters in the novel. Reinforcing traditional customs and conventions of male dominance, Earline's function in the text seems to be limited to helpmate to LaBas and lover to Berbelang. After Berbelang is killed, Earline is possessed by Erzulie, a Haitian loa of eros, and seduces a bus driver. Black Herman subjects Earline to an exorcism in a closed room by feeding the passionate desires of the possessed girl. The function of this possession in relation to the rest of the text remains problematic since it is a theme that is not pursued or explained.

In conclusion, *Mumbo Jumbo* is strongest in its depiction of the Neo-HooDoo aesthetic. Overall, the mingling of fact and fiction in *Mumbo Jumbo* works because it does not err to either side. The politics of the novel may succumb to phallocentrism and exaggeration, yet its themes are presented in such a way as to resist polemic, an attribute Reed has been criticized for in his later work. The central conceit of using a black hoodoo priest as detective holds the novel together and creates a narrative suspense often lacking in Reed's other fiction. In Detective PaPa LaBas, Reed's philosophy of positive African American identity based on both the African past and the creative present is masterfully presented. The book challenges accepted viewpoints on history, literary conventions, and the nature of knowledge, though it fails to consider alternatives to the tradition of male dominance and authority. Overall, *Mumbo Jumbo* continues the tradition of black detective fiction in alteration of detective persona, use of black vernaculars, double-consciousness, and hoodoo while showing that the ability of African American double-conscious hoodoo to create new forms out of old will continue to jes grow.

Reflex and Bone Structure (1975), written by Clarence Major (1936–), is an experimental novel that contributes to the emancipation of black consciousness by confronting the traditional methods of narrative discourse. As Major himself has written, social protest is not the only way to liberate the human spirit: "the novel *not* deliberately aimed at bringing about human freedom for black people has liberated as many minds as has the propaganda tract, if not more" (*Dark and Feeling* 24–25). In "Major's *Reflex and Bone Structure* and the Anti-Detective Novel," by Larry McCaffery and Linda Gregory, Major is quoted as saying: "I set out with the notion of doing a mystery novel, not in the traditional sense, but taking up the whole idea of mystery" (40). In its pursuit of metaphysical themes, its parody of literary and detective forms, and its lack of a final solution, *Reflex and Bone Structure* falls within the anti-detective tradition as defined by Tani and further emphasized by McCaffery and Gregory in their essay.

The novel's experimental narrative form, with its lack of traditional character and plot development, also makes it a metafictional detective story as defined by Tani in *The Doomed Detective*:

> Thus when we get to metafictional anti-detective novels, the conventional elements of detective fiction (the detective, the criminal, the corpse) are hardly there. By now the detective is the reader who has to make sense out of an unfinished fiction that has been distorted or cut short by a playful and perverse "criminal," the writer. (113)

Metafiction in this sense suggests a renewed emphasis on the construction of the text and the artifice of words. Bell points us in this direction when he describes Major as having "a preoccupation with exploring the boundaries of language and imaginative consciousness" (317). Other critics such as Klinkowitz confirm this line of reasoning when they emphasize the nature of the book's construction over its content: "Yet *Reflex and Bone Structure* is a more than conventional detective novel, for every element of its composition—character, theme, action, and event—expresses the self-apparent nature of its making" (108–9). The experimentation with structure, character development, plot, and other literary devices in this novel illustrates Major's preoccupation with the trope of double-conscious detection as applied to a critique of Euro-American literary forms.

Reflex extends the black detective tradition into experimental narrative territory. Houston Baker points out how Major's metafictional novel shares themes with the African American cultural tradition: "The products of Afro-American expressive culture are, frequently, stuttered, polyphonic, dissociative—fragmented, ambivalent, or incomplete. They 'urge voyages' and require inventive response" (*Workings* 100). Much like a sustained jazz solo, *Reflex* improvises on the black detective tradition by further reinventing the four tropes of black detection as well as demanding a creative response from the reader. I see *Reflex* as a form of signifying on appropriated Euro-American cultural literary conventions, such as character, plot, and description, as well as parodying the detective form. In this sense it is a logical extension and further elaboration of the double-conscious detection theme, paralleling Ishmael Reed's experimentation with form.

As well as being a primary character in the text, the Narrator writes the novel *Reflex* and comments on the process of writing it. Although nameless and never described, the Narrator self-reflexively manipulates the plot and characters of this episodic novel. Through his repeated references to the act of writing, we know that the Narrator is playfully deconstructing the text while in the process of composing it. "I'll make up everything from now on. . . . I'll do anything I like. I'm extending reality, not retelling it" (49). The Narrator is whimsical, forgetful, and unreliable. He refuses to tell a consistent story that follows traditional discursive conventions. His method of engagement is self-reflexive in the sense that the reader is continuously made aware of his manipulation of the text. We know little of the personal history of the Narrator other than that he lives in Manhattan. He exists through the act of writing, and his identity is inextricably tied to that process. Throughout the novel the Narrator remains aloof, detached, and fearful of growing old.

The other characters are seen exclusively through the Narrator's eyes. Cora Hull is a black actress who lives in Greenwich Village in Manhattan. At various times she has intimate relationships with the novel's three male characters, the Narrator, Canada, and Dale. She is often in rehearsal for plays but never seems to have any long-term commitments either to the stage or to the other characters. She may have been killed in the mysterious bombing episode that occurs in the beginning of the novel, but because of the convoluted time frame of the plot we can never be sure until the end. She is described as being twenty-five years old, five feet, five inches tall, and weighing between 112 and 125 pounds. She was born and brought up in Atlanta, Georgia.

Canada Jackson is a black male who may be part of a black revolutionary group, but he is also described as having once been a policeman (*Reflex* 2). He is Cora's husband and a rival of both Dale and the Narrator. Canada collects weapons and keeps a gun in the silverware drawer in the kitchen of his apartment. He is also an actor in New York City.

Dale is a black off-Broadway actor who flits in and out of the text with little definition. The Narrator professes to have the most difficult time constructing Dale. Furthermore, Dale threatens the Narrator's sense of self. As Cora's suitor, Dale causes more problems than Canada or the Narrator. The Narrator is very jealous of Dale, and he is often sent on long journeys.

As a detective novel *Reflex* stretches the boundaries of the form by toying with three conventions: the detective, the crime, and the solution. Repeated references to these three conventions give the novel an eerie sense of suspense associated with detective fiction but provide none of the expected behavior or resolutions of the form. A bomb has exploded on the street, and the police are investigating the apparent assassination of two people. Somebody with a suitcase has been murdered, and there are indications that the murder was committed by an unnamed revolutionary group. Hints are given that Canada is a member of a black revolutionary group responsible for the bombing. Canada and the Narrator are fingerprinted as suspects. The nameless police return again and again to the scene of the crime with no apparent success. A Puerto Rican boy with a green shirt flits in and out of the text and says he knows who owned the suitcase that exploded. The Narrator tells us the boy lies. The Narrator also tells us that the crime occurred just outside his apartment. At times, the Narrator says that it was Cora who was killed. "Anyway by now I think you find no problem realizing this is her eulogy" (132). However, even this simple premise is complicated by the Narrator, who claims that it was he who murdered Dale and Cora, suggesting that the murder is a figment of his literary imagination, as are the characters, including the Narrator, and the novel itself.

The interrelationships of these four characters revolve around the murders of Cora and Dale. Due to the fragmented time frame, it is impossible to tell what occurs before or after the murder of Cora. However, Cora Hull is present during most of the novel, which takes place in New York City, except for trips to places such as the Poconos and New England. Since these trips are not described in any detail, we cannot be sure if they really take place. The characters can travel as easily to the South Pole as to the neighborhood theater. The novel is written in the first person, which gives the Narrator complete control over the story, the same method used by hardboiled detective writers such as Hammett and Chandler. However, in this anti-detective novel the first-person format, which was traditionally used for clarity of expression and easy reader identification, is used to confuse and alienate the reader. The issue of control and authorial authority is subverted at every turn. In fact, the Narrator tells the reader that he is unreliable and consciously manipulating the text. He stresses the fact that he and his characters are simply part of his own imagination: "I do not really hate Dale, but respond this way to him out of lack of interest. I mean, I *should* be interested in him since he's one of my creations. He *should* have a character, a personality" (12). Because of these disavowals of control and the episodic, often contradictory form of the novel, the reader's suspension of disbelief is constantly challenged. In fact, there is little certainty about anything in this novel, which is one of the implied intents of the Narrator, who often claims that forgetfulness or simple arbitrariness purposely alters the text.

However, certain motifs recur throughout the text which provide stable points of reference. The primary frame of reference is the Narrator, who tells the reader he is writing a novel while he is writing it. The Narrator comments continually on the problems he has in constructing the text due to his own misinterpretations, his forgetfulness, his difficulty in describing how things appear or are, and his constant flights of fancy. The other characters are at the mercy of the Narrator's whims. They are sent away or drop out of the action depending on the Narrator's moods. Often the Narrator will contradict himself or even blend himself into the other characters. Though the activity of all four characters takes place in a skewed, apparently haphazard time frame, the story obviously centers around Cora Hull. Cora is described in different and often contradictory ways: "Not only was she involved with a militant white group, she was also part of a revolutionary Black group, plus she was branching out into the women's liberation movement" (31); "She was into Mother Dependency. Unweaned creatures" (33). Often she is described as appearing in a play, but the reader learns little about the drama.

Usually Cora is presented in relation to one of the three other characters in an indeterminate time frame. She is the center of the novel, and all the other characters are redefined through her, but she too is endlessly mutable. Commonly, she is the locus of their sexual attention as well as a physical presence to which the Narrator returns again and again. Her moods are unpredictable, but no more so than any of the other characters, including the Narrator. Although Canada, Dale, and the Narrator are fixated on Cora, none of them maintains any long-term relationship. They revolve around each other without really understanding each other. Their closeness is suggested by the interwoven repetition of their personal and sexual encounters, which are presented in matter-of-fact terms. "She got up and came to my side, kissed me. At that moment Canada came in" (46). The Narrator claims they all have problems focusing on anything. At various times they live either in the same apartment or in close proximity to each other. Much of the novel takes place inside apartments, in rooms ill defined and vague. The Narrator complains about this, claiming they stay inside with closed-in thoughts too much.

From the various locales most commonly mentioned, such as Greenwich Village and the Lower East Side, the reader assumes they live in Manhattan. We know that Cora is often at rehearsals or trying out for plays, but Dale and Canada have no known occupations, although they are associated with the theater as actors. The Narrator at one point calls himself a theater director. All of them drift in and out of the timeless plot, sometimes threatening, sometimes friendly, but never really defined. Another recurring motif is the young Puerto Rican boy who wears a green shirt. The boy is seen everywhere and somehow has access to the apartments of the characters. He is mysteriously attracted to Cora and appears at regular intervals throughout the novel without altering the direction of action or having anything to do with the rest of the characters.

The renewed emphasis on the construction of fiction and the ambiguity of the detective presence are part of the postmodern black anti-detective novel. Once again the detective persona is extended and altered, in this case almost reduced to invisibility. It is difficult to determine who the detective is. Is it the Narrator? The police? The reader? Or a combination of all three? Certainly the Narrator must be looked at closely. He, in fact, calls himself a detective in the text: "I'm a detective trying to solve a murder. No, not a murder. It's a life. Who hired me? I can't face the question" (32). However, he may also be the murderer since he describes the murders of both Cora and Dale that occur (or don't occur) at the beginning of the novel as partly his own doing: "Dale gives Cora a hand. At the edge of the desert they step into a city. They step into a house. It explodes. It is a device. I am responsible. I set the device" (145). Furthermore, on the second page of the novel we are also introduced to the cops, who are "real" and "funny" (2). They are hard at work taking fingerprints and scraping up blood spots and "scattered pieces of body" (1). Later on in the novel they place the Narrator and Canada under suspicion, "the rumor is Canada and I are both very much under suspicion and closely watched" (31). And he in turn suspects them. "Anyway I still suspect the law enforcement officers of murdering Cora" (31). The police drop in and out of the narrative, examining, prodding, and probing. They use the methods of forensic investigation, such as fingerprints and lab work, yet their scientific examinations lead to nothing. At one point Cora looks for a book to read and is momentarily fascinated by "something called *Model Criminal Investigation*. Even this she passed up. The cover was dull" (95). This sendup of police procedural methods parodies the rational aspects of the detective's persona extending back to Dupin and Holmes.

This is about as far as we get with solving or understanding the murders of Cora and Dale in terms recognizable to conventional detective texts. Therefore, we are forced to look for other answers. It soon becomes apparent that the process of detection is somehow linked with the process of epistemology or the nature of understanding itself. In fact, the reader becomes the detective of the novel, trying desperately to put all the disparate pieces together. A perverse, unnameable menace seems to keep anything from occurring in ways that can be understood. This menace may simply be the avowed manipulation of the Narrator. Or it may be the intent of the Narrator to suggest that the true nature of existence consists of these seemingly random encounters with people and places in which there is no rhyme or reason.

Major intersperses the text with references to popular crime films and movie stars. Well-known literary and cinematic icons such as Agatha Christie and John Wayne appear. Old movies are mentioned as well as actors from early crime films such as Edward G. Robinson. The cinematic references reflect the Narrator's interest in film and mirror the cinematic quality of the text, where the action occurs in small "takes." There are also a number of sections that consist simply of lists, more often than not lists of black musicians or other well-known African American artists:

> Cora places a stack of records on the record player. For years she listens to Buck Clayton, Thelonious Monk, Bix Beiderbecke, Benny Carter, Hoagy Carmichael, Chico Hamilton. They drench her. She sleeps with the records, dances through the music. (61)

All but two on the above list are black musicians. These lists seem to function as a type of naive empiricism, proving by their very existence that a world outside the text does exist as well as affirming the positive quality of African American vernacular expression.

The most obvious double-conscious theme in the novel is the heightened and highly creative use of language and narrative experimentation. The novel is composed of small vignettes broken into two sections entitled "A Bad Connection" and "Body Heat." Approximately equal in length, these two sections offer no clue as to the meaning of their titles or their function in the overall narrative. There is no discernible change in storytelling method or characters from one section to the next. In fact, the novel ends much as it began with the Narrator slipping in and out of surreal hallucinatory or dream sequences in which the characters blend with each other and into absurd scenarios. The circular movement of the novel revolves around the characters' relationships with Cora Hull. She is the center of attention of the three males, and she in turn flirts with and is attracted to the Narrator, Canada, and Dale. However, as these characters intermingle, connect, and disconnect there is a curious static quality about the text. The reader is never sure if anything happens. The Narrator adds to the confusion by commenting on the characters, including himself:

> Get to this: Cora isn't based on anybody.
> Dale isn't anything.
> Canada is just something I'm busy making up.
> I am only an act of my own imagination. (85)

The theme of double consciousness in black detection texts traditionally deals with the notion of perception, making the values of black perception the most important aspect of the detective process. In *Reflex,* as in *Mumbo Jumbo,* the trope of double consciousness becomes further complicated through the use of literary masking—the ultimate trickster Narrator who uses words to bewilder and deceive. This double-conscious deception is a complex act of communication indicating important African American language acts. The self-reflexive text is directly related to the black expressive art of signifyin(g). Henry Louis Gates, in relation to the two trickster figures of Esu and the Signifying Monkey, writes that

> the central place of both figures in their traditions is determined by their curious tendency to reflect on the uses of formal language. The theory of Signifyin(g) arises from these moments of self-reflexiveness. (*Signifying Monkey* xxi)

The very nature of a Euro-Americentric fictive voice is challenged in this text. The Narrator writes, "I want this book to be anything it wants to be. . . . I want the mystery of this book to be an absolute mystery" (*Reflex* 61). The Narrator manipulates the reader with double-consciousness intent. The novel refers to hoodoo—"He ran in the wrong direction and a hoodoo fell on him" (12)—but its double-conscious detection is more apparent in its magical reinvention of time, place, and action. Major fractures Aristotle's dramatic verities, creating in their place a complex picture of a more primitive nature. With its bare-boned characterization and negligible plot development, *Reflex* becomes an antinovel as well as an anti-detective novel. In fact, if there is a death in this text it is the death of the novel as commonly experienced.

Cora Hull has X-ray pictures of her brain, heart, womb, and bone structure framed and hanging in her living room. The stark, negative images of X rays suggest only the essential outlines of things, and in this sense the novel itself is like an X ray with its four shadowy characters who interact in ambiguous and contradictory ways. Many of the episodes seem to ignite spontaneously from the mind of the Narrator, who assumes a major role in their instigation:

> Canada and I leave town. It's not easy. . . . For spending change, we stick up a mail train, swooping with seven million, which lasts us a few days. . . . we get work at the Palace Theatre and Carnegie Hall. We're a smash success. . . . But by now we're exhausted. We separate. (35)

The plot reads like the reflex reactions of this unreliable Narrator, who puzzles out his existence among characters who may or may not be real. Since everything is consciously filtered through the Narrator's viewpoint, and he tells us he is lying, the reader's response is also much like a reflex reaction. That is, the reader is as bewildered as the Narrator and the other characters.

The Narrator in this sense can be looked at as the houngan trickster creator who displays his talent in the manipulation of the reader's perception. This trickster mysteriously veils the novel in a magical, surrealist poetry of words: "Cricket frogs jump about on the tables. Whistling tree frogs are in our bedroom. Patch-nosed snakes crawl under the bed. . . . blind snakes are in the dirty clothes containers" (76). In example after example, the Narrator weaves his spell of bewildering impossibilities. None of it in the end is ever summed up, given concrete form, or explicated in any degree commonly associated with the recognition scene of the detective novel. "I simply refuse to go into details. Fragmentation can be all we have to make a whole" (17). Given this fragmentation and refusal to accept order, there is only one consciousness left that is capable of making sense out of the book: the reader's. It is the reader who in the end becomes the detective and the real creator of the text.

Indeed, the author, Clarence Major, is quite aware of the conundrums preferred by this type of fiction and gives the reader some warning of what is coming. On the inscription page there is an enjoinder that reads: "This book is an extension of, not a duplication of reality. The characters and events are happening for the first time." The author's preamble suggests the spontaneous quality of *Reflex and Bone Structure*. The very short, most often elliptical, and confusing vignettes bewilder the Narrator as much as the reader. The Narrator is a character in his own narrative, but he does not possess the omniscience of most narrators. The first-person format also contributes to the sense that the story is unfolding immediately in front of the reader. Some of the most obvious conceits of metafiction are included in this novel: a narrator who is unreliable, a text that talks about itself being written, sketchy characters who are confusingly described and often revealed as figments of the narrator's mind, a jumbled plot that repeats and often contradicts itself. Consequently, the abstract quality of the text often forces the reader to play a primary role in fabricating order.

The characters and plot are reduced to essentials like names and forms and never seem to progress beyond that point. It is as if Major is forcing the reader to relearn and rename everything taken for granted in Euro-American novels. Early in the book the Narrator describes Cora:

> Cora switches to a children's program. It's all about P and Y and B and T and G and F and H and E and W and C. It's all about the deep dark secrets of the mind. A boy and girl are exploring a haunted castle called Alphabetical Africa. (5)

Like the children in this program, the reader must confront the elemental aspects of fiction's construction. The act of naming is basic to understandable language use, and the Narrator plays with the concept of naming as a structural device: "It isn't that I myself forget their names. The truth is I do not really give a shit about the names these men have who happen to be cops. One might be called U" (31). The Narrator uses naming as a repetitive motif in the text. "I make too much of names: but then what are things or people *before* they attain names?" (121). Obviously, the Narrator is searching for a preverbal, more primitive method of understanding.

The reference to Africa in the passage quoted above might suggest a new orientation to the Narrator's struggle for meaning. Major has spoken about this reorientation in one of his interviews, where he comments on the importance of art over what he calls "militant rhetoric" and urges a renewal of artistic inspiration:

> I'm not talking about artistic standards based on European-American concepts of excellence. Rather, I'm referring to formative and functional standards that have their origins in African cultures. (*Dark and Feeling* 128)

Keith Byerman, in *Fingering The Jagged Grain,* associates this Afro-centric artistic understanding with the importance of naming: "Crucial to this view of art is the concept of 'nommo,' the word that gives meaning to the object created." Naming gives ultimate meaning. "Thus, a mask of a dead person need have no resemblance to that person because the artist will give it its proper name and thereby its meaning." This emphasis on naming gives all power to the creator, and in *Reflex* this creator is the Narrator, who "like the singers of blues rearrange[s] the verses or invent[s] new ones in order to create a certain mood" (256). *Reflex* can be interpreted in this way as a palimpsest text of mood and feeling with meaning conveyed on a very abstract plain.

Because the story has a crime, detectives, and an investigation, certain rudiments of the detective novel genre are satisfied, and the mood of mystery infuses the text. However, the investigation stalls, and the unsolved crime stands as a metaphor for the rest of the novel in which nothing gets resolved. The reader is forced to assume the detective role, amassing clues that go nowhere. The reader's role as detective also ends in failure since the key to the crime and the book lies with the Narrator, who refuses to relinquish his hold on meaning. The formula of detective fiction as we know it is totally subverted. The details are twisted, the plot is nonexistent, the characters are hardly more than names—nothing can be solved. Order often cannot be imposed, which suggests that the novel might be about the process of understanding itself as well as the nature of language. In the end nothing makes sense but the poetry of the words.

In this way the novel is akin to modern abstract painting, which is self-referential and concerned with the nature of paint and painting rather than the depiction of reality or the illustration of a recognizable object. Major studied painting and painted for many years. Allusions to painting occur in the text: "He takes me on a tour of the museum, showing me various abstract paintings. 'These things are about themselves. Look at the paint.' " (99). The analogy between painting and the experimental text of Major's novel is intriguing. Major has commented on this in relation to his novel *All-Night Visitors:* "I saw the work as a kind of drawing done with words" (*Dark and Feeling* 16). In *Reflex,* words seem to function like paint in the way the characters and episodes sometimes blend into each other. Strange apparitions such as insects and frogs mysteriously appear in large numbers, inhabiting rooms or dropping from Cora Hull's dress. The characters are described as being in a room talking or sadly looking out of windows when suddenly, in the same paragraph, they are transported to some remote beach. This fluid and strangely melting quality of the text reminds the reader of the bizarre fusions and juxtapositions of surrealism. The absurd scenes reel out in seemingly random fashion, as if the Narrator were asleep or hallucinating. None of the characters acts consistently and with purpose, and so the meaning must be contained on a surface level of construction, much as abstract painting refers to the paint and the act of painting before suggesting anything representational.

Furthermore, the representational quotient of the abstract painting is often generated only in the eye of the beholder. In Maly and Dietfried Gerhardus's *Cubism and Futurism,* the nature of perception is discussed in relation to abstract painting. The uncertainty of the viewer in front of such a painting is connected with a history of understanding:

> The main reason for this uncertainty is of course that all our knowledge and experience are determined in some way by our previous linguistic understanding of the everyday world. . . . In other words: we do not learn to perceive, for perception as such is an inherited faculty, but we do learn to distinguish perceptions from one another, and do so precisely by means of linguistic hierarchies and divisions. (8)

The connection between linguistic and visual perception is an area of experimentation in *Reflex.* The book's reduction to essential linguistic elements is mirrored by its visual indeterminacy, that is, its willing inability to construct a linear plot and recognizable characters. Visual and linguistic perception depends on linking known and accepted hierarchies of word and visual clues. The ultimate dissolution of this Euro-American hierarchy seems to be one of the aims of *Reflex.* With its nonlinear time frame, its character and plot dissembling, and its epistemological fragmentation, the novel forces a new perception. William Spanos, in his essay "The Detective and the Boundary: Some Notes on the Postmodern Literary Imagination," makes the same point in relation to the symbolist's deconstruction of language:

> Its purpose was to undermine its utilitarian function in order to disintegrate the reader's linear-temporal orientation and to make him *see* syn-

chronically—as one sees a painting or circular mythological paradigm—what the temporal words express. (158)

In many ways this new perception is based on contradictions. For all its movement and spontaneous transformations, the novel projects claustrophobia and paranoia—or, as Spanos would put it, an existential dread. Nothing is ever done or accomplished in the novel, and none of the mysteries of its text are elucidated. None of the characters change or develop because the reader does not really know who they are. The Narrator continually bemoans his increasing age, but we do not know what that age is. The novel is reduced to an obsession for indeterminacy.

This sense of incompleteness is what people normally fight against by writing books, creating plays, believing in something. This indeed may be the warning of the Narrator in writing such a novel—that we must know ourselves first so that we in turn may know the world. *Reflex and Bone Structure* confronts the accepted Euro-American notions of the novel. In his essay "A Black Criteria" (1967), Major urges a transformation and a breaking away from Euro-American literary structures. Although he later disavowed an "all-encompassing black aesthetic," he nevertheless urges freedom of expression for black writers (*Dark and Feeling* 134). In this sense *Reflex* is a good example of radical fictional experimentation with an underlying theme urging African American expression. It demands to be met on its own terms, which suggests that the key to all reality is elusive and that fiction has a life of its own separate from mimesis or realism.

The novel's pastiche construction, akin to the abstract canvas, forces a new perspective. The text is continuously in a state of rebirth, denying the past, living immediately in the present. Like *Mumbo Jumbo,* it replaces linear time with circular time, always coming back to the essential elements of its own existence. The reader must engage and interact with the text to derive meaning while questioning the nature of fiction and of reality. In this sense I agree with Bernard Bell, who sees Major's work as able to "extend the experimental tradition of the Afro-American novel [through] exploration of sex and language as a ritualistic rebirth and affirmation of self" (320).

Major also extends the black detective tradition by transforming the four tropes of black detective fiction through his use of double-conscious detection. At its most basic level *Reflex* attacks Euro-American control of literary genres and standards of literary excellence, forcing a new awareness of how cultural identity is taught and perceived. Out of this comes a new sense of self and renewal of identity. Stefano Tani, in *The Doomed Detective*, sees the duality of construction/destruction as at the root of the artistic process in Poe's construction of his tales:

> art's process is as much destructive as constructive: to bring back childhood's sense of innocence, beauty, and wonder, to give substance to the artists's dim intuition of what might be or might once have been, the artist violates and destroys what is. (12)

Poe's detective persona, with its essential dualities and complex nature, launched the detective tradition. As we have seen, this sense of self and identity has changed with the development of black detective novels. Major's reduction of detective fiction to the basics of understanding seems to suggest that a new approach to perception and the nature of learning is necessary. This is particularly important to the notion of black identity in America.

The question of African American identity and how it is expressed in the black detective novel has been a primary thesis of *The Blues Detective*. Major has brought us full circle from the first stirring of this expression of black identity through black detective tropes in Pauline Hopkins's *Hagar's Daughter* to a deconstructive extension of those tropes. By reducing the text to its basic elements, Major forces a reassessment of the four tropes of black detection. He uses double-conscious detection experiments to present an alternative viewpoint of the African American experience. He infuses language with new power through radical alterations of conventional detective plots and the detective persona. By so doing he recapitulates and signifies on the very nature of the black detective and the detective text. Through an emphasis on the poetic nature of language, he stresses the beauties of sensual experience and the special artistic perceptions of black Americans. Such elementary reduction also urges a renewal or new beginning, as does the circular time frame of the novel. Bell recognizes this abstract continuity and extension of tradition when he writes that Major attempts "to resolve Afro-American double-consciousness by the subordination of social truth and power for blacks to the expressionistic truth and freedom of the artist" (320). Major presents the viewpoint of a black American in a radically different way. By example, he stresses the importance of an autonomous and distinct African American poetic identity, which opens the way for other black writers to attempt their own revolutionary reinterpretation of African American consciousness. Major's ultimate achievement is his indication of new possibilities of reconstruction for African American artists.

In conclusion, both Reed and Major have advanced African American detective fiction into the postmodern era. Both writers have used the primary conventions of detective fiction in postmodern texts that, in the very nature of their self-reflexivity, signify on the tradition. Furthermore, Reed and Major recognize the four tropes of black detective fiction while transforming them with highly original double-conscious narrative and structural ploys. These creative reinterpretations once again confirm the inexhaustible potential for renewal and affirmation within the black detective tradition as well as in African American culture as a whole.

Afterword

*T*he *Blues Detective* has focused on early African American writers of detective fiction, tracing their influence on each other and the creation of a black detective tradition that extends from the beginning of the twentieth century into the postmodern period. By using vernacular criticism that examines African American and Afrocentric worldviews, I have attempted to analyze black detective writing through the use of four tropes: black detective personas, double-conscious detection, black vernaculars, and hoodoo. In the process I have shown how African American detective writers were consciously transforming detective formulas for particular social, political, and cultural ends. The Euro-American detective form proved extremely useful to black writers, who used the popular culture genre to comment effectively on issues of race, class, and gender. In particular, the transformation of both classical and hardboiled detective conventions by black writers consistently created a new type of detective fiction defined by an insistent inclusion of African American cultural expressions in the text. From early in the history of the genre, black writers have made considerable and consistent use of detective fiction, and for the most part—George Schuyler being a notable exception—they have been interested in experimenting with detective themes for culturally specific ends.

We have seen how black writers used a popular Euro-Americentric literary form to help define a distinctive African American culture. As the earliest known writer of black detective fiction, Pauline Hopkins in *Hagar's Daughter* laid the groundwork that subsequent African American authors were to follow. Her radical transformation of the detective persona from the traditional white, male, middle-class model presented in Euro-American detective novels to a black, female, working-class character establishes the importance of race, gender, and class in the black detective novel. Furthermore, Hopkins showed how black cultural identity could be the definitive theme of black detective fiction, enhancing the crime text in consistent ways. Through her persuasive reexamination of detective tropes, she showed how double-conscious detection redefined the detective's role and stressed the importance of black cultural values and vision. By writing a novel about passing in pre-and post-Civil War southern society, Hopkins also showed how masking and disguise, typical conventions of detective fiction, could be amplified through double-conscious detection. Hopkins demonstrated that the detective novel, traditionally a novel of suspense and intrigue, might be reworked by African Americans in meaningful sociopolitical ways. Through extensive use of black vernaculars and positive references to hoodoo as a shared black worldview, Hopkins created a detective novel that informed its readers about important aspects of African American culture. Her use of the black vernaculars of music, language, and food, coupled with her emphasis on the community values of family and shared black identity, enlarged the capacities of the detective novel in ways not seen before. Her groundbreaking experiments established the bedrock of the black detective tradition while reinforcing the overall perception that African Americans transform literary formulas for cultural survival.

J. E. Bruce, a black author with a highly developed sense of racial and political identity, wrote at about the same time as Pauline Hopkins. His novel *The Black Sleuth,* serialized in the black periodical press, added a new dimension to the black detective tradition through the inclusion of an Afrocentric worldview that celebrated African culture and consciousness. His strong African characters, with their positive sense of family and community, served to create a recognizable and admirable African past for African Americans. Bruce used the formulas of detective fiction to contrast this Afrocentric worldview with a racist Euro-American hegemony. He successfully extended African American self-identification beyond the confines of America and in the process showed how blacks could use the detective persona to illustrate the inherent intelligence, nobility, and pride of their people. His emphasis on the positive aspects of black identity coupled with a militant attitude toward black self-expression, dignity, and survival brought a new awareness of black nationalism to the detective novel. Following Hopkins's lead, Bruce also indicated ways in which a black detective character, with a heightened sense of self and double-conscious awareness, could use the trope of double-conscious detection to advantage. Coupled with the use of masquerade and disguise, Bruce's detective utilized the double-conscious detection trickster theme to amplify the traditional detective tropes of masking. Overall, Bruce's serial novel shows that black writers understood that detective fiction was a useful tool for black expression at a very early date in detective fiction history.

Rudolph Fisher was instrumental in further developing the black detective tradition in his novel *The Conjure Man Dies*. This was the first black detective novel to use all black characters and to take place in the black environment of Harlem. Fisher extended the use of all four of the black detective tropes in his socially satirical novel. His variation on the locked-room murder mystery contains elements of both the classical detective tradition and the modern police procedural. However, Fisher innovatively transformed these tropes by experimenting with the detective persona, creating a novel with an official homicide detective, an unofficial doctor detective, and a split detective persona of a working-class black and a hoodoo priest. In using more than one detective, Fisher compounds the black detective persona, demonstrating how black detective writers can rework and remove themselves from the traditional Euro-Americentric model.

Fisher also showed that the black detective novel could present issues of race and class. He was not afraid to critique all levels of class in black Harlem while generally presenting an urban cityscape infused with elements of black pride and community. Fisher laces his novel with references to black vernaculars and urban rituals, initiating the use of a *blackground* in detective texts that introduces the reader to varied aspects of African American culture while structurally adhering to the detective story format. However, Fisher's main achievement was his clever demonstration of how hoodoo elements might be used in a novel to reinforce black pride. His black conjure man, who was African by birth and American by choice, melded the Afrocentric themes initiated by Bruce with an African American viewpoint. Fisher also amplified the mystical spirituality of hoodoo and conjure, first seen in Hopkins, in a concentrated worldview. The trickster qualities of his conjure man continue the double-conscious detection trope. Fisher deserves his reputation as a primary black detective writer who introduced Harlem Renaissance themes to black detective fiction.

Chester Himes proved to be the most prolific black writer in detective fiction. With the recent posthumous publication of *Plan B* (1993), Himes is responsible for ten detective novels. His creation of the hardboiled detectives Coffin Ed Johnson and Grave Digger Jones provided a vehicle for Himes's exploration of race, class, and social conditions in the black community of Harlem. Himes worked a consistent African American viewpoint and blackground into his novels. Seen as a group, his ten novels provide a wide-ranging review of changing African American behavior and developments in the black community. Himes refuses to fossilize the characterizations of his detectives or to use formulas in his detective plots. The progression of his novels from *For Love of Imabelle* to *Plan B* presents an overview of African American social and political conditions in Harlem. As Coffin Ed and Grave Digger progress toward ineffectuality, frustrated idealism, and eventual death, Himes's plots also mirror the disintegrating social fabric of the community around them. His fractured plots pitch white against black and black against black in an increasingly chaotic world of exaggerated political dimensions.

The social satire cleverly alluded to in the signifying asides of his two detectives in the early novels grows increasingly bitter and vituperative in the last few works. Violence becomes increasingly less comic and more politically motivated until *Plan B,* when black revolution erupts and catapults the community into total bloody chaos. From his first novel Himes shows how the detective plot could be used for political satire. Perhaps his most important discovery was that violence, commonly used for dramatic effect in hardboiled detective fiction, might be applied to African American political ends. All of the novels pinpoint racism as lying at the root of the disorder in the black community, a racism so diffuse and debilitating that blacks end up fighting blacks as whites continue the racist practices that threaten black existence. By the second-to-last novel Coffin Ed and Grave Digger are incapacitated by a systematic repression engineered by their white superiors; by the last novel they are simply useless tools who end up being killed. No longer can they keep the peace in Harlem. And while they are reduced to ineffective characters in the text the politically violent wing of some obscure black nationalist group plunges Harlem into violent revolution.

Himes established the black detective novel as a vehicle for social critique, depicting a madness in Harlem that cannot be cured except by a radical realignment of moral values in the United States. In the process, Himes further demonstrated how important blackground was to African American detective fiction. His descriptions of Harlem illustrate the sociopolitical themes of his novels while his fascinating interiors of bars, nightclubs, and soul-food restaurants depict the exotic and culturally specific environs of the black community. In the end the double-conscious detection of his two detectives proves fruitless in solving the more endemic disease of racism.

Himes proved to be a valuable predecessor for Ishmael Reed's reinterpretation of the detective novel. Reed acknowledges that Himes showed him how to use the detective format for African American themes, but Reed went much further than Himes in his experimental use of the form. Reed almost abolishes both the classical and hardboiled varieties of the detective novel, retaining only the useful structural and iconic portions of detective fiction for his satirical novel *Mumbo Jumbo*. Reed's interest in social satire and historical revisionism displaces the traditional detective format, leaving only the armature of detective fiction on which he hangs the most consistent exploration of African American themes in black detective fiction to date. Reed uses the detective formula to present elements of his Neo-HooDoo worldview and expands elements of the mystery to a metaphysical level. As an affirmative re-creation of African American identity, Neo-HooDoo effectively represents Reed's black-consciousness worldview while at the same time utilizing the four tropes of black detection in a postmodern novel of experimentation. Continuing the theme of detective transformation, Reed's PaPa LaBas is a double-conscious trickster detective who uses his Neo-HooDoo powers to confound white attempts to destroy the black race. His far-ranging powers connect him spiritually to ancient hoodoo themes while presenting a revisionist interpretation of history along Afrocentric lines. Reed confirms the importance of black vernaculars to the healthy creation of a black culture. His greatest contribution to the black detective novel is in showing how the African American hoodoo trope can be innovatively transformed to support social and political ends.

Whereas Reed almost abolishes the detective formula through his alteration of traditional detective tropes, Clarence Major effectively continues the transformation by writing a novel that critiques the very process of writing. In *Reflex and Bone Structure* Major retains only the barest minimum of detective allusions in his novel while forging new connections between reader and text. *Reflex and Bone Structure* challenges conventional notions of time and history while continuing postmodern experimentation as an anti-detective novel. Like Himes and Reed before him, Major contradicts the primary detective conventions, particularly in his refusal to have a positive resolution to the story. Harking back to Poe's theory of ratiocination, Major writes a metafictional novel that suggests the mind cannot solve everything. He uses the detective format to write a novel about perception and language while critiquing the novelistic conventions of characterization, plot, and predictable motivation. Utilizing his background in modern art and his interest in the poetics of prose, Major infuses his complex postmodern novel with African American sensibilities against a backdrop of indeterminant chaos. The black detective novel in this case questions the nature of reality and the function of the written word. Major reverts to the traditional hard-boiled first-person narration but complicates the objective stance of that style with a highly subjective, self-referential, postmodern experimental format. Major's book is written by a nameless narrator whose depiction of crime and detection questions the very nature of perception itself and in the process reworks the tropes of African American detective fiction. Both Reed and Major use double-conscious hoodoo narrative and structural ploys in self-reflexive novels that signify on the black detective tradition.

A recent revival of interest in the detective novel by black writers provides an interesting closure to my study of the African American detective novel. Furthermore, black detective authors have gained a measure of respectability and recognition in the field as readership and acceptance of black detectives has become more diverse. This is especially true concerning black female authors. At the same time these authors have continued a tradition by maintaining an African American cultural viewpoint. Some of these contemporary authors and their books are: Dolores Komo's *Clio Browne Private Investigator* (1988); Barbara Neely's *Blanche on the Lam* (1992) and *Blanche among the Talented Tenth* (1994); Eleanor Taylor Bland's *Dead Time* (1992) and *Slowburn* (1993); Nikki Baker's *In the Game* (1991), *The Lavender House Murder* (1992), and *The Long Goodbyes* (1993);

Valerie Wilson Wesley's *When Death Comes Stealing* (1995); and Walter Mosley's four novels, *Devil in a Blue Dress* (1990), *A Red Death* (1991), *White Butterfly* (1992), and *Black Betty* (1994).

After the publication of Pauline Hopkins's *Hagar's Daughter* in (1901–2), which introduces an amateur black female detective, there are no known African American women writing novels with black female detectives until the publication of Dolores Komo's *Clio Browne* (1988). There is a Chicana detective named Kat, short for Maria Katerina Lorca Guerrera Alcazar, who appears in M. F. Beal's feminist detective novel *Angel Dance,* published in 1977. Kathleen Klein in *The Woman Detective: Gender and Genre* (1988) calls this groundbreaking novel "the earliest of what has become a subgenre of the eighties—the explicitly feminist detective novel usually published by a women's press" (216). Although it is not my express interest in this chapter to discuss the fertile and ever-growing genre of female writers writing novels with female detectives, it is important to note that black female detectives have appeared in print almost concurrently with the renewed interest in female detectives as a whole. It is also important to remember that even though there are no known black female detectives between Hopkins's 1901 novel and Komo's 1988 novel there were a number of black women who were consciously employing the strategies of detective fiction in their more mainstream novels. These writers and novels would include Toni Morrison's *Song of Solomon,* Ann Petry's *The Narrows,* and Gayl Jones's *Eva's Man.*

The history of female detectives has a literary tradition stretching back to 1864 in England with the publication of *The Female Detective* edited by Andrew Forrester and introducing Mrs. Gladden, a police detective, and the appearance of W. Stephen Hayward's *The Experience of a Lady Detective* featuring the female detective Mrs. Paschal. Although both these books have female detectives they are generally considered to be part of the detective memoir category. The first authentic appearance of a female detective in a detective novel written by a woman occurs in United States with the publication of Seeley Regester's *Dead Letter: An American Romance* (1864). This was followed by Anna Katherine Green's *Leavenworth Case* (1878). Both preceded by a number of years the first appearance of Conan Doyle's detective Sherlock Holmes in 1887. The female detective under various guises continued to appear in print throughout the late nineteenth and the early part of the twentieth century. Practioners of the genre include, in Britain Dorothy Sayers, Patricia Wentworth, and Agatha Christie, and, in United States, Mary Roberts Rinehart, Mignon G. Eberhart, and Amanda Cross. The above are only a few names from a field that is extremely large and diverse. While the tradition of the female detective is long and varied, critics such as Kathleen Klein have found much to debate concerning their effectiveness in challenging the male model of the detective. One of the primary ways in which detective authors, both female and male, failed to present convincingly a new type of female detective was by creating a split between the female detective and gender issues. As Klein states, there is no positive correlation between the detective's gender and her professional experience (23). One common pitfall of female authors was modeling their female detectives directly on male models in the genre, giving their heroines similar attributes and traits. "Modeling the female protagonist on a male prototype establishes the conditions for her failure as either investigator or woman—or both" (Klein 162). Another fatal ploy that sabotaged the effective creation of a unique female detective was infusing the detective novel with a typical marriage plot in which the female detective falls in love and gets married, often to a male detective, and consequently gives up her career. The difficulty of having a woman work within the system without co-opting her own feminist principles is one of the great problems of female detective novels. In the early novels the female detective commonly restores the dominant male social superiority and overall male hegemony at the conclusion of the case. Concerning the early period of female detective writing Klein states: "Less important as detective novels, these novels function as cautionary tales for readers about the importance of middle class respectability and its rewards" (79).

Other critics, including Maureen T. Reddy in *Sisters in Crime: Feminism and the Crime Novel* (1988) and Gloria A. Biamonte in her dissertation "Detection and the Text: Reading Three American Women of Mystery" (1991), use greater flexibility in examining early female detective texts, suggesting that they subvert the genre and critique the dominant male viewpoint in indirect but no less meaningful ways. All critics seem to agree that the publication in the 1970s in United States of a number of female detective novelists such as Sue Grafton, Marcia Muller, and Sara Paretsky brought new life to the genre. "Not until the 1970s is there a consciously articulated response to social change by women writers who challenge the sexist assump-tions of hero formation" (Klein 5). These contemporary female novel-ists consciously work within the traditions of the detective genre, predominately the hardboiled school, "exposing the genre's funda-mental conservatism and challenging the reader to rethink his/her assumptions" (Reddy 2). Klein, who focuses mainly on paid profes-sional female detectives, also mentions there are female authors who use amateur women detectives to "consciously and carefully tell women's stories through feminocentric plots and structures which challenge the generic restrictions" (229). These would include such writers as Amanda Cross, Barbara Wilson, Valerie Miner, and Bar-bara Paul.

Contemporary African American female detective writers in United States work out of two traditions—the extended tradition of male and female detective writing and the more circumscribed tradi-tion of black detective writing, as I have outlined in the previous chapters of *The Blues Detective*.

Dolores Komo's *Clio Browne, Private Investigator* revises the male white model of the private investigator by introducing a contempo-rary African American female who inherits a detective agency, the Browne Bureau of Investigation, from her father, who started it in 1947. Clio calls him "the first black private investigator in the city of St. Louis—maybe in the whole country" (2). Clio's pride in her family is evident from the first pages of the novel. She informs us that she kept her maiden name when married, that she has a son who is a fighter pilot in the navy, and that she lives with and is strongly attached to her mother. Her husband, one of St. Louis's first black police officers, was killed in the line of duty. Clio Browne is highly educated and she displays her B.A. and M.A. degrees proudly on the walls of her small midtown office. She mentions more than once her desire to write a definitive history of the black investigator in the United States.

The novel is a comic blend of mishaps and coincidences that echoes variations on the hardboiled novel albeit in a somewhat lackluster manner. Like other hardboiled detectives, Clio Browne has a private practice and accepts cases as a paid professional. She has a female secretary and an office without the modern convenience of comput-ers. But unlike other hardboiled detectives she carries no gun, has no pernicious vices except a desire for fatty foods and ice cream and a fashion/money-consciousness that she tries to keep in check. The issues of money, class, and race enter the story early. On one hand, Clio drives an old Honda Civic when not using the bus, shops for bargain sales, and worries whether a parking attendant will charge her more than two dollars a day if she moves her car. On the other hand she eyes expensive Italian shoes, recognizes exquisite perfume, and envies large limousines. She takes on the case of Serena Scutter-Paschal, from one of St. Louis' richest families, in part because of the large ten thousand dollar retainer and her speculative eye for jewelry (Serena's large Russian-legacy Miroff diamond has been stolen).

In fact, the novel revolves around a series of intentional contrasts. Serena Scutter-Paschal's family, the Scutters, are one of St. Louis' founding families and started their way to fortune "trading beads for beaver skins with the local Indian tribes" (7). Clio informs us that her own family also had its share in St. Louis' history: "Only they had been bought and sold on that great block of limestone under the rotunda of the old courthouse just down the street from Clio's office" (8). The contrasts between the two women are both obvious and subtle. Clio Browne has a black natural while Serena has flaxen hair done in a flawless wedge. Clio's business card is tan with bold brown letters while Serena's is white with an Old English script. Serena's limousine is parked illegally in front of Clio's office protected by a chauffeur against tickets, while Clio's tiny import has been ticketed and impounded for being in the same place.

As a private investigator she has a small, shoddy but clean office and an often absent secretary. She also has a highly developed sense of morality which prevents her from getting involved in domestic cases. She is hired by Serena to gather dirt on Angel Moon, Serena's son's girlfriend who has the heirloom Miroff ring that Serena wants back. Clio's sympathies immediately lie with Angel Moon against the Scutter-Paschals' and when she finds Angel brutally murdered with her ring finger cut off, Clio pursues the case for personal reasons.

Clio solves the case through a combination of coincidence, dogged determination, and good luck. The important aspects of this rather mundane mystery novel lie in the establishment of the detective persona. In this novel the black female detective continues in many ways a tradition in black detective writing as a whole. For example, Clio Browne uses her blackness as part of her detective trade. She often masks herself as a maid to gain entry into houses and she lapses into black dialect when the occasion demands. She is well aware of her difference from detective heroes of the past like Sherlock Holmes, whom she often refers to in contrast. She does not use the ratiocination of classical detectives. Instead she works from gut responses. "In her heart she knew it was true and her gut feeling confirmed it, but what kind of detective relies on human organ responses to determine someone's guilt" (22).

Although without a current boyfriend, Clio Browne, like other black detectives we have studied, works with a group that includes white male detectives who help her out. She is content to be single and speaks highly of her dead husband. She enlists her secretary Tanya and Tanya's boyfriend, Jesse, to help her on the case. Clio Browne is very family oriented and depends on her mother for good down home cooking and solace and support. Her mother, in fact, gets involved in the case by sheltering the prime suspect without Browne's knowledge. Although Tanya and her mother Mrs. Browne account for her closest relationships in the novel, Clio does have male friends, including the white police detective Felix Frayne. *Clio Browne, Private Investigator* is a women-centered novel that mildly criticizes male behavior, both black and white, but saves its strongest critique for white privilege and prejudice. With deft asides Clio informs us of how she and her husband broke the color line by moving to a white neighborhood and how in cases of police investigation the color of one's skin often determined who was believed. As the first black female detective novel in the contemporary period, *Clio Browne* introduces us to a female black perspective in a southern environment that is independent and assimilationist. References to black food and black music and language are made throughout the novel. Written in the third person, it is an important contribution to the tradition of black detective fiction.

Barbara Neely has written two novels featuring Blanche White as an amateur detective. Both *Blanche on the Lam* and *Blanche among the Talented Tenth* are murder mysteries in which Blanche gets involved by circumstance. Blanche White is a domestic who cleans and cares for wealthy white families. In both novels she is not a professional detective although she feels that her occupation has given her the observational skills of one. The two novels show the development in Blanche's consciousness as she moves from a southern environment in the first novel to a sheltered and elite black community in Maine in the second.

Blanche on the Lam provides a contemporary counterpoint to *Hagar's Daughter*, the first novel discussed in this work, because here too the female protagonist uses her position and her blackness for purposes of detection. The novel represents an important viewpoint in the black detective novel because it tells the whole story from the black maid's perspective. Neely's book might be compared to the film *Alice Adams* (1935), which featured Hattie McDaniel as a scene-stealing, gum-chewing maid who subtly criticized her white, upper-class employers. Blanche expands the limited role of Hattie McDaniel's character into a fully developed figure who comments scathingly on the progressive disintegration of southern white aristocracy. There are many interesting similarities between the black female detective figures of Clio Browne and Blanche White. Like Clio, Blanche finds herself pitted against a southern white aristocratic family. Clio and Blanche are both closely connected to their families and unabashedly express their love and emotional bonds in the first pages of the novels. Both are single women with family ties and close girlfriends, but neither has a permanent relationship with a male. Clio and Blanche, coming out of a working-class environment, express knowledge of black culture, African history, and women's rights that is predominately self taught.

In the first novel Blanche White hides out from the police by posing as a domestic in a white household. In the second, *Blanche among the Talented Tenth,* Blanche is on holiday with her dead sister's two adopted children. Amber Cove, the exclusive Maine resort which is the scene of the novel, is a black aristocratic community where issues of class and gender play a major role. There are no white people in this novel, but the gradations of skin color among the vacationers provide ample opportunity for an insidious internal prejudice and the resort is a microcosm of the class and color antagonism in black society at large. Along with this critique of class consciousness based on color, the novel provides a running commentary on relationships between black males and females. Blanche is a confirmed single person whose ex-boyfriend marries someone else after Blanche refuses him. Blanche's mistrust of Stu, a handsome black man who courts her, provides an important subtext of the plot. Blanche is strongly critical of men in both books and black and white males wither under her scathing attack. Blanche's best female friend, Ardell, and a hoodoo priestess, Madame Rosa, are her most important influences. Blanche retains only a slight hope in the possible success of heterosexual relationships and she has no interest whatever in having children. Nonetheless, she is a good mother to the nephew and niece she has adopted. Blanche is also much less interested in assimilation than Clio Browne, devoting her attention to the black community and leaning toward a black separatist viewpoint. She also voices strong support for black culture and believes in the power of hoodoo and its spiritual connection to ancestors and Africa.

Clio and Blanche are similar in their lower socioeconomic status and their frugality. Both detectives rely on their mothers for financial and moral support. They take buses often and are not adverse to shopping for sales. More interesting, both women detectives disguise themselves as domestic help in the pursuit of their cases. Clio reflects on "how invisible the maid became as secrets were openly discussed or classified materials were left carelessly about" (9). Blanche actually earns a living as a domestic despite her mother's disapproval. Blanche sees a connection between her domestic status and the folk tradition of African American culture. "Men like Nate and women like her were the people, the folks, the mud from which the rest were made. It was their hands and blood and sweat that had built everything . . ." (*Blanche on the Lam* 149). It is this pride in her background and black skin that provides the anchor for her personality as well as the fulcrum for her investigative behavior. In *Blanche among the Talented Tenth,* murder and blackmail provide the motivations for plot development in the novel, but the story has more to do with social frictions among African American presented in an insular and intense environment. The novel skewers false behavior among blacks, both male and female, who see a hierarchy of social position based on skin color and occupation. From her viewpoint, at the bottom of the social totem pole, Blanche provides a sweeping perspective and an incisive social commentary, which indicate new ways that the detective novel can be used to explore contemporary issues of African American culture.

Both Dolores Komo and Barbara Neely continue the African American detective tradition by altering and extending the detective persona with black female consciousness. Their novels also use black vernaculars liberally, constantly apply double-conscious detective techniques, and make some use of hoodoo awareness in rounding out an African American viewpoint.

Three other black female novelists, Nikki Baker, Eleanor Taylor Bland, and Valerie Wilson Wesley are not quite as successful in this capacity. Although these authors are supportive of African American culture, their novels are more concerned with female identity in the changing sociopolitical climate of contemporary United States. Nikki Baker has written three detective novels featuring Virginia Kelly, a proud African American lesbian, as an amateur detective. The three novels take place in Chicago, Provincetown, and the small midwestern town of Blue River, Indiana, where Virginia Kelly was brought up. Virginia lives in the fast lane of contemporary urban life and works as a well-paid investments options broker for a Chicago firm. Her first-person narratives are told from a distinctive viewpoint that outlines contemporary issues of sexuality and class for a well-educated and ambitious black women. Virginia Kelly is a liberated, black female involved in an on-again, off-again relationship with Emily. Amidst numerous affairs and interactions with other women and a few men (mostly white), Virginia struggles to define her place in American society, first as a lesbian and then as a black women. Virginia leans toward a lesbian separatist attitude, yet hides her sexuality in her work place and fights with her parents who cannot accept her choice. Less crime novels than social critiques, Baker's three novels explore the insular world of lesbian politics in explicitly sexual and gay terms. At the same time they present an interesting picture of the corporate world, contemporary materialism, and a growing awareness and need for more avenues for the expression of spirituality, anti-materialism, and African American identity in a predominately white environment.

Eleanor Taylor Bland's two novels feature Marti MacAlister, a Chicago homicide detective. Marti is a liberated black female, a widow with two children, who has struggled to attain recognition and appreciation from her professional associates as well as from the people she deals with as a homicide detective. Marti has a male white partner who provides an effective counterpoint to her black female perspective. Both novels are written in the third person and reinterpret police procedural formats by introducing contemporary social themes filtered through the consciousness of an African American policewoman. Likewise, Valerie Wilson Wesley's *When Death Comes Stealing* concerns a single mother, Tamara Hayle, who is a private investigator in Newark, New Jersey. This contemporary murder mystery deals with African American society, written from a black female perspective.

Walter Mosley's *Devil in a Blue Dress* (1990), *Red Death* (1991), *White Butterfly* (1992), and *Black Betty* (1994), confirm the continuity of the male black detective tradition and provide the best example of how that tradition has developed in the last quarter of the twentieth century. His four novels feature the detective Easy Rawlins and take place predominantly in the Watts area of Los Angeles. Mosley has consciously set out to write a series of detective novels that span a historical period of black development in the United States. Each novel takes place in a specific year, 1948, 1953, 1958, and 1961, and depicts the changing historical and cultural milieu. At the same time, each novel shows the progression of Easy Rawlins's self-development, as the detective reveals more and more about himself and his growing black consciousness. His personality in some ways mirrors the changes in society around him. The novels feature some of the same characters in an ever-evolving scene in Watts. Easy Rawlins is a black veteran of World War II who is part of the black southern migration to the West Coast. He becomes a detective because his blackness allows him entry into certain areas of society where whites have little access. Easy is an amateur detective who turns semiprofessional as the books progress. He works for money but does not retain an office nor does he have any official status as a detective. His first-person narration harks back to the heyday of hardboiled detective fiction, yet his character retains important elements of the black detective tradition. Contrary to most hardboiled fiction, this detective's personal life and connection to the black community are integral to the progression of the plot. In the first novel Easy is a bachelor with a shady past and a drinking habit. In the third story Easy is married with a daughter and son. The son is adopted and is a character from the first novel. By the end of the novel Easy is separated and Easy Rawlins's former affair with the wife of one of his best friends has an important function to the plot. Easy's struggle for identity through social and political associations in the black community becomes an important theme of the novels. His personal life is not static as is the case in most hardboiled detective novels.

This extension of the black detective persona continues a tradition I have outlined in *The Blues Detective*. Mosley effectively comments on the flux of black American life without sacrificing important tropes of the detective tradition. His cast of black characters and a growing sophisticated perception of black consciousness cleverly reinterpret double-conscious detective themes. Mosley also has an acute eye for black vernacular detail. His descriptions of the bars and clubs of Watts are reminiscent of Himes's interiors while they concentrate the reader's attention on such vernacular elements as language, food, music, and religion.

Finally, Komo, Baker, Bland, Neely, and Mosley show that the black detective tradition continues as a viable force in contemporary detective fiction. The black female authors apply new varieties of expression to the detective novel, making social statements influenced by both a feminist and an African American consciousness. In the best of these books the authors emphasize the survival skills of black females in contemporary culture. All of these authors demonstrate how the primary figures of a black female and a black male detective persona, initiated by Hopkins and Bruce at the beginning of the century, still exert an influence on black detective writers in the modern period. In fact, the popularity of black detective fiction continues to grow, as witnessed by President Bill Clinton's recent purchase of an Easy Rawlins novel.

In summary, I hope to have demonstrated in *The Blues Detective* how black detective fiction as a tradition has grown through a common sharing and reworking of themes and tropes. Blacks challenged the limited use of the detective form and showed ways in which it could be used. Black detective fiction in this sense reinforces Henry Louis Gates's point concerning repetition and continuity through a series of texts as integral to the African American literary tradition. This tradition established a number of important points about black detective fiction, including a refutation of the accepted view that blacks rely solely on Euro-American culture for identity. Black detective fiction shows that the African past has an influence on the African American present. It shows that blacks were not completely fragmented and destroyed as a group when brought to America and that they nurtured a culture that was important to their survival. Black detective writers learned from each other and kept alive in their succession of works important themes that speak specifically to and about black culture in the United States.

The works I have studied range from an early examination and critique of society during the Civil War period to novels that reflect political concerns that kept pace with historical events, such as black nationalism and Black Power. Furthermore, black detective fiction has proven to be an important contribution to detective fiction as a whole. By showing ways in which detective fiction can challenge sociopolitical viewpoints, black detective fiction has opened up the form and widened its thematic concerns. Finally, black detective fiction suggests that the values of black perception are important aspects of the detective process. Black detective fiction acknowledges the continuous regeneration of the African American presence in United States culture by celebrating black consciousness and black cultural expressions.

Notes

Introduction

1. The terms "detective" and "mystery" are almost interchangeable when applied to genre works. Generally, the term "detective" connotes a work in which a detective is actually part of the cast of characters. "Mystery" is a more universal term for genre works that use the typical conventions of suspense, action, physical danger, and intrigue; a detective may or may not be part of the plot. I use the term "detective" loosely to describe the whole genre of what is commonly called mystery/suspense fiction. This would include all the aspects of literary works that contain elements of mystery/suspense and detective conventions.

2. It must be noted here that there is one black author who wrote black detective fiction with a series of black detectives that I have chosen not to examine. George Schuyler (1895–1977), best known for his novel *Black No More* (1931), wrote six detective short stories for the *Pittsburgh Courier* during the years 1933–39. These stories were published under his own name as well as under the pseudonyms William Stockton, Samuel I. Brooks, and Rachel Call. After reviewing this detective fiction, I found that Schuyler's work proves the rule of African American detective tropes by way of exception. Schuyler's detective fiction does feature a series of black male detectives, but they hardly break new ground in African American detective personas, as they are usually "tall, powerful and handsome" with no other defining characteristics. The stories themselves are routinely executed in the classical detective mode in the most elementary fashion. Schuyler wrote these stories without a modicum of the satire, comic relief, or insight into black life that make his novel *Black No More* so interesting. Some of the stories take place in Harlem but add nothing to the depiction of that community or its culture. Most troublesome is Schuyler's negative depiction of aspects of African American and African culture. In "The Beast of Broadhurst Avenue: A Gripping Tale of Adventure in the Heart of Harlem" (*Pittsburgh Courier,* Mar. 3, 1934-May 19, 1934), Schuyler, writing as Samuel I. Brooks, describes a hoodoo ceremony as "rigmarole," full of "grotesqueness."

He tells us that an African tribe, the Guro, were "recently cannibals" and that an African sculpture was an "amazingly ugly African image about 3 feet high." The evil professor of the story, trying to transplant an African American brain to the skull of a great dog, says, "Yes, the female Negro brain because of its small size was best adapted for my purposes." A complete list of Schuyler's short fiction published in the *Courier* is given in the reprinted issue of Schuyler's novel *Black Empire* (1991).

3. By "worldview" I mean a philosophical and socioreligious awareness of the affirmative as well as negative qualities of one's culture in relation to the rest of society and the world. The term "Euro-American" or "Euro-Americentric" is used to refer to literary structures, philosophical worldviews, and moral judgments based on white European and American models. I use "Afrocentric" in the broad sense of the term, suggesting the importance of African cultural attributes and worldviews to African American perspectives and the direct use or mention of Africa, Africans, or Africanisms in the text. For an interesting discussion of Afrocentrism, see *Newsweek*, Sept. 23, 1991, in particular the articles by Molefi Kete Asante and Henry Louis Gates, Jr.

4. This quotation is from a current literary magazine called the *Hungry Mind Review*, no. 17 (Spring 1991), in an article by Gerald Early, entitled "Rhythm-a-nings: Two Notes towards a Definition of Multiculturalism" (10). To find such a quote in a literary review in an article written by an educated black man seems strangely perverse, considering all the recent critical work done by black writers to prove just the opposite.

5. This language creation is a process that continues in black culture. The recent evolution of rap music is a case in point. See the *New York Times* arts section for Feb. 2, 1992, pp. 8–9, for an article by John Russel called "Rap, the New Message."

6. There are any number of essays and articles on African American music. However, for immediate emotional delivery I suggest James Baldwin's "Of the Sorrow Songs: The Cross of Redemption," originally published in the *New Edinburgh Review*, Aug. 1979, and republished in *Views on Black American Music*, no. 2 (Amherst: University of Massachusetts, 1984). Also in that same issue is "The Afro-American Musician: Messengers of a Unique Sensibility in Western Culture" by Playthell G. Benjamin, in which he writes: "No single development in the history of modern culture surpasses—both in artistic achievement and cultural effect—that of the musical tradition created by the Afro-American musician" (13).

7. Zora Neale Hurston was one of the first anthropologists to recognize, as she puts it in *The Sanctified Church*, the way "the American Negro has done wonders to the English language" (51). She sees the greatest contribution to the language in "(1) the use of metaphor and simile; (2) the use of the double descriptive; (3) the use of verbal nouns"

(51). But this is not the only way blacks influenced American English. Robert Farris Thompson in *Flash of the Spirit* writes about the adaptation of African words into black vernacular language: "More important than the impact of Ki-Kongo on the languages of blacks throughout the Americas, though, is the influence of Kongo civilization on their philosophic and visual traditions" (105).

1. The Paradigmatic Gesture

1. "Among the thirty top best-sellers from 1895 to 1965, seven were by Spillane. Only such super best-sellers as Dr. Spock, *Peyton Place, Gone with the Wind*, and *The Carpetbaggers*, have exceeded the sales of *I, the Jury*, and *The Big Kill*. Such superb hardboiled stories as Chandler's *Farewell, My Lovely* and Hammett's *The Maltese Falcon* have sold just over a million copies, while Spillane's books average four to five million" (Cawelti 183). Also, see Carolyn Heilbrun's "Keep Your Eye on Whodunit: The Mysterious Appeal of the Mystery," *Harper's Bazaar*, Nov. 1985, 200.

2. A discussion of the origins of the rogue or *picaresque* novel and its relation to crime fiction is beyond my ability here. There are many good works on the subject—for example, Michael McKeon's *Origins of the English Novel, 1600–1740* (1987). Also, my unpublished essay, "Moll Flanders: Mistress of Words," discusses Defoe's *Moll Flanders* in relation to Mikhail Bakhtin's theory of narrative discourse in the novel.

3. There are a number of important histories of detective fiction, including Howard Haycraft's *Murder for Pleasure, The Life and Times of the Detective Story* (1941). Alma E. Murch's *Development of the Detective Novel* (1958), and Julian Symons's *Bloody Murder: From the Detective Story to the Crime Novel* (1985). The debate as to what constitutes a detective novel and how far back in literary history one needs to go to find its traces is very complicated and not necessary for this work.

4. H. Bruce Franklin's *Victim as Criminal and Artist* (1978), contains an excellent chapter on criminal narratives, stressing the origins in England and the United States of the popular form; see chap. 4, "A History of Literature by Convicts in America."

5. Two important books on female detectives are Kathleen Gregory Klein's *Woman Detective: Gender and Genre* (1988) and Maureen T. Reddy's *Sisters in Crime: Feminism and the Crime Novel* (1988). See also Jane C. Pennell, "The Female Detective: Pre-and Post-Women's Lib," *Clues*, Fall/Winter (1985); and Gloria A. Biamonte's dissertation, "Detection and the Text: Reading Three American Women of *Mystery*" (University of Massachusetts, 1991). Biamonte's chapter, "The Blurring of Separate Spheres: Renegotiating Boundaries in Seeley Regester's *The Dead Letter*," is particularly interesting on the issue of early American detective writing in relation to female authors.

2. The Tropes of Black Detection

1. For further information on signifying and related speech acts, see Claudia Mitchell-Kernan, "Signifying as a Form of Verbal Art," in *Mother Wit from the Laughing Barrel,* ed. Alan Dundes (1973). See also Roger D. Abrahams, *Talking Black* (1976).

2. For an overview of this subject, see the introduction to David Geherin's *Sons of Sam Spade* (1980).

3. See Dennis Porter's chapter, "Backward Construction and the Art of Suspense," in his *Pursuit of Crime* (24–52). Besides Dennis Porter on this important aspect of detective fiction, see Pierre Macherey's "Front and Back," in his book *A Theory of Literary Production;* and Tzvetan Todorov's "Typology of Detective Fiction," in his *Poetics of Prose.*

3. Early African American Adaptations of Detective Conventions

1. Frankie Bailey's *Out of the Woodpile: Black Characters in Crime and Detective Fiction* (1991) is the first comprehensive look at African American characters as they appear in both English and American detective fiction. It is a primary text for anyone interested in the subject. At the end of the book the author notes that "most of the images of blacks in crime and detective fiction have been created by white writers. Only a few writers who can be identified as black write (or are published) in the genre. Why this is so is a question the author has not been able to answer, but would suggest that black writers may perceive participation in genre fiction as: (a) increasing their marginality as writers and/or (b) too restrictive—although Ishmael Reed in *Mumbo Jumbo* (1972) does use the genre as a vehicle for a discourse on black culture and white racism" (120). Bailey adds to this difficulty somewhat by being vague about whether or not writers are African American; see her directory, "V. Black Detectives in Genre Fiction" (161–64), for a list that includes both white and black writers of detective fiction.

2. The offensive nature of much hardboiled detective fiction in regard to gender is one of the drawbacks of the genre. A historical examination of hardboiled fiction shows the consistency of white, male prejudice until after World War II. Janey Place's article "The Black Widow: Women in Film Noir," in *Women in Film Noir,* ed. Ann Kaplan (1980), is an excellent review of how film noir reflects hardboiled detective patterns of gender discrimination. Recent trends in detective fiction have shown many particularly strong female characters written by females. Also, detectives such as Robert Parker's Spenser suggest a more sensitive male approach. See Biamonte's dissertation, "Detection and the Text," for a detailed overview of female detective novelists.

3. The first known use of the word "stereotype" occurred in the

Colored American, Mar. 4, 1837): "We are written about, preached to, and prayed for, as *Negroes, Africans* and *blacks.* All of which have been stereo typed as names of reproach, and on that account, if no other, are unacceptable." For definitions of stereotype, see the *OED, Webster's Collegiate Dictionary,* and separate glossaries by Abrams. Frankie Bailey relies on William F. Wu's definition of stereotype as published in his book *The Yellow Peril: Chinese American in American Fiction,* 1850– 1940: "the word *stereotype* refers to descriptions of Chinese Americans that . . . are based on race and ethnicity rather than on serious attempts by the author at characterization" (see Bailey xiii).

4. There was also a proliferation of detective magazines and pulps. The first pulp devoted exclusively to detective stories was *Detective Story,* Oct. 5, 1915 (see Goulart 11). Others were *Detective Fiction Weekly, All Star Detective Stories, Best Detective, The Underworld,* and *Ten Detective Aces* (see Goulart 19).

5. Detective fiction was also of interest to and had an influence on other African American writers, including Richard Wright in *Native Son,* Toni Morrison in *Song of Solomon,* Ann Petry in *The Narrows,* and Gayl Jones in *Eva's Man.* Michel Fabre, in *The World of Richard Wright* (1985), details Wright's literary influences, correctly pointing out Wright's fascination with the detective form: "But cheap pulp tales, detective stories, and Sunday supplements attracted him as much as the classics he borrowed from the public library" (3).

6. In my essay delivered at the MLA Annual meeting in Washington, D.C., 1989, "Narrative Discourse in Charles Chesnutt's *The Conjure Woman,*" I attempt a structural analysis of one of Chesnutt's Uncle Julius tales. It is interesting to see how the trickster themes of the Uncle Julius character are amplified and paralleled by the narrative tricks of the author.

7. For the political aesthetics of black periodical literature, see *Propaganda and Aesthetics: The Literary Politics of African American Magazines in the Twentieth Century* (1979), written by Abby Arthur Johnson and Ronald Maberry Johnson. Their chapter 1 is an excellent review of *Colored American,* among other African American magazines, and specifically discusses Pauline Hopkins's contribution as editor and writer. See also Hazel Carby's *Reconstructing Womanhood* (1987).

8. I am greatly indebted to Professor John Gruesser of Kean College of New Jersey for background information on John E. Bruce and for his help in locating a complete copy of *The Black Sleuth* from the New York Public Library's Schomburg Center for Research into Black Culture. The Schomburg possesses the only known copy of this novel culled from microfilm records of *McGirt's Magazine.* Due to the serial nature of the seventeen installments, I follow Professor Gruesser's lead in numbering the pages 1 through 64 for the sake of convenience.

9. John Gruesser personal communication, Dec. 24, 1992.

4. Detective of the Harlem Renaissance: Rudolph Fisher

1. For an intelligent discussion of the concepts of ancestralism and primitivism as they relate to the Harlem Renaissance, see Bell's *Afro-American Novel and Its Tradition* (112–16). See also Robert A. Coles and Diane Isaacs, "Primitivism as a Therapeutic Pursuit," in *The Harlem Renaissance* (1989).

2. Alain Locke's anthology of African American writers and artists, *The New Negro* (1925), was instrumental in gaining recognition for new black writers and artists of the period and awakened interest in African American culture on the part of both whites and blacks. Locke continued to write extensively on African American arts for the rest of his life. For an excellent collection of his essays, see *The Critical Temper of Alain Locke,* ed. Jeffrey Stewart (1983).

3. Langston Hughes wrote many essays about the Harlem Renaissance; see, for example, the collection of Hughes's journals called the Langston Hughes Review. Vol. 4, no. 1 (Spring 1985), contains "The Negro Artist and the Racial Mountain," "Harlem Literati in the Twenties," "The Twenties: Harlem and Its Negritude," and "The Task of the Negro Writer as an Artist."

4. For a comprehensive discussion of African American speech patterns, see William Labov's *Sociolinguistic Patterns* (1972) and Labov "Some Features of the English of Black Americans," in *Varieties of Present-Day English,* ed. Richard W. Bailey and Jay L. Robinson (1973). Another excellent book is Geneva Smitherman's *Talking and Testifying: The Language of Black America* (1986). Among other books and articles dealing with the complicated subject of black English are J. L. Dillard, *Black English;* Sumner Ives, "A Theory of Literary Dialect"; Henry Louis Gates, Jr., "Dis and Dat: Dialect and Descent," in *Figures in Black;* and Tremaine McDowell, "Negro Dialect in the American Novel to 1821."

5. See Kathy J. Ogren, "Controversial Sounds: Jazz Performance as Theme and Language in the Harlem Renaissance," in *The Harlem Renaissance,* which provides an interesting discussion of jazz's position in Harlem Renaissance literature.

6. Often the final recognition scene involves an interpolated narrative of some length. This pattern was established early on in detective fiction. See Michael Atkinson, "Type and Text in *A Study in Scarlet:* Repression and the Textual Unconscious," *Clues,* Spring/Summer 1987. *A Study in Scarlet,* Arthur Conan Doyle's first detective tale, provides an example of an interpolated text that both enhances and redefines the main narrative.

7. As N'Ogo Frimbo the servant plays only an incidental role, all references to Frimbo denote N'gana Frimbo, the conjurer, unless otherwise noted.

8. For an interesting discussion of the concept of Afrocentrism in literature, see Abiola Irele, "Negritude-Literature and Ideology," by *Journal of Modern African Studies* 3, 4 (1965): 499–526.

5. City within a City: The Detective Fiction of Chester Himes

1. The question of absurdity in Himes's detective fiction is a constant theme in much of the critical work. Gilbert H. Muller, in *Chester Himes* (1989), is perhaps most explicit on the subject: "This study of Himes offers a coherent assessment of the author's evolving vision of contemporary absurdity, beginning with the early novels in which characters attempt to affirm middle-class values and lives and ending in urban apocalypse as Himes's Harlem cycle (nine novels 1957–69) comes to a close with *Blind Man with a Pistol* and 'Plan B' " (x).

2. See, for example, Gilbert H. Muller, *Chester Himes* (1989); Stephen F. Milliken, *Chester Himes: A Critical Appraisal* (1976); James Lundquist, *Chester Himes* (1976); and Robert E. Skinner, *Two Guns from Harlem: The Detective Fiction of Chester Himes* (1989). We also have the two-volume autobiography, *The Quality of Hurt* (1972) and *My Life of Absurdity* (1976).

3. The issue of criminality and its relation to writers of detective fiction is an interesting one. The hero of *Vidocq's Mémoires* was a criminal who turned police informant and then became a detective. Edgar Allan Poe, although eccentric, alcoholic, and desperate, never actually committed a crime. Arthur Conan Doyle was an upstanding member of the middle class, as was Agatha Christie. Dashiell Hammett, who worked for a number of years as a Pinkerton detective, never was himself a criminal. Raymond Chandler, although eccentric, alcoholic, and desperate, threatened only to kill himself. And Georges Simenon, who, possibly, has written more detective and crime novels than any writer ever, claimed near the end of his life that he had never even received a parking ticket, never mind committed a crime.

4. For further information on Himes's years in France, see chapter 14 in Michel Fabre's *From Harlem to Paris* (1991).

5. For an interesting discussion of how Samuel Goldwyn, Jr., Ossie Davis, and Himes worked together to try to get detective character differences into the movie *Cotton Comes to Harlem,* see pp. 360–64 in the second volume of Himes's autobiography (*MLA*). Milliken, while agreeing that Coffin Ed and Grave Digger are "shadowy and elusive figures" in the novels, finds that the "hypnotic strength" of Godfrey Cambridge and Raymond St. Jacques in the movie makes the problem irrelevant (227–28).

6. A very good book on the subject of the African American folk hero and badman is John W. Roberts, *From Trickster to Badman* (1989). Also see Lawrence W. Levine, *Black Culture and Black Consciousness* (1977), chap. 6.

7. In his essay "Brer Robert: The Bluesman and the African American Trickster Tale Tradition," Bennett Siems sees the bluesman and the mythic folklore built up around the bluesman as based on the trickster traditions: "Trickster, hoodoo man, lone wolf, the devil's son-in-law, too

lazy and too proud to work for a living" (143); see *Southern Folklore* 48. no. 2 (1991); 41.

8. For a more comprehensive plot analysis of eight of the nine novels, see Skinner, *Two Guns from Harlem*. Skinner doesn't consider *Run, Man Run* part of the detective series since Coffin Ed and Grave Digger do not appear in that story. I have included the novel in my analysis because it transforms detective conventions in important ways while extending Himes's black detective worldview.

9. Himes worked on *Plan B* in the last years of his life. In the novel he planned to show that violent revolution was the only logical action for blacks who had suffered so long under racism. Grave Digger would kill Coffin Ed, and thousands of whites would die by violent means. See *MLA* 361, and Muller, chap. 7. In 1983 Michel Fabre gathered Himes's material and created a version that was published in France by Lieu Commun. In 1993 a new version, edited and with an introduction by Michel Fabre and Robert E. Skinner, was published by the University Press of Mississippi.

6. The Black Anti-Detective Novel

1. "The anti-detective novel" is a phrase used by Larry McCaffer and Linda Gregory in their article, "Major's *Reflex and Bone Structure* and the Anti-Detective Tradition," *Black American Literature Forum*, Summer 1979, 39–45. Also see Bell's chapter 8 (318–20), in which he analyzes Major's novel in relation to postmodern themes.

2. "Metaphysical detective" is an alternative way of describing the attributes of what I prefer to call the anti-detective novel. For a complete discussion of the development of the anti-detective novel and its relation to the metafictional anti-detective novel, see Tani, *The Doomed Detective*.

3. For a more complete and exacting examination of *Mumbo Jumbo* in relation to detective texts as defined by Tzvetan Todorov, see "On the Blackness of Blackness: Ishmael Reed and a Critique of the Sign," in Gates, *The Signifying Monkey*. I find Todorov's attempt to break down the detective novel into three different types of structures somewhat specious and impossible to defend considering the hybrid nature of the form.

Bibliography

Abrahams, Roger D. *Talking Black*. Rawley, MA.: Newbury House, 1976.

Abrams, M. H. *A Glossary of Literary Terms*. New York: Holt, Rinehart and Winston, 1981.

Alewyn, Richard. "The Origin of the Detective Novel: Probleme und Gestalten." 1974. In *The Poetics of Murder: Detective Fiction and Literary Theory*, ed. Glenn W. Most and William W. Stowe, 62–78. New York: Harcourt Brace Jovanovich, 1983.

Atkinson, Michael. "Type and Text in *A Study in Scarlet:* Repression and the Textual Unconsciousness." *Clues*, Spring/Summer 1987.

Awkward, Michael. *Inspiriting Influences: Tradition, Revision, and Afro-American Women's Novels*. New York, Columbia University Press, 1989.

Bailey, Frankie Y. *Out of the Woodpile: Black Characters in Crime and Detective Fiction*. New York: Greenwood Press, 1991.

Baker, Houston A., Jr. *Workings of the Spirit: The Poetics of Afro-American Women's Writing*. Chicago: University of Chicago Press, 1991.

———. *Modernism and the Harlem Renaissance*. Chicago: University of Chicago Press, 1987.

———. *Blues, Ideology, and Afro-American Literature: A Vernacular Theory*. Chicago: University of Chicago Press, 1984.

———. *The Journey Back: Issues in Black Literature and Criticism*. Chicago: University of Chicago Press, 1980.

Baker, Nikki. *Long Goodbyes*. Tallahassee: Naiad Press, 1993.

———. *The Lavender House Murder*. Tallahassee: Naiad Press, 1992.

———. *In the Game*. Tallahassee: Naiad Press, 1991.

Bakhtin, Mikhail. *The Dialogic Imagination*. Austin: University of Texas Press, 1981.

Baldwin, James. "Of the Sorrow Songs: The Cross of Redemption." *New Edinburgh Review*, Aug. 1979. Reprinted in *Views on Black American Music*, no. 2. Amherst: University of Massachusetts, 1984.

Bell, Bernard. *The Afro-American Novel and Its Tradition*. Amherst: University of Massachusetts Press, 1987.

Benjamin, Playthell G. "The Afro-American Musician: Messengers of a Unique

245

Sensibility in Western Culture." In *Views on Black American Music,* no. 2. Amherst: University of Massachusetts, 1984.

Berghahn, Marion. *Images of Africa in Black American Literature.* London: Macmillan, 1977.

Bernel, Albert. *Farce: A History from Aristophanes to Woody Allen.* Carbondale: Southern Illinois University Press, 1990.

Biamonte, Gloria A. "Detection and the Text: Reading Three American Women of Mystery." Ph.D dissertation, University of Massachusetts, Amherst, 1991.

Bland, Eleanor Taylor. *Slow Burn.* New York: Signet, 1993.

———. *Dead Time.* New York: Signet, 1992.

Blauner, Robert. "Black Culture: Myth or Reality?" In *Afro-American Anthropology,* ed. Norman E. Whitten, Jr., and John F. Szwed. London: Free Press, 1970.

Bone, Robert. *The Negro Novel in America.* New Haven: Yale University Press, 1958.

Bontemps, Arna Wendell. *The Harlem Renaissance Remembered.* New York: Dodd, Mead, 1994.

Butterfield, Stephen. *Black Autobiography in America.* Amherst: University of Massachusetts Press, 1974.

Byerman, Keith E. *Fingering the Jagged Grain: Tradition and Form in Recent Black Fiction.* Athens: University of Georgia Press, 1985.

Carby, Hazel. *Reconstructing Womanhood: The Emergence of the African American Woman Novelist.* New York: Oxford University Press, 1987.

Castle, Terry. "The Carnivalization of Eighteenth-Century Narrative." *PMLA* 99, no. 5 (1984): 903–16.

Cawelti, John G. *Adventure, Mystery, and Romance: Formula Stories as Art and Popular Culture.* Chicago: University of Chicago Press, 1976.

Chandler, Raymond. "The Simple Art of Murder: An Essay." In *The Simple Art of Murder,* 1–21. New York: Ballantine, 1934.

Christianson, Scott R. "Language as Power in American Detective Fiction." *Journal of Popular Culture,* Fall 1989, 151–62.

Coles, Robert, and Diane Isaacs. "Primitivism as a Therapeutic Pursuit: Notes towards a Reassessment of Harlem Renaissance Literature." In *The Harlem Renaissance: Revaluations,* ed. Amritjit Singh, William S. Shiver, and Stanley Brodwin. New York: Garland Press, 1989.

Cooke, Michael. *Afro-American Literature in the Twentieth Century: The Achievement of Intimacy.* New Haven: Yale University Press, 1984.

Craig, Patricia and Mary Cadogan. *The Lady Investigates: Women Detectives and Spies in Fiction.* New York: St. Martin's Press, 1981.

Dance, Daryl Cumber. *Shuckin' and Jivin': Folklore from Contemporary Black Americans.* Bloomington: Indiana University Press, 1978.

De Jongh, James. *Vicious Modernism: Black Harlem and the Literary Imagination.* Cambridge: Cambridge University Press, 1990.

Dillard, J. L. *Black English: Its History and Usage in the United States.* New York: Random House, 1972.

Dove, George N. *The Police Procedural.* Bowling Green, OH: Bowling Green State University Popular Press, 1982.

Du Bois, W. E. B. *The Souls of Black Folk: Essays and Sketches.* 1903. Reprinted in *Three Negro Classics.* New York: Avon Books, 1965.

Durham, Philip. "The *Black Mask* School." In *Tough Guy Writers of the 30s,* ed. David Madden. Carbondale: Southern Illinois University Press, 1968.

Ellison, Ralph. *Shadow and Act.* New York: Random House, 1964.

Equiano, Olaudah. *The Life of Olaudah Equiano, or, Gustavus Vassa the African Written by Himself.* 1789. Rpt. Harlow: Longman Press, 1989.

Fabre, Michel. *From Harlem to Paris: Black American Writers in France, 1840–1980.* Urbana: University of Illinois Press, 1991.

———. *The World of Richard Wright.* Jackson: University Press of Mississippi, 1985.

Fisher, Rudolph. *The Conjure Man Dies: A Mystery Tale of Dark Harlem.* 1932. Rpt. New York: Arno Press, 1971.

Fox, Robert Elliot. *Conscientious Sorcerers: The Black Postmodernist Fiction of Leroi Jones/Amiri Baraka, Ishmael Reed, and Samuel R. Delany.* New York: Greenwood Press, 1987.

Franklin, H. Bruce. *The Victim as Criminal and Artist: Literature from the American Prison.* New York: Oxford University Press, 1978.

Frazier, E. Franklin. *The Negro Family in the United States.* Chicago: University of Chicago Press, 1939.

Frye, Northrop. *Secular Scripture: A Study of the Structure of Romance.* Cambridge, MA: Harvard University Press, 1976.

Fuller, Hoyt. "Traveler on the Long, Rough, Lonely Road." *Black World,* Mar. 1972, 4–22, 87–98.

Gates, Henry Louis, Jr. *The Signifying Monkey: A Theory of Afro-American Literary Criticism.* New York: Oxford University Press, 1988.

———. "Dis and Dat: Dialect and Descent." In *Figures in Black,* 167–95. New York: Oxford University Press, 1987.

———. "A Wealth of Material on Black Literature Discovered by Periodical Fiction Project." *Chronicle of Higher Education.* Oct. 23, 1985.

———. "The Blackness of Blackness: a Critique of the Sign and the Signifying Monkey." In *Black Literature & Literary Theory,* ed. Gates. New York: Methuen, 1984.

Gayle, Addison. *The Way of the New World: The Black Novel in America.* Garden City, NY: Anchor Press, 1975.

Gayle, Addison, and Larry Neal, eds. *The Black Aesthetic.* Garden City, NY: Anchor Books, 1972.

Geherin, David. *The American Private Eye: The Image in Fiction.* New York: Ungar, 1985.

———. *Sons of Sam Spade.* New York: Ungar, 1980.

Gerhardus, Maly, and Dietfried Gerhardus. *Cubism and Futurism: The Evolution of the Self-sufficient Picture.* Oxford: Phaidon, and New York: Dutton, 1979.

Gilbert, Peter, ed. *The Selected Writings of John Edward Bruce, Militant Black Journalist.* New York: Arno Press, 1971.

Glazer, Nathan, and Daniel P. Moynihan *Beyond the Melting Pot: The Negroes, Puerto Ricans, Jews, Italians, and Irish of New York City.* Cambridge, MA.: MIT Press, 1964.

Goulart, Ron. *The Dime Detectives.* New York: Mysterious Press, 1988.

Grella, George. "The Hardboiled Detective Novel." In *Detective Fiction: A Collection of Essays,* ed. Robin Winks. Englewood Cliffs, NJ: Prentice-Hall, 1980.

Haycraft, Howard. *Murder for Pleasure: The Life and Times of the Detective Story.* New York and London: Appleton-Century, 1941.

———, ed. *The Art of the Mystery Story: A Collection of Critical Essays.* New York: Grosset & Dunlap, 1947.

Heilbrun, Carolyn. "Keep Your Eye on Whodunit: The Mysterious Appeal of the Mystery." *Harper's Bazaar,* Nov. 1985, 200.

Herskovits, Melville. *The New World Negro.* Bloomington: Indiana University Press, 1966.

———. *The Myth of the Negro Past.* New York and London: Harper and Brothers, 1941.

Himes, Chester. *Plan B.* Edited by Michel Fabre and Robert E. Skinner. Jackson: University Press of Mississippi, 1993.

———. *The Collected Stories of Chester Himes.* Edited by Calvin Hernton. New York: Thunder's Mouth Press, 1991.

———. *My Life of Absurdity: The Autobiography of Chester Himes.* Vol. 2. New York: Doubleday, 1976.

———. *Black on Black: "Baby Sister" and Selected Writings.* New York: Doubleday, 1973.

———. *The Quality of Hurt: The Autobiography of Chester Himes.* Vol. 1. New York: Doubleday, 1972.

———. *Blind Man with a Pistol.* 1969. Rpt. London: Allison & Busby, 1986.

———. *The Heat's On.* 1966. Rpt. New York: Berkley Publishing, 1972.

———. *Run, Man Run.* New York: G. P. Putnam's Sons, 1966.

———. *Cotton Comes to Harlem.* 1965. Rpt. New York: Dell, 1970.

———. *All Shot Up.* New York: Avon Books, 1960.

———. *The Big Gold Dream.* 1960. Rpt. New York: Berkley Publishing, 1966.

———. *The Real Cool Killers.* 1959. Rpt. New York: Berkley Publishing, 1966.

———. *The Crazy Kill.* 1959. Rpt. New York: Berkley Publishing, 1966.

———. *For Love of Imabelle.* 1957. Rpt. Chatham, NJ: Chatham Bookseller, 1973.

Holquist, Michael. "Metaphysical Detective Stories in Postwar Fiction." In *The Poetics of Murder: Detective Fiction and Literary Theory,* ed. Glenn W. Most and William W. Stowe. New York: Harcourt Brace Jovanovich, 1983.

Hopkins, Pauline. *Hagar's Daughter: A Story of Southern Caste Prejudice.* 1901–2. Reprinted in *The Magazine Novels of Pauline Hopkins.* The Schomburg Library of Nineteenth-Century Black Women Writers. New York: Oxford University Press, 1988.

Huggins, Nathan. *Harlem Renaissance*. New York: Oxford University Press, 1971.

Hurston, Zora Neale. *Tell My Horse: Voodoo and Life in Haiti and Jamacia*. New York: Perennial Library, 1990.

———. *The Sanctified Church*. Berkeley: Turtle Island Press, 1983.

———. "Hoodoo in America." *Journal of American Folklore*, 1931.

Hutcheon, Linda. *A Poetics of Postmodernism*. New York: Routledge, 1988.

Irele, Abiola. "Negritude-Literature and Ideology." *Journal of Modern African Studies* 3, 4 (1965): 499–526.

Ives, Sumner. "A Theory of Literary Dialect." *Tulane Studies in English* 2 (1949–50): 137–82.

Jameson, F. R. "On Raymond Chandler." In *The Poetics of Murder: Detective Fiction and Literary Theory*. ed. Glenn W. Most and William W. Stowe. New York: Harcourt Brace Jovanovich, 1983.

Johnson, Abby Arthur, and Ronald Maberry Johnson. *Propaganda and Aesthetics: The Literary Politics of African American Magazines in the Twentieth Century*. 1979. Rpt. Amherst: University of Massachusetts Press, 1991.

Klein, Kathleen Gregory. *The Woman Detective: Gender and Genre*. Urbana: University of Illinois Press, 1988.

Klinkowitz, Jerome. *The Self-apparent Word: Fiction as Language/Language as Fiction*. Carbondale: Southern Illinois University Press, 1984.

Knight, Stephen. *Form and Ideology in Crime Fiction*. Bloomington: Indiana University Press, 1980.

Komo, Dolores. *Clio Browne, Private Investigator*. Freedom, CA: Crossing Press, 1988.

Labov, William. *Sociolinguistic Patterns*. Philadelphia: University of Pennsylvania Press, 1979.

———. "Some Features of the English of Black Americans." In *Varieties of Present-Day English*, ed. Richard W. Bailey and Jay L. Robinson, 236–56. New York: Macmillan, 1973.

Langston Hughes Review 4, no. 1 (Spring 1985).

Levine, Lawrence W. *Black Culture and Black Consciousness: Afro-American Folk Thought from Slavery to Freedom*. New York: Oxford University Press, 1977.

Locke, Alain. *The Critical Temper of Alain Locke: A Collection of His Essays on Art and Culture*, ed. Jeffrey Stewart. New York: Garland Press, 1983.

———. *The New Negro*. 1925. Rpt. New York: Atheneum, 1968.

Lott, Rick. "A Matter of Style: Chandler's Hardboiled Disguise." *Journal of Popular Culture*, Winter 1989, 65–76.

Lundquist, James. *Chester Himes*. New York: Ungar, 1976.

Madden, David, ed. *Tough Guy Writers of the 30s*. Carbondale: Southern Illinois University Press, 1968.

Major, Clarence. *Reflex and Bone Structure*. New York: Fiction Collective, 1975.

———. *Dark and Feeling*. New York: Third Press, 1974.

———. "A Black Criteria." In *The Black Aesthetic*, ed. Addison Gayle and Larry Neal. Garden City, NY: Anchor Books, 1972.

————. ed. *The New Black Poetry.* New York: International Publishers, 1969.

Malmgren, Carl Darryl. *Fictional Space in the Modernist and Postmodernist American Novel.* Lewisburg, PA: Bucknell University Press, 1985.

Mandel, Ernest. *Delightful Murder: A Social History of the Crime Story.* Minneapolis: University of Minnesota Press, 1984.

Mann, Jessica. *Deadlier Than the Male.* New York: Macmillan: 1981.

Margolies, Edward. *Which Way Did He Go? The Private Eye in Dashiell Hammett, Raymond Chandler, Chester Himes, and Ross Macdonald.* New York: Holmes & Meier, 1982.

Martin, Reginald. *Ishmael Reed and the New Black Aesthetic Critics.* New York: St. Martin's Press, 1988.

McCluskey, John, Jr. *The City of Refuge: The Collected Stories of Rudolph Fisher.* Columbia: University of Missouri Press, 1987.

McDowell, Tremaine. "Negro Dialect in the American Novel to 1821." *American Speech 5* (April 1930): 291–96.

McKeon, Michael. *The Origins of the English Novel, 1600–1740.* Baltimore: Johns Hopkins University Press, 1987.

Milliken, Stephen F. *Chester Himes: A Critical Appraisal.* Columbia: University of Missouri Press, 1976.

Mitchell-Kernan, Claudia. "Signifying as a Form of Verbal Art." In *Mother Wit from the Laughing Barrel: Readings in the Interpretation of Afro-American Folklore,* ed. Alan Dundes, 310–28. Englewood Cliffs, NJ: Prentice-Hall, 1973.

Mosley, Walter. *Black Betty.* New York: Pocket Books, 1994.

————. *White Butterfly.* New York: Pocket Books, 1992.

————. *A Red Death.* New York: Pocket Books, 1991.

————. *Devil in a Blue Dress.* New York: Pocket Books, 1990.

Most, Glenn W., and William W. Stowe, eds. *Poetics of Murder: Detective Fiction and Literary Theory.* New York: Harcourt Brace Jovanovich, 1983.

Muller, Gilbert H. *Chester Himes:* Boston: Twayne, 1989.

Murch, Alma E. *The Development of the Detective Novel.* 1958. Rpt. New York: Greenwood Press, 1968.

Murphy, Joseph. *Working the Spirit: Ceremonies of the African Diaspora.* Boston: Beacon Press, 1994.

Myrdal, Gunnar. *An American Dilemma: The Negro Problem and Modern Democracy.* 1944. Rpt. New York: Harper & Row, 1962.

Neely, Barbara. *Blanche among the Talented Tenth.* New York: St. Martin's Press, 1994.

————. *Blanche on the Lam.* New York: Penquin, 1992.

Nye, Russel. *The Unembarrassed Muse: The Popular Arts in America.* New York: Dial Press, 1970.

Ogren, Kathy J. "Controversial Sounds: Jazz Performance as Theme and Language in the Harlem Renaissance." In *The Harlem Renaissance: Revaluations,* ed. Amritjit Singh, William S. Shiver, and Stanley Brodwin. New York: Garland Press, 1989.

Olsen, Lance. *Circus of the Mind in Motion: Postmodernism and the Comic Vision.* Detroit: Wayne State University Press, 1990.

Ostendorf, Berndt. *Black Literature in White America.* Sussex: Harvester Press, 1982.

Pennell, Jane C. "The Female Detective: Pre-and Post-Women's Lib." *Clues,* Fall/Winter 1985.

Perry, Margaret. *Silence to the Drums: A Survey of the Literature of the Harlem Renaissance.* Westport, CT: Greenwood Press, 1976.

Phillips, Ulrich Bonnell. *American Negro Slavery.* 1918. Rpt. Baton Rouge: Louisiana State University Press, 1966.

————. *Life and Labor in the Old South.* 1929. Rpt. Boston: Little, Brown, 1946.

Place, Janey. "The Black Widow: Women in Film Noir." In *Women in Film Noir,* ed. Ann Kaplan. London: BFI, 1980.

Porter, Dennis. *The Pursuit of Crime: Art and Ideology in Detective Fiction.* New Haven: Yale University Press, 1981.

Propp, Vladimir. *Morphology of the Folktale.* 1932. Rpt. Austin: University of Texas Press, 1968.

Puckett, Newbell Niles. *Folk Beliefs of the Southern Negro.* New York: Dover, 1969.

Reddy, Maureen T. *Sisters in Crime: Feminism and the Crime Novel.* New York: Continuum, 1988.

Reed, Ishmael. *Writin' Is Fightin': Thirty-seven Years of Boxing on Paper.* New York: Atheneum, 1988.

————. *Shrovetide in Old New Orleans.* Garden City, NY: Doubleday, 1978.

————. "Chester Himes Writer." In *Shrovetide in Old New Orleans.* New York: Doubleday, 1978.

————. *Conjure: Selected Poems, 1963–1970.* Amherst: University of Massachusetts Press, 1972.

————. *Mumbo Jumbo: A Novel.* New York: Atheneum, 1972.

Roberts, John W. *From Trickster to Badman: The Black Folk Hero in Slavery and Freedom.* Philadelphia: University of Pennsylvania Press, 1989.

Routley, Eric. "The Case against the Detective Story." In *Detective Fiction: A Collection of Critical Essays,* ed. Robin W. Winks. Englewood Cliffs, NJ: Prentice-Hall, 1980.

————. *The Puritan Pleasures of the Detective Story.* London: Gollancz, 1972.

Sayers, Dorothy, ed. *The Omnibus of Crime.* New York: Payson & Clarke, 1929.

Schulz, Max F. *Black Humor Fiction of the Sixties.* Athens: Ohio University Press, 1973.

Schuyler, George. *Black Empire.* Boston: Northeastern University Press, 1991.

————. *Black No More.* New York: Macaulay, 1931.

Settle, Elizabeth A., Thomas A. and Settle. *Ishmael Reed: A Primary and Secondary Bibliography.* Boston: G. K. Hall, 1982.

Skinner, Robert E. *Two Guns from Harlem: The Detective Fiction of Chester*

Himes. Bowling Green, OH: Bowling Green State University Popular Press, 1989.

Smith, Robert, Jr. "Chester Himes in France and the Legacy of the Roman Policier." *CLA Journal* 25 (Sept. 1981): 18–27.

Smitherman, Geneva. *Talking and Testifying: The Language of Black America.* Detroit: Wayne State University Press, 1986.

Spanos, William V. "The Detective and the Boundary: Some Notes on the Post-modern Literary Imagination." *Boundary* 2 (Fall 1972): 147–68.

Stampp, Kenneth. *That Peculiar Institution: Slavery in the Ante-Bellum South.* New York: Knopf, 1956.

Sudarkasa, Niara [Gloria A. Marshall]. "African and Afro-American Family Structure." In *Anthropology for the Eighties,* ed. Johnnetta Cole, 133–60. New York: Free Press, 1982.

Symons, Julian. *Bloody Murder: From the Detective Story to the Crime Novel.* 1985. Rpt. New York: Mysterious Press, 1992.

———. *Mortal Consequences: A History from the Detective Story to the Crime Novel.* New York: Harper & Row, 1972.

Tani, Stefano. *The Doomed Detective: The Contribution of the Detective Novel to Postmodern American and Italian Fiction.* Carbondale: Southern Illinois University Press, 1984.

Thompson, Robert Farris. *Flash of the Spirit: African and Afro-American Art and Philosophy.* New York: Random House, 1983.

Todorov, Tzvetan. *The Poetics of Prose.* Ithaca, NY: Cornell University Press, 1977.

Turner, Lorenzo D. *Africanisms in the Gullah Dialect.* Ann Arbor: University of Michigan Press, 1949.

Van Deburg, William. *A New Day in Babylon: The Black Power Movement and American Culture.* Chicago: University of Chicago Press, 1992.

———. *Slavery and Race in American Popular Culture.* Madison: University of Wisconsin Press, 1984.

Van Dine, S. S. [Willard Huntington Wright]. "Twenty Rules for Writing Detective Stories." In *The Art of the Mystery Story: A Collection of Critical Essays,* ed. Howard Haycraft, 189–93. New York: Simon & Schuster, 1946.

Weatherford, W. D. *Negro Life in the South.* Miami: Mnemosyne, 1969.

Williams, John A. "Chester Himes—My Man Himes." In *Flashbacks: A Twenty-Year Diary of Article Writing.* Garden City, NY: Anchor Press, 1973.

Winks, Robin W. *Detective Fiction: A Collection of Critical Essays.* Englewood Cliffs, NJ: Prentice-Hall, 1980.

Wintz, Cary D. *Black Culture and the Harlem Renaissance.* Houston: Rice University Press, 1988.

Wu, William F. *The Yellow Peril: Chinese American in American Fiction, 1850–1940.* Hamden, CT: Archon Books, 1982.

Index